WHAT'S LEFT?

*Marxism, Utopianism,
and the Revolt against History*

Jack Lawrence Luzkow

University Press of America,® Inc.
Lanham · Boulder · New York · Toronto · Oxford

Copyright © 2006 by
University Press of America,® Inc.
4501 Forbes Boulevard
Suite 200
Lanham, Maryland 20706
UPA Acquisitions Department (301) 459-3366

PO Box 317
Oxford
OX2 9RU, UK

Library of Congress Control Number: 2006927251
ISBN-13: 978-0-7618-3545-5 (paperback : alk. paper)
ISBN-10: 0-7618-3545-8 (paperback : alk. paper)

To Yelena
For sharing the journey

Contents

Preface

More than a decade ago, when the Soviet Union collapsed, I thought like many others. Utopia was dead forever. Moreover, it deserved to be dead. Marxist-Leninist utopianism had only led to totalitarianism. It had never produced the happy life of legend and promise. Soviet Marxism had been used to legitimize the deaths of tens of millions, produced the gulag for millions of others, and terrified the citizens of what had become instead the nightmare of Stalinism.

My first trip to the Soviet Union in 1989 made what I had feared abstractly appear even worse in practice. All I could think of was that the Cold War was based on a mythology, just as Soviet Marxism was. For it was almost impossible to imagine a Soviet state in a nuclear war with the United States. The Soviet Union couldn't even afford to feed its citizens. It could not build decent roads. Even the quickest glance revealed a country that was on the verge of imminent collapse, though nobody predicted it at the time. Any foreigner arriving in Moscow for the first time could see the entire bankruptcy of the Soviet system the moment he got his first good look.

As for the Chinese experiment with Maoist utopianism, I remember sitting in a hotel café in Poland, talking with correspondents from the *Christian Science Monitor* about the impending elections in Poland the following day. The excitement was visceral. Poland was moving toward something, toward Europe, toward democracy, toward freedom, maybe even toward social democracy. The following days, in Prague, I watched the events of Tien'anmen Square unfold before my eyes on the screen. By then it had become clear. Maoist utopianism had long withered away. What was left was the power of the state, still holding onto a dead ideology. Unlike Poland, China was not moving toward democracy, or toward socialism, or toward anything. Instead it was defending an old faith. Or it was defending the party in power that rationalized its hold on power in the name of an old faith. Which in fact was no longer a faith at all.

In 1992 I was in the midst of writing an essay that included a long section on Marxism and utopianism. I quietly discarded the part of that essay which dwelled on the topic of utopianism. I did not agree with Francis Fukuyama's thesis, and still don't, that history had 'ended' because no better system could be devised than liberal democracy. Or that liberal democracy as a system of thought was the endpoint of human history. But clearly something had ended. What exactly has preoccupied me ever since. To be sure, Marxism-Leninism as a world system capable of moving millions had ended. Marxism-Leninism as a political force had surely failed to resolve poverty, eliminate class conflict, or bring about equality even in the states where people who called themselves Marxists were in power. Work in Communist Russia was even more alienating than in the capitalist West. Marxism-Leninism as anti-Western inspiration no longer mobilized masses outside the West or anywhere. Marxism, in its Russian and Chinese versions, had failed as a great experiment in non-market economics. Neither country could keep up with economic development in Western Europe or in the United States. Even as early as the 1960's it was clear that Russia had lost its global contest with the United States. The Cold War ended that decade, but nobody knew it, or wanted to know it, certainly not in Russia.

It was even worse than that. Marxism-Leninism had failed because of Marxists. They made promises they never kept. They turned Marxism into a religion, putting Utopia further and further onto a distant horizon. Or they turned it into a science, proclaiming themselves as master theoreticians. Or they turned it into a morality play, proclaiming that they knew best the interests of the working classes in whose interests they exercised power. And they murdered millions because they were capitalists. Or would be capitalists. Or bourgeois, or enemies of the state or left wing deviationists or Trotskyites or . . . something.

It was easy to turn away in disgust from all that. It had to be called what it really was, not seen for the ideals that it proclaimed. These were long forgotten. Russian Communism was a kind of inverted nationalism. Inverted because of the ideological baggage that had been used to justify and rationalize the Soviet Communist Party and its hold on the Soviet state. The ideals were gone, but the Party remained.

Yet all that was Soviet (or Maoist) Marxism. Whatever it was, it was hardly the communist Utopia of Marx. Lenin may have been inspired by Marx, including what he took to be Marx's proclamation of the dictatorship of the proletariat, but focusing on Marx's notion of 'dictatorship' of the proletariat and ignoring his lifelong stress on humanity seemed to cloud the issue. And in the West, the Marx who fought to humanize humanity, Marx the humanist, was practically unknown at all. In the West, Marx was deliberately confused with Marxism-Leninism, and that was indeed different. Marx became the bogeyman, the totalitarian. He was denigrated as a would-be dictator. Suddenly the West discovered that Marx was Lenin or Stalin. The sins of the sons were put on the father. Within several years of the so-called end of history, history returned with a vengeance. The widely heralded peace dividend did not even survive the Clinton years in the White House. It was difficult to make sense of the world that was emerging after the Cold War. Communism was collapsing and was dead, but liberalism as a world beating philosophy? People wanted freedom, they wanted political choice, and they rejected Big Brother. But they had many different ideas about the kind of democracy they wanted. Muslims everywhere talked about Islamic democracy. In some countries when militant Islamism came to power democratically, in Algeria for example, it was abruptly turned out of power. In Algeria, Islamic victory was snatched away by a Westernized Algerian military. The West did not complain. It preferred a secular power to an Islamist state. On the other hand, in Westernized Turkey, Muslims came to power, led by Prime Minister, Recep Erdogan, who had been imprisoned for many years because of his Islamist views. He at once defended democracy, democracy with Islamic values, Islamic democracy.

Europe also has not embraced liberal democracy, at least not since World War II. This is no surprise. Europe tried liberal democracy in the nineteenth-century. The result was World War I. Then World War II. Liberal democracies were dramatic failures, inherently unstable, inherently unequal, unable to build consensus, anything but fraternal, that famous catchword of the liberals in 1789. The liberal democracies of Europe failed to prevent war, or to stand up to nationalism, or to stop Mussolini or Hitler. World War II was a good lesson. Europe knew the weaknesses of liberal democracy; it understood the horrors of nationalism. It preferred social democracy with many of the distinguishing features of socialism. The state accepted responsibility for its citizens. All people were entitled to human dignity: to medical care, housing, jobs, old age pensions. Europeans still do not believe that the so-called free market can be used to solve all human problems. It can be a powerful engine of development, but it can also dehumanize, divide society into rich and poor, create income and wealth gaps that are unprecedented, deprive people of basic human rights. Today, once again, parts of Western Europe have turned toward the left, including England and Spain.

Several years after the collapse of the Soviet Union and the end of the Cold War, it became clear that the collapse of communism did not mean a bonanza for the poor nations of the world. Half the citizens of the world are still living on two dollars a day or less in the year 2006. For them the issue is not democracy but survival. Latin America, practically bludgeoned by the World Bank and the United States into liberal democracy and free market values, is still staggering along. In Latin America market values mean little, only endemic and growing poverty, no meaningful land reform, the loss of indigenous lands, farmers who can only survive by growing coca. Not surprisingly, it is in Latin America that pockets of Maoists still survive, the Shining Path for example, in countries where ancient grievances and loss of lands have never been addressed. In Chiapas, Mexico, indigenous peoples hold out against the state for autonomy, if not independence.

In Eastern Europe, socialism has been resurgent. Socialists, many of whom were previously communists, have been returned to power everywhere. Practically every one of the states that were spun out of the Soviet Union, Turkmenistan, Tadzhikistan, Uzbekistan, Belarus, Ukraine (until its democratic revolution), are Stalinist in tone, though they are more moderate than the Soviet system. Russia itself elected Boris Yeltsin, a former communist, as President, following the collapse of the Soviet Union. His designated successor, Vladimir Putin, was head of the Soviet intelligence system and a former high-ranking member of the Party. Today, he is a Russian nationalist, nominal democrat and ex-communist. But he remains tied to the erstwhile communist bureaucracy and is reluctant either to turn westward or to embrace market economics. Especially if and when it conflicts with Russian nationalism.

It may be that Marxism, especially Marxism-Leninism, will disappear from the world scene altogether. But it is equally apparent that socialism will endure as a utopian dream and political and social objective. The anti-US sentiments that have emerged in so many parts of the world demonstrate the strong resentment toward American individualism.[1] Many of the poor nations of the world feel vulnerable to market economics. They feel threatened by the raw power of the United States, the only remaining superpower, when it uses loans from the World Bank, or from the US, or from both, to impose market economics. They do not feel reassured by democracy, especially when democracy means putting everything up for grabs on the free market, eliminating all forms of state subsidies for the poor, privatizing the wealth of the state, eliminating protective tariffs, eroding already low environmental standards, offering little or no protection for labor, and turning over entire state industries to foreign control. Russia, not among the poorest nations, provides a good example of how 'democracy' and the 'free market' have set a country further back. Here a market economy and 'democracy' have meant a new class of bandit millionaires, the elimination of many social guarantees, the rise of unemployment, the erosion of living standards, a slide toward authoritarianism.

Soon after 'history ended', I became convinced that Utopia was bound to return. Or that it had never left. The gap between the West and the rest was widening, not narrowing. The United States, with 5 percent of the world's population, was consuming 25 percent of the world's energy and owned the same percentage of its wealth. Half the globe was undernourished and hungry. Much of the world population was vulnerable to the least disturbance of nature, as we all found out from the giant tsunami in the Indian Ocean. What was astonishing was not the magnitude of the tsunami, but the fact that the victims were for the most part the poor, many of whom had been forced off the best lands in the highlands in their respective countries by the more prosperous. It wasn't just nature that was catastrophic, or demographics. It was the social system that had forced the poor to ring the coastline, making them dependent on the sea.

As Vincent Geoghegan has pointed out, the "utopian impulse is not necessarily politically progressive."[2] The twentieth-century has been a graphic illustration of this. Hitler's Third Reich was meant to be a thousand-year Utopia for good Aryan Germans. Hitler was himself a nationalist, a national socialist and utopian. He did not believe these terms contradicted each other. He took it for granted that the good German nationalist was also a utopian believer in the biological community, the German nation. The inevitable consequence of this utopian vision was Auschwitz.[3] That Auschwitz followed from Hitler's vision is generally agreed. That all utopias must end in Auschwitz is widely disputed.

J. L. Talmon, a modern critic of Utopia, pointed to Stalin's Russia. He argued that the gap between rhetoric and reality in Communist Russia was as great as in Hitler's Germany. He had no illusions about the utopianism of the Soviet Union. It was based on fanaticism, self-righteousness and elitism. His conclusion was unavoidable. The gulag was the inevitable result of Soviet and Stalinist exclusivism, proof that Marx and Marxism-Leninism, and utopianism in general, could only create dystopia, the very opposite of the original utopian impulse.[4] Talmon was correct up to a point. He had described the system of Marxism-Leninism and Stalinism exactly as it was. That the gulag followed from Marxism-Leninism and Stalinism is no longer in serious dispute. But the connection between the work of Marx and the gulag is still widely disputed. It is the argument of this book that they are a disconnect. To blame Marx and the ideal of Utopia in general for the gulag is much like blaming Christ for the German Christians who followed Hitler.

The idea of Utopia has been around for centuries. Plato's *Republic* was a kind of Utopia, it envisioned an elite of guardians who would have a monopoly of power, but as philosopher kings they would put the interests of the citizens of the republic above those of their own. They were to be totally disinterested in power or wealth.[5] The Renaissance gave us several utopias, notably Thomas More's *Utopia*, which presented a kind of Christian socialist alternative to incipient capitalist England in which, More proffered, sheep received better care than human beings.[6]

More's *Utopia* presented the good alternative, a society without want and in perfect balance. Utopia was stuffed with ideals that would alleviate human suffering, and it measured those ideals against the imperfect present. Reason, education, and the slight reorganization of society could bring about the good life for all. More was convinced that if an entire society worked, and shared its production as equals, then the working day could be reduced to six hours or less. Moreover, the impulse toward Utopia was already at hand. More's Utopia was located in the present, but in some other part of the world. The implication was clear enough. Utopia wasn't a distant dream. It was in some distant place, but not in a distant future. Utopia was desirable because it was rational, it was possible because it was desirable, and it was already somewhere.[7]

For More it was a matter of restoring mankind to its rightful place in the cosmos. Thomas Campanella, sharing similar assumptions, thought that the citizens of Utopia would need to work only a four-hour workday.[8] Denis Diderot, writing in the eighteenth-century, in *Supplement to the Voyage of Bougainville*, thought Utopia achievable by limiting the needs of mankind.[9] Fewer needs meant less labor time to produce them. He compared modern society, unfavorably, to more primitive societies that minimized labor time because their needs were minimal. The result was that needs were met effortlessly, allowing much more time for leisure. Diderot's point was a simple one. Men enslave each other by wanting too much. Implicit in Diderot's argument was a primitive labor theory of value. Modern man worked long hours but had little to show for his work. The reason was that he labored to meet the needs of others. Diderot's vision, however, was of another kind. He did not look toward a future communist society, but backward toward a return to nature. For Diderot, the new science and technology would not make mankind happy, it would only enlarge its needs.

Like so many of the eighteenth-century utopias, Diderot's Utopia was a yardstick enabling him to judge the present, not a blueprint for changing society. Diderot's contemporary, Jean-Jacques Rousseau, in the *Social Contract*, provided yet another measure against which to judge the France of the eighteenth-century. Like earlier utopias, Rousseau's theory was a-historical and static. It was intended as a model for moral regeneration.[10] But like later utopians, Rousseau felt that the root of all evil, the great corrupter, was private property. Eliminate that, and mankind could be restored to its libertarian beginnings. Change institutions and human nature could become perfected, mankind could live in harmony. Rousseau's *Social Contract*, then, was prescriptive, it contained a recipe to cure social ills, but it was not necessarily a recipe for the future. It was a concoction based on first principles, a notion of Utopia in a hypothetical golden age, a normative structure that beckoned mankind to unshackle itself. Not for man to return to nature, but to return to himself and to his human essence. Mankind must return to its roots prior to the debacle of civilization that had only enchained men by forcing them to serve those who had private property.[11]

Henri de Saint-Simon (1760-1825) was a utopian socialist with an ironic twist. He was a realist, the father of sociology and a believer in technocratic engineering. He was also a socialist who believed that capitalist entrepreneurs could and would lead the way toward Utopia. As socialist and utopian, as capitalist and realist, Saint-Simon thought the future had arrived. It was only a matter of the reorganization of society. Society was after all a machine. It had only to be oiled and cared for properly by social engineers. Society could be reorganized rationally on the basis of productive labor. Saint-Simon believed that the emerging industrial class included everyone from common laborers to owners of industrial factories. They were all productive. The group that was not productive, leftovers from the aristocratic old regime, were nothing more than parasites whose privileges blocked society from being rationally managed by the industrial class.[12]

This was not all. For just as Saint-Simon believed that priests and Christianity had provided the impetus and *raison d'etre* for the medieval period of history, so science and scientific knowledge would bind together and help to improve modern society. Scientists, bankers, industrialists, artists, writers and intellectuals would be the priests of the modern era. They would replace the clergy as the new elite. Even more importantly, they had the management skills that would enable them to reorganize society on the basis of the new science and industry. The rational management of society implied a science of society, the notion that a rational society could be planned and implemented. And it implied that the new class of managers and intelligentsia had no self-interest other than the rational management of society. At last, thought Saint-Simon, utopian dream and scientific realism were merging.

Charles Fourier (1772-1837), Saint-Simon's contemporary, thought he had a recipe for the future. In fact it was Fourier who thought he had found the key to human nature itself, and therefore the key to human happiness. So much so that he termed his work a new "Social Science," whose key insight was that individuals were naturally attracted to what they found most fulfilling. Fourier believed that God had instilled in human beings sensual, emotional and intellectual passions that were fundamentally beneficial. Human nature did not need to be transformed, it needed to be fulfilled. Fourier did not counsel the abolition of private property to accomplish this. Instead he advised the (re)channeling of the creative passions so that individuals could perform the functions that best matched their desires. Anticipating both Ernst Bloch and Herbert Marcuse, Fourier argued that mankind's fantasies and passions needed to be unloosed in order to make individuals free. Individuals would be fulfilled when their passions were matched with the functions that they wanted to perform, when their creative passions were unleashed within properly organized, collaborative institutions.[13] Children for example, because they were attracted to filth, could be used to clean sewers.

Fourier has been widely skewered for this belief. But he thought he was offering humanity a means to transform work into pleasure, and to transform life into fulfillment by making labor satisfying and cooperative and not just a means of subsistence. Match work to desire. Liberate all the creative passions. Allow citizens to perform varied work, to divide the functions they perform. Human labor would cease to be alienated work because it could fulfill the passions, it would afford the individual variety in work and life, unchain him from the drudgery of a job.[14]

It was Karl Marx who applied the term utopian in a derisive way to indicate that nineteenth-century thinkers like Saint-Simon and Charles Fourier were dreamers, not realists. The implication was that their ideas were a-historical and based only on their own fantasies. They contemplated just (socialist) societies, but had no ideas about how to achieve them. Marx represented his own ideas as scientific, based on the actual movement of history, on the historical struggle and practice of the proletariat in its struggle against the bourgeoisie. He also tried not to fantasize or dream about what a socialist society should look like when it was achieved. By denying that we could know the precise look of a communist society in the future, he abandoned what has always been most appealing about utopias. Namely, why we should want to achieve them, or why we need to be utopians if we want to be happy human beings.

Despite his denial, Marx has given us some of the most idealized visions of an ideal future communism, of a harmonious human society. Even in his revolutionary pamphlet, *The Communist Manifesto*, his call for universal suffrage, the emancipation of women and universal education demonstrated that he had a vision of the future, a vision, moreover, that was a realistic dream, though a dream that was based more on hope than on science. It was this Marx, the visionary, egalitarian and utopian, the Marx who dared to dream the future, who inspired later thinkers like Herbert Marcuse.

Karl Marx thought that Saint-Simon, Fourier and the socialists of the early nineteenth-century were utopian because they lacked a roadmap to the future. Yet he was the greatest utopian of all. Not in the modern pejorative sense of utopianism, but because he believed that humanity could at last become free. Man could achieve his full individuality, he could liberate himself from the stress of economic needs, overcome alienation from other men. Marx was driven by a sense of messianism, a hope for deliverance, and he uttered his beliefs and hopes with biblical passion. It was prophecy not science. Marx was driven by a thirst for justice. He strove for an unalienated society based on love:

Let us assume *man* to be *man* and his relation to the world to be a human one. Then love can only be exchanged for love, trust for trust. . . . If you love without being able to evoke love in return . . . if you are not able by the *manifestation* of yourself as a loving person, to make yourself *a beloved person*, then your love is impotent and a misfortune.[15]

Love ought to be the foundation of society, but what should be its aim according to Marx? Marx rejected the materialism of the industrial culture around him. It generated needs in individuals that turned them into consumers of life and robbed them of true being. The commodity-man only knew one way to relate to the world, and that was to consume it. Modern man had sold his soul, had defined himself by having and using, had let himself become defined by false needs. Moreover, the man who became subject to his alienated needs was *"a mentally and physically dehumanized* being . . . the *self-conscious* and *self-acting commodity*.[16] For Marx, sounding more and more like a thundering prophet, human alienation had a direct relation to having and using. "The less you *are*, the less you express your life, the more you *have*, the greater is your *alienated* life and the greater is the saving of your alienated being."[17]

Marx saw man as increasingly lonely and alienated, a victim of his own creations. He saw man as a creature that had not achieved his possibilities, as a creature moreover who was alienated from other men, from himself and from nature. He believed mankind could only realize its essence by understanding and removing the source of its own alienation. Marx's cure was socialism, not as the end of history, but as the condition in which mankind could realize its essence to be free, creative and loving; free from the bondage of economic necessity, free to be self-determining and fulfilled. Socialism was the means through which mankind at last became transcendent, at last achieved the utopian by simply discovering its humanity. Paul Tillich, hardly an orthodox or even unorthodox Marxist, found Marx's utopian vision compelling. It was "a resistance movement against the destruction of love in social reality."[18] Marx's socialism, his utopian vision, was of a society in which man was not subordinated to the state, or to a bureaucracy, or to other men, but was fully in control over what he produced, fully involved in planning society and in the execution of the plan. Socialism, Utopia, meant being fully invested in industrial and political democracy.[19] Socialism was freedom. "Freedom is so much the essence of man," said Marx, "that even its opponents realize it. . . . No man fights freedom; he fights at most the freedom of others. Every kind of freedom has therefore always existed, only at one time as a special privilege, another time as a universal right."[20]

The task of socialism was to awaken man from illusory false needs, to make conscious his real needs, to awaken him to his real possibilities should he live in a society where he no longer felt alienated. It was precisely this kind of awakening, be it plumbing of the unconscious mind, be it making conscious man's dream visions, that inspired Walter Benjamin to explore the dream world of the nineteenth-century, the better to understand the alienation of the twentieth. The better to understand, as well, the kind of anguish and existential protest against industrial capitalism ingested in Marx's own prophetic Utopia. Ernst Bloch saw the prophetic vision in Marx as a kind of protest against the spiritual malaise of mankind caught in the alienated web of class society. He made the connection between the spiritual Christian mission based on universal love and Marx's attempt to overcome modern alienation by creating a communism of love. Marx's protest was against the lovelessness of industrial capitalism. Herbert Marcuse, echoing these sentiments, saw in Marx's hopeful visions an existential protest against the falsification of mankind's true nature, a revolt against the exploitation of man by man.[21]

Marx's socialism was in fact biblical. His philosophy of history, and notion of socialism, were akin to the hopes of the Old Testament prophets. Marx shared in common with the prophets the idea that history was meaningful, that man would perfect himself within the historical process, and that he would create a utopian society of complete harmony and justice in the fullness of time. Marx also shared with the biblical prophets the notion that the love of justice was the very essence of humanity. The historical process was for Marx the self-discovery by mankind of itself, the development in man of his human qualities, the powers of love and understanding. Mankind's spiritual aims, far from being something that Marx denied and abhorred, were the basis of his desire to transform society. Politics and moral values were merged in the process of mankind's self-realization. Only the political transformation of the world could lead to the original Christian vision of man living in harmony with himself, other men and nature, a veritable return to Eden.[21] Thus, Marx's vision was characterized by Messianic time, the notion that the Messianic idea could not be separated from the secular world in which it was rooted. Eric Fromm, who appreciated this characteristic in Marx, made the linkage between the prophetic tradition and Christian thought explicit: "What is common to prophetic, thirteenth-century Christian thought, eighteenth-century enlightenment and nineteenth-century socialism, is the idea that State (society) and spiritual values cannot be divorced from each other; that politics and moral values are indivisible."[22]

This book argues that the impulse toward the utopian has been pervasive throughout human history, and that without the vision of Utopia mankind would have had a far poorer history. Utopia has historically been the dream of the future without which the present would be unbearable. Thus, Utopia informed the Christian vision, at least when Christian ideas challenged or criticized secular authority. It was present during the Renaissance in Thomas More and among the Protestant rebels in central Germany, led by Thomas Munzer. It was present in the ideas of the *philosophes* in the eighteenth century. It inspired the ideas of the utopian socialists, among them Saint-Simon and Charles Fourier. And it formed the philosophical and spiritual underpinning of Marx. In the twentieth-century it helped inspire the political catechism of V. I. Lenin and Mao-Tse-tung, both of whom blended it with their idiosyncratic ideas of political revolution and revolutionary messianism, both of whom distorted the theoretical idealism of Utopia and developed their own versions of 'scientific socialism'.

In the twentieth-century Marx inspired another kind of utopian. Walter Benjamin believed that the utopian impulse could be seen in the cultural artifacts of humanity, often even disguised from the cultural workers themselves. But Benjamin believed that deep in the unconscious one could plumb the dreams, ambitions, hopes and drives toward the utopian. It was the aim of the culture worker to dislodge these deep dreams and incoherent longings, to discover what humanity itself really longed for and often stated in, consciously and unconsciously, its dream works and cultural expressions.

Ernst Bloch went even further. He believed that the utopian impulse pervaded all forms of popular culture, anything from fashion and travel to architecture and gardening. Everywhere and at all times mankind had hope eternal. It clung to the belief that it would recover the biblical Eden that it had lost. At the bottom of these wish-fantasies was the deep-rooted desire for justice and for human happiness which Bloch thought would never be fulfilled in modern capitalist and class divided society.

Herbert Marcuse perhaps did more than anyone to stress that mankind had an instinct for the utopian, which no amount of social and political repression could crush. He took Freud as his departure and turned him upside down. He urged mankind to unleash its instinctual energies. These would lead to the recovery of liberty and a liberated society. Mankind would turn work into pleasure, life would be something more than the unmitigated duty prescribed by Freud. Mankind, said Marcuse, should not repress itself for the good of civilization, for in fact repressed humanity is uncivilized and often barbaric precisely because it has allowed its own repression.

Andre Gorz also followed the road toward Utopia. He disclaimed against the classical proletariat because it was clearly not revolutionary. Yet he was still swept along by Marx's prophetic visions of utopian society. Influenced by the New Left, Gorz believed that socialism would fill the gaps in the cracks left by liberal democracy. He envisioned parallel societies in which socialism, as a superior ethical system of beliefs, would simply win out over an unjust industrial capitalism which he thought would crack open because of its inherent class divisions, income disparities and moral chaos.

Utopia can be practical or impractical, realistic or unrealistic. It can be liberating or authoritarian. It is not likely to disappear. Moreover, it is impossible to characterize it as purely fantastic and unrealizable, since it can and often has been quite realistic. At one time, the dream of the nineteenth-century to create democratic republics seemed remote at best; today it is taken for granted. Once universal suffrage was called hopeless dreaming. So were women's liberation and universal schooling and comprehensive health care. It is the argument of this book that Marx's utopianism stretched in two different directions, one the so-called scientific socialism and the other messianic utopianism; it was the latter version of Marx that edified and provided mankind with a glimpse of its liberated, utopian future. That his vision has been put to malignant use in Russia and China, as Marxism-Leninsm and Maoism, is not an indictment of a moral vision that asked for no more and no less than the completion of human hope.

Marx, then, like Fourier before him and Benjamin, Bloch, Marcuse and Gorz after him, was affected by a utopian impulse. His work was a rejection of the Fall and of human original sin. If mankind's essence was its fallen nature, then the impulse toward Utopia was futile. If the human animal was inherently sinful and weak, incapable of natural virtue without divine intervention and religion, then humanity could not be utopian. Thus, Marx had something in common with other utopians, the belief that mankind could scale the moral heights by using natural powers to see the light and to restore man to his command prior to the Fall.[23]

Jack Lawrence Luzkow
St. Louis, Missouri
March 15, 2006

Acknowledgments

My first debt of gratitude goes to my wife, Yelena Vardzigulova, for her tireless and unselfish support and encouragement that have sustained and guided me in bringing this book to print. Her intuitive understanding and deep knowledge of life and learning, her companionship and conversation across several continents have made my understanding of the world and its history much deeper and better. I am also deeply indebted to my friend and colleague John Rex Van Almsick, whose thirst for learning and understanding the past and contemporary events has often kept me abreast of developments and their implications in various parts of the world, especially Russia.

Several of my professors have played a significant role in shaping my education. If this book has any merit at all it is because of them. Roberto Giammanco, former professor of history at Wayne State University, was an extraordinary thinker and teacher. He introduced me to the world of art, literature and history and opened horizons and worlds that might otherwise have been closed to me forever. In many ways, my professional life has been a conversation with him. Theodore H. Von Laue played a similar role for me at Washington University, where in despair that his graduate students would never see the relevance of history, he adopted the *New York Times* as our textbook and graphically demonstrated the relevance of the past for the contemporary world. In so many ways his kind and gentle spirit, and his extraordinary intellect, made my education possible.

My former colleague and enduring friend, Ali Arshad, has contributed mightily to my understanding of the world, past and present. I am indebted to him for the long and sensitive conversations we have had over the years. His keen intellect has helped me avoid many pitfalls of misunderstanding. I cannot measure the innumerable ways in which he has helped me clarify and sharpen my ideas, many of which appear in this book. I am also indebted to my lifelong friend, Larry White, for his friendship and sharp intellect. Larry helped provide the impetus to write this book, although he would not have imagined it at the time.

I am also grateful to Patti Belcher of the University Press of America. She has helped me through the wilderness preparing the manuscript for publication and has helped prevent innumerable errors of commission and omission. Many thanks also to the librarians at Fontbonne University for checking references and offering bibliographic advice. I am especially indebted to John Baken and Julie Portman for helping me run down bibliographic details.

Part I
From Marxist Utopianism to Socialist Totalitarianism

Chapter 1
Karl Marx: The Last Great Utopian

Marxism was offered by founders and disciples alike as a 'science of history', but from its birth there was an element of utopian thinking, even in the hard-headed, calculating and 'scientific' Marx. Marx not only reprised prophetic and biblical expectations of the future, he incorporated, in secular dress, the Christological expectations of a final salvation. For Marx, history took on a kind of sacred shape, complete with ritual penitence and final redemption. In the end all was rectified, human alienation was transcended, the solitary human being was rescued in a reconstitution of the human community, purged of bourgeois sin, emancipated by deified, world-shattering and apocalyptic philosopher kings. For Marx, communism was not a state of affairs which would inevitably eclipse what he believed were the contradictions of capitalism, it was a superior moral ideal which was already present in the consciousness of the present and which stood as clarion call to the future. Thus, communism, Utopia, was morally desirable even before it could be proven to be historically inevitable. The ideal preceded the 'science'.

The ambiguity of the term Utopia has been present since its inception. Sir Thomas More's *Utopia*, published in 1516, distinguished between Utopia, meaning the 'good place', and outopia, which signified 'no place'. The distinction between the possible discovery of a 'good place' projected into the future, as against the futility of searching for 'no place', suggested an ironic – and perhaps hopeful – relationship between Utopia and history. Utopia, as fantasized future and projected wish, suggested a moral ideal that transcended historical reality and acted as critique of the historically imperfect present. A historical tension resulted from the dichotomy of the fantasized ideal and the actual historical present: "It is the consciousness of that lack of correspondence which gives utopian thought its sense of moral pathos and its historical ambiguity. Morally, Utopia may be 'the good place', but historically it may be 'no place'."[1]

Defenders of the 'good place' have always abounded. Both Max Weber and the Marxist German philosopher Ernst Bloch believed that Utopia generated a sense of hope for the future, producing a tension between the insufficient present and the desire to transform the world into the 'good place'. History itself was shaped by the tension between the possible and the given. Moreover, the striving for Utopia generated not only the dynamic of history, but historical optimism as well. When Utopia arrived it would mark the end of history.

It was the belief in a foreseeable and realizable utopian future, particularly the optimistic belief in the imminence of the 'good place', that inspired many Marxist and socialist critiques of 'really existing capitalism' and of the West in the twentieth-century. Herbert Marcuse, the doyen of radicalism in the 1960's, understood the revolutionary power of fantasy in the summoning of Utopia. In his synthesis of Marx and Freud, Marcuse believed that fantasy was a direct projection of the pleasure principle, Eros, of human desire and the search for happiness. Girded by Eros, fantasy overcomes repression in the present, it

> Restores imagination to its rights. As a fundamental, independent mental process, fantasy has a truth-value of its own – namely, the surmounting of the antagonistic human reality. Imagination envisions the reconciliation of the individual with the whole, of desire with realization, of happiness with reason.[2]

For Marcuse, fantasy was the bridge between the irrational capitalist present and the glorious future. Fantasy made human happiness possible by projecting a society in which human repression was no longer necessary or tolerable. Fantasy exposed illusion, and posed perfection. It was liberating because it offered an escape from the inequities of the capitalist West, an alternative to the suppression of human instincts. Utopia was hope, and hope sprung from the dream – the diurnal dream in Ernst Bloch's case, the dreamwork of the 'authentic' as he called it, an outline of a better world.

Utopia has had no lack of defenders in the modern age, though the aftermath of 1989 might have stinted its prospects. Historian Vincent Geoghegan has argued the case for the 'dreamwork of the authentic'. Utopia, he anticipated, was plausible, compelling and liberatory. Geoghegan looked forward to its "flagrant otherness":

> The classic utopia anticipates and criticizes. Its alternative fundamentally interrogates the present, piercing through existing societies' defensive mechanisms. . . . Its unabashed and flagrant otherness gives it a power that is lacking in other analytical devices. By playing fast and loose with time and space, logic and morality, and by thinking the unthinkable, a utopia asks the most embarrassing questions. Utopia can be seen as the good alternative, the outline of a better future, an 'ought' to the current 'is'. The possibility of such a future helps undermine the complacency and overcome the inertia of existing society by showing that it is neither eternal nor archetypal but merely one form among many.[3]

In the West, where Utopia has often been identified for more than a century with Marxism-Leninism, Stalinism and Maoism, Utopia has taken on pejorative connotations. It has been denigrated as the quest for the magic talisman, for 'no place', an unrealizable fantasy and therefore useless to strive for, an illusion at best. And, at the worst, not just hopeless but dangerous because of the fanaticism often instilled in its pursuit. Among the pejorative terms attached to Utopia by its enemies in the West have been 'unrealistic', 'irrational', 'naive', 'unscientific', 'escapist', 'messianic' and 'elitist'. For critics, the pursuit of Utopia inevitably descends into totalitarianism, not only because it is irrational and escapist, but because of its inherent elitism. Justified by faith alone, Utopia must be administered by the 'trustees of writ and of posterity'. By combining imaginary perfection, personal asceticism and historical transcendence, Utopia has always – inevitably – ended in political totalitarianism.

Norman Cohn, not a true believer in Utopia, argued in his pathfinding book, *The Pursuit of the Millennium*, that the revolutionary messianism of the Middle Ages can been directly linked to most revolutionary upheavals since the seventeenth-century. Utopia was the prologue to the revolutionary disturbances of the twentieth-century and to modern totalitarianism.[4] Adam Ulam, once a fellow traveler of Utopia, asserted that "the utopian character of much of socialist thinking represented . . . a kind of rearguard action which withdrawing radicalism conducted against the triumphant march of industrialism and liberalism"[5] in the West. The utopian 'menace' was withdrawing to areas where modern industrialism and liberalism had yet to triumph. Thus, the utopian tradition withdrew eastward as the West became more prosperous, liberal and democratic. In Ulam's rhetorical conclusion he wondered whether "all utopian thinking and much of socialist thought [is] but a critique of the values and traditions of the West?"[6] Twentieth-century radicalism occurred in non-Western areas only because industrialism and liberalism had yet to triumph there.

One of the most vehement critics of the modern utopian tradition, historian J. L. Talmon, traced a straight line from Robespierre to Lenin, Stalin and Mao, a straight line from the French Revolution to totalitarian democracy and modern communism. The 'messianic revolutionaries', the appellation Talmon gave to the Jacobins and the Babouvist communists of the French Revolution, claimed to be "the trustees of posterity," and as such they thought themselves merited "in employing whatever means were necessary for the inauguration of the Millennium: subversion when in opposition, terror when in power."[7] The revolutionary Jacobin defense of the rights of the individual was originally enforced to help inaugurate the millennium. The collectivist utopias that matured later as socialism and Marxism in the nineteenth and twentieth-centuries issued from the same premises as Jacobin individualism:

> Extreme individualism thus came full circle in a collective pattern of coercion before the eighteenth-century was out. All the elements and patterns of totalitarian democracy emerged or were outlined before the turn of the century. From this point of view the contribution of the nineteenth-century was the replacement of the individualist premises of totalitarian democracy by frankly collectivist theories. The natural order, which was originally conceived as a scheme as absolute justice imminent in the general will of society and expressed in the decisions of the sovereign people, was replaced by an exclusive doctrine regarded as objectively and scientifically true, and as offering a coherent and complete answer to all problems. . . . Whether approved by all, by a majority, or by a minority, the doctrine claimed absolute validity.[8]

Talmon concluded that the two deepest yearnings of humanity, the desire for salvation and the love of freedom, were incompatible. A messianic creed that had pretensions to transcendent universalism and that claimed to be salvationist would eventually resort to coercion. Messianic creeds were by their very nature totalitarian. Salvationist creeds were born of the noblest impulses, but they were exclusive, defensive and therefore constantly in peril, only able to retain power by recourse to coercion and terror.[9] Ultimately, all utopian thought tended to be totalitarian because its claims to transcendence divided society into two communities, those with the unchallengeable knowledge of the creed of perfection and those who remained in ignorance of the holy truth, there were only the masters and the sycophants.

Talmon's arguments were conceived in the framework of the Cold War but they proved prescient. There was a relation between the repression of the communist regimes of Eastern Europe – and China – and Marxist-Leninist utopian eschatology, replete with its promise of an egalitarian future. Marxism-Leninism, in the hands of its practitioners in the twentieth-century, was a veritable sociopolical religion, a theologico-historical system that not only claimed to be morally justified and superior in terms of ultimate goals, but which also was touted by true believers as a virtual annunciation that was historically inevitable and morally irreproachable. Here was rhetoric in which – it was believed – the scientific understanding of history coincided with apocalyptic expectations for the future.[10]

The belief that Utopia was inherently totalitarian eventually became commonplace in the West, not only due to the Cold War, but especially because of the utopian, anti-Western bias of Marxist-Leninist ideology which flourished in many parts of the Third World well into the 1980's. The congruity between Marxism-Leninism and anti-Westernization, both expressions of anti-imperialist and anti-modernist sentiments of societies which saw themselves as unwitting victims of the West, made the adoption of a messianic ideology, with its utopian eschatology, popular vehicles in the combat for the 'good place'. This was not simply a justification for the holding of political power on behalf of some desirable goal, it was an expression of true belief, an exaltation and anticipation of an all-embracing framework for the movement of History. History became religious dramaturgy, a dialectical struggle of good and evil, a metaphysical drama.

Of course there has been no lack of defenders of Utopia. The spectrum runs from true believers to earnest philosophers and 'scientific' historians. Historian Michael Meisner, for one, has argued that Western scholars have erred in associating all forms of radicalism and totalitarianism with utopian thought. Utopia and totalitarianism, he argues, are neither synonymous nor necessarily logically connected in historical practice. The Kuomintang regime in China, which ruled prior to the Communist victory in 1949, had no utopian ideology, nor even a program for social reform, though it was emphatically totalitarian. The Soviet Union became totalitarian only after the decline of the radical utopianism of Lenin that had inspired the Bolshevik revolution. In China the eclipse of Mao's radical utopianism occurred in the late 1960's, but China remained, well after the end of utopian experimentation, a society that many in the West still characterized as totalitarian. Utopia, Maurice Meisner admonished, could not be faulted if it offered hope for the future and the promise of historical progress.[11]

The fault lay with the brutalization of Utopia, the ritualization of utopian goals and hopes, the metamorphosis of the symbols of emancipation into the cruelties of ritualized slogans and the manipulations of the bureaucratic-totalitarian state. George Lichtheim, who knew the pitfalls and the false glitter of Utopia all too well, also defended it: "Civilizations are founded upon utopian and messianic promises that are never fulfilled, but without which there would have been no progress."[12]

Despite these more auspicious renderings of Utopia, the twentieth-century edition of communist Utopia was more akin to the bureaucratic-totalitarian variety than to the innocuous version of Thomas More's *Utopia* or the modern, purely descriptive literary landscapes of the imagination. The Soviet and the Chinese utopian visions of communism proved unrealizable. Neither found a way to separate the theory of perfection from its imperfect historical edition, or to build paradise without men who were themselves imperfect. Both Marxism-Leninism and Maoism were inherently flawed. They represented movements permeated by millenarianism and the prophetic notion of their inevitability and infallibility; the belief they were modern revelations justified by their perfect faith and wisdom, superior to the common run of humanity on whose behalf they were, hypothetically, acting.

Although modern revolutionary movements inspired by Marxism-Leninism and Maoism have been avowedly secular, they have been permeated by messianic and millenarian expectation, not unlike the Christian-inspired revolutionary peasant movements of medieval Europe. The millenarian movement inspired by Thomas Munzer in sixteenth-century Germany, for example, has much in common with its more secular-minded modern counterparts. Widely admired by *fin-de-siecle* German Communists like Karl Kautsky, it was messianic, religious and social in tone, inspiration and substance. Kautsky recognized the similarities between Munzer and Marx in ways that his successors chose to ignore or deny. Both had millenarian expectations, aimed at transcendence and traced their inspiration to trans-historical goals. Both employed revolutionary fervor to rant against the authority of a foreign power or the rule, and the ideology, of a superordinate class.[13] And both prescribed a revolutionary activism, whether in Munzer's sixteenth-century or Marx's nineteenth-century Germany.

Mao Tse-tung had a similar prescription for twentieth-century China. Here a future millennium was imminent, Utopia was under construction. Like Lenin before him, Mao began with millenarian preachments and egalitarian hopes, with the expectation of Utopia, but ended by constructing the edifice of dystopian totalitarianism. If radical utopian movements in the twentieth-century began as revolutionary opposition movements based on egalitarian inspiration and millenarian expectation, inevitably they became ritualized and deradicalized once they attained power.

Marx and Utopianism

Not only was utopian speculation not absent from Marxist debates in the nine-teenth-century, it constituted one of its most enduring legacies, so much so, that Marx himself has been categorized in modern debate as the progenitor of the anti-utopian utopian tradition par excellence. The parlous language employed by Marx's successors still conjured a religious imagery that was redolent with apocalyptic expectations. Marx, of course, claimed that his sober hopes for his socialist project of the future were based on a science of history and ranted about the pejorative connotations he normally associated with the term 'utopian'. Both Marx and Engels spared no effort in driving a distinction between their 'scientific socialism' and the 'utopian socialism' of thinkers like St. Simon and Charles Fourier whose a-historical theories, as Marx put it, made it unlikely that they would discover the link between the rejected present and the visions of their imagined utopias. Utopia became a highly charged term that served as a convenient label for the opposition. All those who did not employ the 'scientific' terms of Marx and Engels were relegated to the philosophical scrapheap of utopians, the original sin to orthodox Marxists. There was to be no future specu-lation according to the keepers of script. Marx's analysis was an anatomy of the contradictions of capital, so it was argued, not a predictive 'science' based on speculation about a future which was better consigned to dreamscapes than to the serious work of analyzing the anatomy of the present.

Marx's own work did nothing to discourage such conclusions. Scientific so-cialism, the notion that history was a social science, seemed to be at the core of his thought. One could find in Marx the assertion of a relationship between eco-nomic progress and human emancipation, between the cumulative logic of the natural and historical sciences and the progression of the idea of human free-dom, between the advance of science and technology and the advent of commu-nist man. Marx's work was sprinkled with the notion that the scientific under-standing of nature could be applied to a science of man and of society, the laws of the natural sciences to an understanding of the social behavior of human be-ings. Moreover, Marx believed that human consciousness had a direct relation to technological progress, and he thought he had a historical explanation for how this worked. Industrial capitalism, because of its social and economic inequities, created an alienated class whose self-interest coincided with the creation and building of socialism. Industrial capitalism contained within itself its own nega-tion, the working-class. Marx was confident that the working-class would de-velop a socialist consciousness, the inevitable result of its own exploitation. So-cialism, through a dialectical unfolding of history based on the conflict between labor and capital, seemed a foregone conclusion. The laws of capital were self-evident, the laws of history as predictable as the natural sciences.

Yet, Marx generally reached such conclusions only in his more polemical works, when he intended that his writing should make a contribution to the emergence of a socialist consciousness. Marx understood that there was no his-torical necessity, no inevitable historical endpoint. Human consciousness was not bound by natural laws. Human beings were not predictable, nor did they behave according to any prescribed or presumed logic of capital, or any cumulative logic of history. Workers were not inevitably driven toward socialism, nor were they inherently revolutionary. Marx's historical works, such as *Class Struggles in France*, as well as his utopian writings in *Economic and Philosophical Manuscripts of 1844* and *Grundrisse*, made this abundantly clear.

Neither Marx and Engels, no matter how much they protested the anticipation of Utopia, were able to repress the urge to concoct something like the edifice of the future. Marx's work in the 1850's and 1860's, especially in the *Grundrisse* and the *Critique of Political Economy*, was a fascinating glimpse into the future after the abolition of capitalism. It bore traces of Marx's earlier quest to end human alienation, explored in *The Economic and Philosophic Manuscripts of 1844*, and prefigured Marx's anticipation of the 'end of history'. There emerged a kind of schizophrenia between denying that the future could be known or prefigured in a 'scientific' sense, and the need for an illumined apocalypse that informed the present as the object of human liberation. There was an instinct in Marx and Engels for an orientation toward the future, and that instinct was not based on 'science' so much as a passionate drive toward and biblical anticipation of earthly justice.

Thus, it was as a visionary with an apocalyptic bent that Marx fitted himself into the nineteenth-century notion of progress, following in the footsteps of the German philosopher G.W.F. Hegel and strangely mirroring the work of Charles Darwin in the natural sciences. Moreover, embracing biblical and apocalyptic expectation, Marx fulminated against the West in a language that was in the tradition of prophetic hope and Christian eschatology. It was not science but human redemption, not the logic of history but utopian millenarianism that provided the impetus for Marx's theoretical work. Ironically, the thundering, atheistic Marx retained a unifying scatological vision that bore a distinct resemblance to Saint Augustine and the early Catholic Church. History was the evolution of human hope, a narrative of universal redemption, a drama of good and evil, an existential struggle in the pursuit of personal salvation.

In the nineteenth-century G. F. W. Hegel provided much of the theoretical underpinning for Marx's utopian idealism. For Hegel, History was an evolution of ideas, the movement of human self-consciousness, reflexive and purposive, ultimately realizing its final goal and thereby attaining to the mind of God. History was the realization and completion of the idea of human freedom that, in Hegel's ponderous terminology, meant the convergence of human self-consciousness and the Absolute – or the mind of God.

Hegel rejected the Augustinian interpretation of History, for while it pointed to the 'end of history' and contained a soteriology that pointed to a sacred history, it also implied a historical dualism in the parallel communities of the sacred and the profane. It was Hegel's quest to unify the two realms, to resolve the problems of human emancipation and historical necessity, to demonstrate that human freedom was realized within the secular, mundane process of History itself. For Hegel human freedom arrived in the form of the 'liberating' French Revolution. The French Revolution, with its proclamation of the "Rights of Man and Citizen," its assertion of the absolute rights and freedoms of humanity and its insistence on constitutionally defined liberties, seemed to prove, in Hegel's mind, that history was dialectically unfolding toward the realization of human freedom, the endpoint of human history.

The evolution of the French Revolution into Napoleonic despotism did not dissuade Hegel from his basic schema of History. But whereas he had formerly built on the adulation of Napoleon, the world-liberator who unconsciously acted out his 'world-liberating' role, that role now fell to the Prussian state on which Hegel urged, in his riper years, resistance to Napoleonic – and French – despotism. Paradoxically, the spirit of liberty would now come to be realized – and defended – by the Prussian state, an unlikely conclusion for a thinker who had searched for a universal history based on the unity of mankind, but no odder than the belief that the liberal program of the French Revolution represented the ultimate in achieving a universal human emancipation. Still, Hegel never lost his fundamental faith that the grand narrative of History was a dialectical unfolding of Mind, which conferred a leitmotif of intelligibility and unity on the historical process, a process in which historical necessity and human freedom were finally resolved and merged.[14]

Marx demurred against Hegel's sense of metahistory, but he remained indebted to the philosophical master. If Christian (divine) intervention and ineluctable imperial decay were the motors of historical advance to Augustine, and the evolution of Mind or Spirit accounted for historical evolution and progress for Hegel, for Marx it was the industrial proletariat, the community of the dispossessed, that would play the role of Spirit. But there was an important distinction in Marx's mind. History was not composed of moments in the progression of Mind up to the penultimate realization of human self-consciousness. Rather History – still seen as grand narrative by Marx – was moved along by class struggles. Even here, however, Marx remained the idealist as well as the materialist. For class struggles were not only about economic issues, they were about grand moral imperatives as well. In Marx's lexicon this suggested that the development of consciousness included the evolution of Mind becoming self-conscious of its human possibilities. The development of human consciousness did not take place in a historical vacuum but in a struggle over material advantage. Human consciousness developed in the context of wealth and power. For Marx this suggested a primordial conflict between the capitalist employers who controlled the means of production and their 'dispossessed' employees who had to sell their labor-power to survive. History became a dramaturgy between these two forces of good and evil in which Marx's elect were predestined to destroy the forces of evil. History was above all rectification. The industrial proletariat embodied the principle of moral rectitude, it would sweep away the money changers in the temple.

Both Marx and Hegel accepted that History was linear and intelligible, either because of the progression of Spirit in Hegel or because of a prophetic moral vision in Marx. Both imagined that History had a higher purpose that would be fulfilled at the 'end of history', either as Hegel's Absolute Idea or as Marx's communist Utopia.

Ironically, then, for both Hegel and Marx, it was the moral vision of the future that moved History. For Marx, science became the handmaiden of vision. His projected future was clearly a moral vision first, his point of departure a kind of existential humanism whose purpose was to redeem mankind by recovering man before the Fall. Thus, Marx thought communism the only goal worthy of mankind, the ultimate humanization of humanity. Marx the social scientist was first and foremost the communist utopian. Marx, full of hopes and dreams, became the thundering biblical prophet hoping to restore the Golden Age, a utopian striving to overcome the alienation of humanity divided against itself.

Oddly enough, Marx, a critic of nineteenth-century utopian socialists St. Simon and Charles Fourier because of their lack of historical 'realism', developed a consummate utopianism that was strangely at odds with his hypothetical science. He was certain that the proletariat would develop a revolutionary socialist consciousness. Once the revolution succeeded there would be a post-revolutionary convulsion in which the state would wither away. Humanity would be redeemed; it would leap out of the realm of necessity into the realm of freedom. The fully human society would be born.

Marx has been criticized for anticipating and hoping for Utopia so zealously. The criticism has been used not only to denigrate his science, but to attack his utopianism as well. A virtual army has attacked Marx's thinking as fantastic, unrealistic, delusionary, even dangerous because of the apocalyptic hopes that Marx raised.[15]

Yet, Marx was perhaps the last and the greatest of all utopians, not because he thought and wrote in the realm of the fantastic, but because he continued a tradition of critical utopian thinking that presupposed an ideal of freedom as the foundation of a truly human society. Communism, to Marx, meant a society without alienation, a society that ended the prehistory of mankind and unleashed it so it could freely determine its own history. Communism was the condition in which humanity freed itself from the curse of economic scarcity by putting the vastly expanded productive forces under the collective control of society. Set free from the realm of necessity, individuals could at last develop their full individuality. Moreover, free men were like natural artists, for unlike the animal kingdom, unalienated "man constructs in accordance with the laws of beauty."[16] Thus, Marx's communism was a kind of humanism, a utopian hope and projection toward a harmonious future; a future, moreover, in which mankind's collective happiness became the objective of its own history. In the *Economic and Philosophical Manuscripts of 1844,* Marx made this explicit:

> *Communism* is the *positive* abolition of *private property*, of *human self-alienation*, and thus the real *appropriation of human* nature through and for man. It is, therefore, the return of man himself as a social, i.e. really human, being, a complete and conscious return which assimilates all the wealth of previous development. Communism as a fully developed naturalism is humanism and as a fully developed humanism is naturalism. It is the *definitive* resolution of the antagonism between man and nature, and between man and man. It is the true solution of the conflict between existence and essence, between objectification and self-affirmation, between freedom and necessity, between individual

and species. It is the solution of the riddle of history and knows itself to be this solution.[17]

This kind of prophetic wishing and apocalyptic expectation was not limited to Marx's early work. He had a similar description of communist Utopia at the end of the third volume of *Capital*:

> The realm of freedom only begins, in fact, where that labor which is determined by need and external purposes ceases; it is therefore, by its very nature, outside the sphere of material production proper. Just as the savage must wrestle with Nature in order to satisfy his wants, to maintain and reproduce his life, so also must civilized man, and he must do it in all forms of society and under any possible mode of production. With his development the realm of natural necessity expands, because his wants increase; but at the same time the forces of production, by which these wants are satisfied, also increase. Freedom in this field cannot consist of anything else but the fact that socialized mankind, the associated producers, regulate their interchange with Nature rationally, bring it under their common control, instead of being ruled by it as by some blind power, and accomplish their task with the least expenditure of energy and under such conditions as are proper and worthy for human beings. Nevertheless, this always remains a realm of necessity. Beyond it begins that development of human potentiality for its own sake, the true realm of freedom, which however can only flourish upon that realm of necessity as its basis. The shortening of the working day is its fundamental pre-requisite.[18]

This prophetic note, rooted in Marx's moral ideal of a communist future, envisioned a liberated mankind no longer bound by the realm of necessity. Thus, by expanding free time, the realm of freedom, the individual could develop fully his species-being. In this sense Marx viewed human history in much the same way as Hegel, history was the growth of humankind through self-consciousness and self-mastery. As man developed historically, technologically, intellectually and culturally, as he developed self-consciousness, he understood his potential as a rational, creative, free and autonomous being.

In this way Marx came to understand communist Utopia as the precondition that allowed mankind to see its potential. It was the condition of developed self-consciousness in which self-mastery replaced the realm of necessity. It was the historical point at which humanity understood that the division of labor no longer corresponded to necessity, the point at which mankind no longer needed to be divided between manual and intellectual workers, between town and country, between a bourgeoisie and a working class. Ironically, it was here that Christian theology and Marxist philosophy coincided. Marx's vision of communism as emancipated and fulfilled humanity, as the point where humanity overcame the division of labor, bore an uncanny resemblance to the Christian notion of overcoming Original Sin and the Fall. Once the original rupture created by Original Sin was overcome by accepting Christ, humanity was restored to itself; the break between the divine and the human was reconciled in the fulfillment of the human species. In Marx, once the original sin of capitalism and the division of labor were overcome, mankind could at last realize its potential and get beyond the mundane realm of material production.[19] Man was not a producer alone, Marx admonished, but a being of multiple creative dimensions:

> As soon as labor is distributed, each man has a particular, exclusive sphere of activity, which is forced upon him and from which he cannot escape. He is a hunter, a fisherman, a shepherd, or a critical critic, and must remain so if he does not want to lose his means of livelihood; while in communist society, where nobody has one exclusive sphere of activity but each can become accomplished in any branch he desires, society regulates the general production and thus makes it possible for me to do one thing today and another tomorrow, to hunt in the morning, fish in the afternoon, rear cattle in the evening, criticize after dinner, just as I have a mind, without ever becoming hunter, fisherman, shepherd or ctitic.[20]

In Marx's future communist Utopia, socially necessary work and free creative activity would find their synthesis in communal society. A common humanity would emerge because the scope of alienated and necessary labor would be compressed, while the enlargement of free creative activity would mean the full florescence of the individual. In one of Marx's most celebrated visions, he spoke rhapsodically of the communist future in explicitly utopian terms:

> Suppose we had produced things as human beings: in his production each of us would have twice affirmed himself and the other. (1) In my production I would have objectified my individuality and its particularity, and in the course of the activity I would have enjoyed an individual life: in viewing the object I would have experienced the individual joy of knowing my personality as an objective, sensuously perceptible and indubitable power. (2) In your satisfaction and your use of my product I would have had the direct and conscious satisfaction that my work satisfied a human need . . . (3) I would have been the mediator between you and the species and you would have experienced me as a reintegration of your own nature and a necessary part of yourself; I would have been affirmed in your thought as well as your love. (4) In my individual life I would have directly created your life; in my individual activity I would have immediately confirmed and realized my true human and social nature. . . . My labor would be a free manifestation of life and an enjoyment of life. Our productions would be so many mirrors reflecting our nature.[21]

In the *Grundrisse*, Marx's sketch of *Capital*, he enlarged on this theme, arguing that the realm of freedom could grow from within the realm of necessity. With the advance of technology, necessary direct labor was no longer the basis of production or the source of wealth. As a result, man was set free to round himself as an individual. The automation of production meant that the work process no longer stood above him as something inhuman and alien to which he had to adjust. On the contrary, automation meant that mankind could engage creatively with a work process that it now controlled. The individual, rather than being reduced to an hourly wage or exchange value, could transform himself into a genuinely human being even within the realm of necessity. Thus, Marx was describing a perfectly utopian condition in which compulsion of any kind was absent from society. On the contrary, humanity had become its own goal in history; it was free and self-determining. Society could become genuinely social and free because individuals could become collaborators in satisfying their mutual needs, freed from the constraint of meeting only the needs of the few at the expense of the many. And in this freedom Marx saw the full development of the artistic, creative individual:

> Labor no longer appears so much to be included within the production process; rather the human being comes to relate more as watchman and regulator to the production process itself. . . . He steps to the side of the production process instead of being its chief actor. In this transformation, it is neither the direct human labor he himself performs, nor the time during which he works, but rather the appropriation of his own general productive power, his understanding of nature and his mastery over it by virtue of his presence as a social body – it is, in a word, the development of the social individual which appears as the great foundation-stone of production and wealth. . . . As soon as labor in the direct form has ceased to be the great well-spring of wealth, labor time ceases and must cease to be its measure, and hence exchange value must cease to be the measure of use value.[22]

This was not the endpoint of Marx's argument, however. It was not enough to humanize work or to share its rewards equally or to harness nature to meet human needs. Marx's utopian vision went much further. He envisioned the transformation of human nature itself. In resolving the contradictions between man and man, between man and nature and man and society, which Marx believed would occur with the adventism of communism, human nature could become genuinely social and society could become genuinely human.[23] Communism, therefore, in Marx's estimation, implied an almost mystical togetherness in which individuals were in harmony with each other because everything that alienated them before had been abolished. For Marx, man was instinctually a social being, a human being who would once again become fully human by discovering his real social nature, which was none other than his natural association with other men such as it had once been prior to the institution of private property.[24]

Chapter 2
From Marxism-Leninism to Stalinist Utopianism

In Karl Marx there was a kind of tension between the laws of scientific socialism and a utopian longing for a socialist end of history, between a science of
history and a prophetic hope based on a moral and ethical ideal. Marx's work
was schizophrenic, driven by a logic of history that culminated, inevitably, in
the necessity of communism, and a prophetic longing for the moral ideal of Utopia.

Following Marx, it was the German Marxist, Karl Kautsky, who embodied
this political schizophrenia most perfectly. On the one hand he invoked the laws
of socialist science which specified the 'necessity' and the 'inevitability' of socialism, and on the other hand he doubted Marx's confidence in the proletariat's
world-historical mission to establish socialism. Kautsky was neither willing to
leave the future to the proletariat nor to rely on a science that did without goals,
but a major theoretical dilemma occurred when Kautsky described socialism,
and the class struggle, as separate developments which arose simultaneously but
did not issue out of one another. Kautsky surmised that:

> Modern socialist consciousness can arise only on the basis of profound scien-
> tific knowledge. . . . The vehicle of science is not the proletariat, but the bour-
> geois intelligentsia: it was in the minds of the individual members of this stra-
> tum that modern socialism originated, and it was they who communicated it to
> the more intellectually developed proletarians who in turn, introduce it into the
> proletarian class struggle where conditions allow that to be done. This socialist
> consciousness is something introduced into the proletarian class struggle from
> without and not something that arose within it spontaneously.[1]

Kautsky added that "what the workers ask of the academics is knowledge of the
goal,"[2] as though the workers were neither capable of identifying goals nor providing the necessary leadership to achieve them.

Espousing the need for intellectuals to identify socialist goals, while simultaneously disavowing recipes for the future, must have been a difficult balancing
act for Kautsky. Moreover, Kautsky's fears and premonitions had already been

anticipated by Marx who had argued against elitist vanguard theories in the *Theses on Feurbach* because they tend to "divide society into two parts one of which is superior to society."[3]

Marx's admonitions notwithstanding, Kautsky retained his belief that socialist goals would have to be communicated 'downwards' by intellectuals to their subalterns, the proletariat. Yet there remained persistent doubts about raising an intelligentsia above the rest of society, the very kind of doubts that Kautsky himself raised on the occasion of the Bolshevik Revolution. It is as if the Revolution of 1917 scored all of Kautsky's suspicions, while he intuitively resisted what appeared a providential, authoritarian Utopia, designed by a class of intellectual betters for their 'acknowledged' inferiors.

For a variey of reasons Kautsky applied the term 'utopian' to the Bolshevik Revolution, intending his meaning to be in the most unflattering and pejorative terms.[4] He remained the orthodox Marxist in asserting that the Bolshevik revolution was utopian because it was premature and built on an inadequate base. True socialism, he admonished, could only be built on the basis of an advanced working class, as in the West, where a majority of the population was working-class. In the Russian Empire, where the working-class was small, undeveloped, pre-Marxist and hardly revolutionary, he theorized that it would not be possible to build socialism unless it was led by a Bolshevik faction that claimed to represent a movement still in embryonic form. The Bolsheviks' natural constituency would be a proletariat that they would have to create and whose ideal interest, in the interim, they would represent. But this meant inevitably that Bolshevism would serve a narrow Party interest rather than issuing from society's – and history's – own movement, and that the Bolsheviks would have to use dictatorial methods in order to preserve their vision and their power against the realities and claims of society. The problem of pure utopianism, opined Kautsky, could be distilled to the following insight:

> The idea that the only task of a socialist government is to put socialism into practice is not a Marxist but a pre-Marxist, Utopian ideal. It represents socialism as an ideal picture of a perfect society. Like all ideal conceptions, its nature is very simple. Once it has been thought out, only the necessary power is required to realize this ideal everywhere and under all circumstances. When power does not produce this result immediately, it is due to treachery or cowardice. The only task of a socialist government is to put into practice the ideal conception of socialism. The more absolute its power, the sooner will it be able to do so.[5]

Kautsky could only conclude that Utopia, as an ideal which transcended actual people and insisted on measuring them as they ought to be when they were perfected, was inherently totalitarian, all the more so when such visionary expectations were applied by one part of the population to another.

Kautsky's nightmare vision of Russia's future turned out to be prescient. His belief that intellectuals would play a vanguard role would not be lost on Lenin who reproduced the idea in his 1902 treatise, *What is to Be Done?* For Lenin the idea of an intellectual vanguard was simply tacked onto a science of society and history, although he was aware also of Kautsky's reluctance to "invent recipes for the kitchens of the future."[6] In Lenin, substitutionism began early, a result of the backwardness of Russia perhaps, but also of the scientific socialism that Lenin insisted was already implied by the work of Marx. Thus, for society and the state Lenin substituted the Party, and for the Party, driven by ideology and the need to adapt that ideology to the conditions of backward Russia, Lenin substituted himself.[7]

In both Lenin and Stalin, the Communist Party controlled by the Bolsheviks was held to embody a superior scientific insight. It was designated a vanguard above the common run of mankind, replacing the actual desires of human beings with the prophetic, infallible visions of the Party. The Party's superior 'science', they argued, gave it the right to play the leading role in the revolution and afterwards. The state, which was controlled by the Party, embodied a higher truth that was unchallengeable.

Here was the foundation of Stalinism itself, the basis of a Utopia that arrogated to itself the right of final judgment and which made of the state a rough equivalent of the City of God, a City that was to be led by the divinely righteous political 'elect'. *The History of the Communist Party of the Soviet Union*, which bore the imprimatur of Stalin when it was published in 1939, canonized the state, defended a vanguard role for the Party, and denied any role for the spontaneous movement of the working-class. It explicitly endorsed a "socialist ideology [which] arises not from the spontaneous movement, but from science."[8] Socialist consciousness had to be imparted from outside the actual movement of the working-class. It had, therefore, to be injected as though the workers had to be inoculated before they could enter the kingdom of human perfection.

Ultimately, 'science', as Kautsky had feared, produced a single truth, an irreproachable truth, a truth beyond all mediations, the Truth. And if there is one truth, then society must be guided by a single vision, guided, that is, by the custodian of that universal truth. Again the *History* completed the creed that accompanied the ascendancy toward these higher certainties. After asserting that true knowledge was "based on the laws of development of nature," and that such laws had the "validity of objective truth" and were knowable as such, it followed that "the laws of development of society" were authentic and had "the validity of objective truths." After mastering the 'science' of the history of society there arrived the possibility "of making use of the laws of development of society for practical purposes."[9] The only question that remained was: who should make the applications of "objective truths." The *History* did not delay long in providing the answers:

> The Party of the proletariat should not guide itself in its practical activities by casual motives, but by the laws of development of society and by practical deductions from these laws. Hence Socialism is converted from a dream of a better future for humanity into a science.[10]

He who mastered the science, he alone possessed the key to the future and had foreknowledge of the future Utopia. That very person was the 'master theoretician', Stalin himself. The scaffolding was now in place, as it had been since

Stalin conquered power in the late 1920's. The *History* was an official endorsement of what Stalin had been building since the early 1930's. It was Stalinist science building a 'better future for humanity'. Utopia legitimized science, but science conferred on Utopia a mantel of inevitability as well as an aura of legitimacy.

Just as Bolshevik power was consolidated in the Soviet Union after the Revolution, first under Lenin and then under Stalin in the late 1920's, so did the 'Russian viewpoint' come to dominate the Communist International (Comintern) after it was established in March 1919. The Bolsheviks felt justified in superimposing the 'Russian viewpoint'. Did not the survival of the Revolution depend on its extension to the West? And there were many in the West, convinced communists and fellow travelers, eager to accept the lead of the Russian Bolsheviks.

However, after revolutions had failed to materialize, or to succeed elsewhere, the Comintern sounded a retreat in 1921. The new global situation demanded peaceful coexistence with the Western capitalist states. Obtaining Western capital had become more important than either political orthodoxy or revolutionary purity.[11] The export of Utopia would await another day, it had first be built in Russia. The preference for coexistence coincided with the imperative of reigning in the communist parties in the West; the better to secure the primacy of Soviet interests by insuring that no communist parties in the West would be too independent.

This mirrored Bolshevik domestic policy in 1921 when Lenin sought to manage growing internal discord – the Kronstadt rebellion and widespread peasant dissatisfaction forced a revision in theory and practice – by adopting a ban on all factions within the Party. The measure banning factions was formally adopted at the Tenth Party Congress in 1921. Although intended by Lenin as an interim emergency measure, the principle became a permanent feature of Soviet life. From here the rest seemed an inexorable logic. In 1927 Stalin used the ban on factions to expel Trotsky from the Party. Two years later he expelled Trotsky from the country. Looking backward Trotsky summed up Stalin's meteoric rise to power. "Nowadays," noted Trotsky, "all ideas and actions of man are divided into two categories: absolutely correct ones, that is, those that comprise the 'general line', and absolutely false ones, that is, deviations from this line. This, of course, does not prevent what is absolutely correct today from being declared absolutely false tomorrow."[12]

The Stalinization of the Soviet state, which was already being accomplished by 1930, was matched by the Sovietization of the Comintern. Just as 'unorthodox' opinion disappeared from the tribunes of the Party, so did it disappear from the debates of the Comintern, especially after the Sixth Congress in July 1928. Between 1928 and 1934, under direct orders from Moscow, communist parties abroad were advised to avoid coalitions with other political parties. For Stalin the explanation was simple: communists were engaged in class struggle abroad and at home, there could be no compromise with the class enemy, no coalitions with the devil. This was partially a political convenience; Stalin took the opportunity in the late 1920's to designate even potential political opponents at home as class enemies. But he also noted that the West, in the throes of depression and anarchy, did not look so invincible after all. Perhaps it was time to renew and promote class struggle in the West.

But, as Trotsky had indicated, what was absolutely correct in 1928 was absolutely false in 1934. Stalin was forced to change his mind about Comintern strategy and about his diplomatic policies toward Europe. Hitler and Mussolini made it necessary for him to support a Popular Front strategy in which communists everywhere were urged to enter into coalitions with any 'progressive' groups or parties, the better to resist further fascist victories. Cooperation, not class war, was the new marching order for communists abroad. The capitalist powers France and Britain, by force of circumstance, had become 'friends' in the new geopolitics of Europe. But the threat posed by Hitler and the increased danger of war because of Nazi Germany meant that dissent within the Party would be tolerated less than ever. The Party was certain to be engaged in a hard fight in the future against a powerful enemy. Hence the Party had to maintain an 'iron discipline', everything had to be sacrificed for the sake of unity. There must be no 'tendencies', for tendencies led to factions and factions led to splits. International crisis required a change in strategy, but it also served as pretext for Stalin to take ideological uniformity and conformity to new heights, to exact an unprecedented servility in the name of both self-defense and the self-proclaimed nobility of communist goals.

By the Seventh Congress of the Comintern in 1935, Stalin's hold over the Comintern was virtually complete and unchallengeable. He had already removed Trotsky and Zinoviev from the citadel of power. His main rival, Sergei Kirov, had been assassinated on 1 December 1934. In the midst of the very real threat from fascism, stern taskmaster Stalin began to spin new webs to solidify his total authority and to establish total mastery over the Party, the better to galvanize the nation for the arduous tasks that lay ahead. Now it was not enough for a minority to accept the will of a majority. There was to be no minority. If opinions diverged, it was not enough to bow to the opinion of the majority. It was necessary to *think* like the majority. The Bulgarian, George Dimitrov, was able to complete the final epigraph to this diet of ideological cordon bleu. All enemies of the people were to take heed, "*the first and highest law of Bolshevism* was the unity of the Party . . . [dissenters against the Party were the] enemies of the people."[13] In the new Stalinist order he, Stalin, would do all the thinking. The principal duty of the revolutionary, to help change the world and to realize communism, was not to think. The lead of the 'master theoretician' was sufficient.

By 1936 Stalinist substitutionism was virtually complete. The Party, somehow, mystically embodied the will of the people. The master theoretician was now the mystical embodiment of the Party. Yugoslav anti-Stalinist, M. Djilas, characterized the system that finally emerged. For 'dogmatic idealists', Djilas' term for Stalinists and other fellow travelers who accepted the Bolshevik talisman, history could offer no rejoinder. "Communism, they insisted, never had been immune to error, but, being 'scientific', it was self-correcting: loyalty to the final goal always had, always would, guarantee that mistakes would be corrected and the true path found again."[14] Stalin had persuaded himself that his 'science' was infallible, his course inevitable, his cause irreproachable.

For Stalin the question of ideology was never merely a pedantic exercise. Stalin was a Russian nationalist, but he remained a true believer in the communist catechism and in its ultimate goals. The defeat of the capitalist West, class struggle until the ultimate victory of communism, remained part of Stalin's political lexicon, part of his revolutionary conviction.

In 1929, on the eve of Stalin's titanic struggle with and ultimate liquidation of much of the Russian peasantry, he invoked the centrality of class struggle, perhaps as much to justify his recent purge of the left and right elements of the Party as to justify his coming struggle with the Kulak and any other 'recalcitrant' elements in or out of the Party. To explain the continuing struggles, Stalin developed the thesis that the internal class war grew more intense with the approach of socialism.

This thesis bore Stalin's imprint, though it had some ancestry in Lenin who, in 1919, stated that the destruction of classes would follow a long, hard class struggle that would overthrow the power of capital, destroy the bourgeois state and establish the 'dictatorship of the proletariat'. At the pitch of Stalin's struggle with the Right opposition in January 1929, Stalin published one of Lenin's previously unpublished articles, originally written by Lenin in January 1918, in the *Pravda* issue of 20 January 1929. In this essay Lenin condemned the "rich," the "crooks," the hooligans and "dregs of humanity . . . this ulcer that socialism has inherited from capitalism. [Lenin advised] no mercy to these enemies of the people . . . the enemies of the toilers . . . war to the bitter end on the rich [and on] bourgeois intellectuals."[15] Here was a testament that put the struggle within the Party and against the 'bourgeois' elements outside the Party within the larger context of historic class struggle, a suitable pretext to act against 'class enemies' to be sure, textured with an element of ideological rectitude.

International politics offered similar opportunities for Stalinist ideological rectitude. Had not Lenin understood the relation between communist revolution and international war? Had not Lenin understood that the communist revolution resulted from the first imperialist World War? Under Stalin the relation between international war and communist revolution became axiomatic. Should war come, Stalin trumpeted to the Seventeenth Party Congress in 1934, it would be a most dangerous game for the bourgeoisie. Some of the governments of the bourgeoisie, Stalin confidently predicted, would be missing on the morrow of war.[16]

Stalin, in fact, had anticipated the eventuality of international war as early as 1925. In January 1925, while addressing the Party's Central Committee, he claimed a world historical role for the Soviet army which, should war break out, would throw its decisive weight in the scales. This remained the official Stalinist view into the 1930's when Stalin fleshed it out by seeking an agreement with Hitler that would allow Stalin to literally tip the scales. That agreement became the Nazi-Soviet pact of August 1939, a prelude to what Stalin expected would be a long drawn out war between the Axis states and the Western alliance. Stalin expected a war that would bleed both and which would allow him (Stalin) to intervene at his pleasure with (he believed) the decisive weight of the Soviet army.[17]

Despite Stalin's miscalculations about the strength of France and the length of the war, Russia eventually defeated the Axis powers and, in the aftermath of war, a number of communist revolutions followed that strengthened, in Stalin's mind, the relation between international war and the spread of communism. Flushed with confidence, Soviet pronouncements during Stalin's final years admonished that a third world war would lead to the final collapse of the world capitalist system and its replacement by a new communist world order. Stalin himself argued, in his final published work of 1952, *Economic Problems of Socialism in the U.S.S.R.*, that wars would continue so long as imperialism continued to exist, implying the inevitability of ideological struggle between the Western democracies and Soviet inspired communism. "To eliminate the inevitability of war it is necessary to abolish imperialism."[18] In Stalin's view of history, Soviet Communism continued to occupy the moral center; its war with the Western capitalist powers was inevitable. Such a war would be the final prelude to the end of history and the entry into a communist Utopia.

Russian nationalism, the imperatives of Cold War diplomacy and the rhetoric of Marxist ideology all dovetailed nicely in Stalin's mind. In the *History of the Communist Party*, Stalin had given himself considerable authority in advancing the 'science' of Marxism and enriching "it with new experience in the new conditions of the class struggle of the proletariat."[19] After the Second World War he became the self-acknowledged authority, the 'great steersman' of the masses in economics, history, philosophy, music, and on the overall direction of Soviet society and world communism. The rhetoric of Marxist ideology coincided with the assertion of Russian national priorities. In Stalin ideology and nationalism went together. Stalinist brutality undergirded both communist goals and the defense of the country. Both were linchpins in Stalin's attempt to lift the Soviet Union up by the bootstraps, the better to match and subdue the West.

In the 1920's Stalin had opted for 'socialism in one country' because the international revolution had failed, nor did it appear that it would succeed in the near future. Moreover, Trotsky's scenario of the Permanent Revolution in which the more advanced (and soon to be communized) West would come to the aid of 'backward' Russia was the kind of idea that made Stalin (and many Bolshevik subalterns) bristle. Stalin's scenario of 'socialism in one country' was the kind of conception that could be fitted into traditional Russian nationalism, as Stalin discovered during World War II. Yet during this entire period, even during the struggle between Trotsky and Stalin during the 1920's, when the debate over 'socialism in one country' and Permanent Revolution was fought out, Stalin never lost sight of the relation between international war and the global success of communism. Stalin's vision remained complex until his death in 1953: long-term, utopian goals extracted from Marx and Lenin were uncomfortably but inseparably juxtaposed with short-term pragmatic and national objectives.[20] It was easier to demand national sacrifices when national objectives were put into the context of global class struggle, or when national deprivation was rationalized or relativized by reference to the paradise that would follow the Soviet victory in the Cold War. Thus true belief remained a part of Stalin's mentality as well as an integral part of scientific socialism. It complemented and even helped guide the national prerogatives that Stalin set for the Soviet Union. Until the end Stalin remained a convinced utopian, though a utopian in the Orwellian sense of totalitarian excess, and a scientific socialist, using the laws of 'science' to fit and buttress the needs of Russian nationalism.

The Reception of Soviet Utopia

Of course not everybody longed for the Utopia of Lenin and Stalin, not all were intimidated by Leninist or Stalinist vituperation. There were always some detractors of the Revolution, some who were willing to speak bluntly. These included those once among the true believers who later had the courage to become the apostates of the Revolution, however much they might rue their departure from Utopia. For them it was necessary to be as ingenuous as possible. Political rectitude demanded the suspension of true belief; truth demanded the constant interrogation of history, not the supine reception of 'true belief' or received creed. One such interlocutor was Russian writer Maxim Gorky, once a favorite of Lenin's, who chose the route of apostate and stern critic of the Bolshevik Revolution as early as 1917. Even during the First World War Gorky's reactions to the war were markedly different than Lenin's. Lenin celebrated the war as the instrument of historical providence, an instrument that would likely produce the collapse of capitalism and herald the advent of socialism. Gorky mourned the war, it was the "suicide of Europe" and a universal crime, it did not herald proletarian internationalism but held the promise of mere perfidy and continued Russian slavishness. Mob violence in Petrograd in the summer of 1917 did not convince him that Utopia was at hand, only that expectations for the future should be more modest than the epic salvation through revolution anticipated by Lenin. Salvation, Gorky was convinced, would come only with the slow flame of culture, a modest hope indeed compared to the universal conflagration planned by Lenin.[21]

Gorky was not prepared to serve one party, though by 1917 he had already been a social democrat for seventeen years. Never the true believer, he could only consider himself a heretic to all parties and creeds. As editor of *New Life*, a predominantly Menshivik magazine, Gorky prefaced a different vision, in 1917, of the road to the future socialist Utopia: the democratic basis of the Soviets would have to be strengthened, the Constituent Assembly must be convened and the minority dictatorship must be ended. All of Gorky's earnest protests produced little more than revulsion among the Bolsheviks who were eager to build the revolution and were openly contemptuous of 'bourgeois democracy' which had always been perfectly compatible, they argued, with Western imperialism and foreign intervention.

The debate over democracy reached epic proportions by November 1917, only days after the Revolution. The arrest of the Cadet members of the Provisional Government moved Gorky to offer his prognosis. "[Lenin's] pitiless experiment will destroy the best forces of the workers and will arrest normal development of the Russian revolution for a long time to come."[22] It was not long before Gorky dismissed Lenin as more in the 'Nechaev-Bakuni' tradition of destructive anarchy, an image which Gorky thought was confirmed by Lenin's ruthless dissolution of the Constituent Assembly, despite the fact that for a hundred years the 'best people of Russia' had dreamed of representative democracy. Gorky's more Promethean conception of the revolution and the future of socialism was imbued with a different sense of global cosmopolitanism than Lenin's militant, mechanical idealism and strident proletarianism. In Gorky's mind, Lenin's vision was a degradation of the human spirit and was motivated more by petty vengeance and class hatred than by universalizing perfection. The confection that Gorky was offering, David Caute perceptively tells us, was:

> Spiritual heir to the whole history of ideas seeking the ultimate perfection of man's relationship to man. Wishing to spiritualize the minds of men, resorting to physical coercion only in the last resort, untouched by motives of petty vengeance and striving to achieve a single family of worker-owners, this authentic revolutionary would be completely satisfied by no existing system.[23]

Gorky had no inconsiderable utopianism of his own, yet his admonitions alerted all to the pitfalls of 'master theoreticians'. He raised doubts about the self-proclaimed 'scientists' who claimed that they alone understood the 'laws of history'. Gorky's quixotic search for Utopia was more romantic than Lenin's hardboiled, pragmatic approach. Gorky spoke of a universe of perfection, a universe that precluded politics and power. In abandoning the human content of the Revolution, Gorky admonished, Lenin was resorting to the same methods of brutality that had always characterized the Russian political landscape. Better eternal rebellion, however romanticized, than this sorry Utopia. Gorky rendered his final verdict, symbolized by his exile to Sorrento. Expressing revulsion for politics, he evinced an instinctive denial that the proletarian masses could eliminate the slavishness of the Russian past. The work of human emancipation could only be carried out by the Russian intelligentsia, the future he counseled should be based on intellect installed by force of reason and not compelled from above by master theoreticians with knowledge of a superior science.[24] Gorky looked West for the salvation of Russia. But there were many disgruntled intellectuals in the West who looked toward the East, with all their hopes for the emancipation of humanity pinned on the communist Utopia of Lenin.

It was not a difficult matter to find sycophants of Utopia, the very glitter was all the more illumined against the subterranean depths to which humanity had sunk in the Great War. Hope summoned the beatified image of Stalin. By the 1930's he was already a cultic figure of mythic proportions, fortified by Western fellow travelers in search of an Olympia which could deliver them from the sordid realities of what they believed was a hopelessly decadent and dissolute West. Driven by the Depression and by the disconsolate masses, later by the accession to power of Hitler, the Russian utopia that was under construction seemed the surest, if not the only, inspiration, left in a world that appeared intent on self-destruction. Ironically, the 'end of history' was proclaimed by numerous

Western intellectuals who thought the final legacy of the West was destitution and dissipation on a global scale. For many this included both moral and physical privation. The long episode of rhapsodic admiration for the utopia being created by Stalin leaves the modern reader almost breathless from the dizzying heights that were scaled by some as they entered the kingdom of the future. Of course, admiration was best done at a distance.

This warning in mind, the legions came to the offertory to give their blessing. Bernard Shaw, visiting Russia shortly after the great crash of 1929 expressed an almost euphoric mood when comparing Russia to the West. Leaving the Hotel Metropole in Moscow he surmised, "tomorrow I leave this land of hope and return to our Western countries of despair."[25] These were not the sentiments of a solitary fellow-traveler. The American novelist Theodore Dreiser observed no corruption, jobbery or sales deception in Russia, Russian Communism was incorruptible. "No summer sales of lots that in winter are under water,"[26] he noted, here was a nation unblemished by warts and tics, at last the true harmonious society. The compelling need for Utopia overwhelmed natural incredulity. Irish playwright Sean O'Casey beat the drums to an even more euphoric froth: "Red mirror of Wisdom, turning the labor in factory, field and workshop into the dignity of a fine song. . . . Herald of a new life, of true endeavor, of common sense, of a world's peace, of man's ascent, of things to do bettering all things done."[27]

So strong was the will to believe that the first Five-Year Plan itself entered the pantheon as self-proclaimed god. Socialism became production, and the more that was produced so much was socialism superior to capitalism. Western sycophants worked tirelessly on behalf of the revolution. "Factories, percentages, machinery, tractors poured from the pens of Louis Fischer, Anna Louise Strong, Walter Duranty, Sherwood Eddy, John Strachey, Ella Winter, Harry F. Ward and many others."[28] The normally sardonic Bernard Shaw managed to conquer his irascible skepticism long enough to add that the success of the Five-Year Plan was the only hope of the world. Intoxication seemed the better part of valor still, but it was what kept Utopia alive when much of the Western world was hungry and when hope had all but vanished.

But what about after the plan, after the deportations, the killings, the trials, the liquidations, what then of Utopia? Had not the image at least become a trifle tarnished, was there not then a reckoning with Stalin and perhaps a repentance or a renunciation? Some, like the American Corliss Lamont were prepared to be ingenuous up to a point: "I am repelled by the dictatorial and repressive aspects of the Soviet Union."[29] But this was uttered only in 1952 and, even at that, his point was directed at the use of repression against the 'enemies of socialism', as though repression was solely the result of extenuating circumstances. Much earlier, in 1933, writer Maurice Hindus, a Jewish immigrant who had been born in Russia and later emigrated to America, castigated "the small group of men who rule the country,"[30] but he seemed to believe that this was a political necessity.

Legions of others had already begun the cultic process of lionizing Stalin and his work of 'advancing the cause of humanity'. British socialists Beatrice and Sidney Webb, not normally given to panegyrics, could hardly control their ardor for Stalin in *Soviet Communism: A New Civilization?* that the Webbs researched between 1932-1934, after the completion of collectivization; a second edition dropped the question mark. Here they borrowed evocatively from one of their intellectual ancestors, Jean-Jacques Rousseau, though one might have expected more sobriety from the normally measured Webbs. Not only did the Party not impose its will over the nation, "but the term dictatorship is surely a misnomer for this untiring corporate inspiration, evocation and formulation of a General Will among so huge a population."[31] Despite an avalanche of criticism, the Webbs remained undaunted, carrying the cross up to Golgotha. Several years later, in *The Truth About Soviet Russia*, they concluded that the Soviet Union had become fully democratic. The Webbs had in fact committed egregious mistakes, though they erred on behalf of socialist rectitude. Given the Webbs' glib elitism, David Caute's sardonic surmise was hardly unfair: "only facts, statistics and blueprints interested them, although their life's work was dedicated to the emancipation of the working class, which is commonly supposed to consist of people."[32] But if their prognosis of Stalin's work was incorrect, the diagnosis of problems in the capitalist West made of the Webbs honest brokers, if not entirely perceptive or ingenious ones. Their 1923 tome, *The Decay of Capitalist Civilization*, dwelled on the recurrent themes of the penury of the Western working classes and the monopoly of power enjoyed by narrow cliques in the capitalist democracies, themes that were hardly limited to the Fabian socialist circles inhabited by the Webbs. The need to cohabit Utopia was in direct relation to the enervating penury still experienced in the West, and this would be especially relevant after the Depression.

It was small wonder then that Utopia had to be defended against the incursions of the Western capitalist countries. There was a virtual catalog of motives. There were the endemic economic disasters of the post-Depression era, the weakness of social democracy, most notably the failure of Ramsay Mac-Donald's British version of social democracy, and the decrepitude of the National Government that he headed in the 1930's. And there was the growing reality of fascism to which the capitalist democracies seemed so vulnerable. Finally, there was the need to defend socialism, the most just means, it was thought by the legions of socialists and fellow travelers in the interwar period, to combat the inevitable privation of the capitalist countries and to resist the spread of fascism. There remained as always the last codicil of the creed of the fellow traveler, that the Soviet experiment was preferred, partially it seemed, because it remained abroad. Western socialism, when it arrived, would have to appear in different dress.

This having been duly noted, fellow traveler Westerners could reprise their idealism and hope for a socialist moral regeneration against the degenerate individualism of the West, or in some cases they could defend a hidebound realism and a moral rectitude that was put in bold relief against Western decadence. By the end of the 1930's a virtual messianic moral fervor had turned into a library of devotional literature. Utopia seemed well in hand and Stalin's position in the Russian pantheon assured for time immemorial.[33] To be admitted into Stalin's presence seemed to assure unmitigated adulation and credulity. American evangelist Anna Louise Strong, the first woman to earn a doctorate at the University of Chicago, having been granted an audience in the Kremlin, assured all who would listen: "His [Stalin's] eyes were kind yet grave, giving rest and assurance."[34] British historian Bernard Pares, not one normally given to wondrous idolatry, added historical perspective to the recipe: "He has shown that his heart is in his own country, that he has set his reputation on a purely practical object of vast scope, [Russia's] radical transformation for the benefit of all."[35] No less a personage than Hewlett Johnson, the Dean of Canterbury, having been granted an audience near war's end, subscribed to a similar testimonial: "Stalin was calm, composed, simple. Not lacking in humor. Direct in speech, untouched by the slightest suspicion of pomposity. There was nothing cruel or dramatic . . . about Stalin's face. Just steady purpose and a kindly geniality."[36] Here was the avuncular Stalin, Uncle Joe, anything but the oriental despot. And soon afterwards, from within the citadel itself, from within the citadel of the citadel, came the tremulous adulation of New York Times' Moscow correspondent Walter Duranty, a Pulitzer prize-winning British journalist. Yes, it was true that "there arose in full measure the dictatorship of Stalin and the Politburo," just as the opponents of Stalin had noted:

> Yet, significantly, 1936 was the year chosen for the introduction of a new constitution, and the first general election under it was held in 1937. Thus, by one of the paradoxes so frequent in Russia, authority was wholly centralized and concentrated at the top of the Soviet pyramid while its base was enormously extended at the bottom. Foreigners might be convinced that the benefits and pledges of the constitution were illusory and existed only on paper, and that the peoples of Russia were cowed and brow-beaten under the rifles of the G.P.U , but the average peasant and worker, the members of the former "subject races" in Central Asia and the Caucasus, the little men and especially women regarded it differently. For the most part they had faith in their new constitution.[37]

Then the Soviet Union had achieved democracy? No, but it might have. "It is a purely academic question to wonder whether the supreme and unlimited authority which the Politburo had now acquired would have diminished or transferred to organs of government if the international situation had improved," for the simple reason that the international situation did not improve. Then, Russia would have been similar to the Western democracies had circumstances permitted? Of course. "The only difference in Russia was that Stalin already had the possession of powers conferred upon President Roosevelt and Winston Churchill by the emergency of war."[38]

Such language was modest compared to the paeans that were sung to Stalin with rousing messianic fervor by Hewlett Johnson, who recognized in the Constitution of 1936 an important step toward the completion of communism. Stalin, the noble shepherd, beckoned Russia toward a blissful future:

> Stalin is no oriental despot. His new constitution shows it. His readiness to relinquish power shows it. His refusal to add to the power he already possesses shows it. His willingness to lead his people down new and unfamiliar paths of democracy shows it. The easier course would have been to add to his own

power and develop autocratic rule. His genius is revealed in the short, simple sentences which enshrine the Basic Law of the U.S.S.R. . . . Here is a document which ranks amongst the greatest in all human documents in its love of humanity and its reverence for human dignity.[39]

Indeed, writing in 1938, Johnson pleaded that Stalin had already established socialism in Soviet Russia: "The completed socialist system of society automatically creates the classless society, and with the abolition of classes the need for one class to predominate ceases. That stage has been largely completed within the brief space of twenty-one years."[40]

One can only wonder what would have happened to this state of bliss had Johnson been aware of the atrocities that had just been committed under cover of the document of the "love of humanity." In retrospect, the ironies of the late thirties seemed limitless. Novelist Lion Feuchtwanger, another noble fellow traveler, may have summed up best the sentiments of the typical fellow traveler when he proclaimed, in 1937, the following virtues of Stalin's creation. In Russia there "was the individual's feeling of complete security, his comfortable certainty that the State is really there for him and not he for the State. . . . Indeed everywhere in that great city of Moscow there was an atmosphere of harmony and contentment even of happiness."[41] Tragically, it was precisely in this period that the 'state was really there' for the ubiquitous show trials of Nikolai Bukharin and Mikhail Tomsky and much of the leadership apparatus of the Stalinist Utopia.

Hindsight, of course, is perfect. Hegel recognized this in admonishing that the owl of Minerva flies at dusk, wisdom only comes late. Fellow travelers, like true believers, were neither duplicitous nor insincere devotees of Utopia. Moreover, the intellectuals who expressed their admiration for Stalin's experiment were among the most intelligent and perceptive observers of their generation, and there was no lack of motives to move them in what appeared an unjustified critical support of Stalin to later generations. There was, first of all, the political climate of the 1930's and the felt need to fight fascism, a need that became dire as the decade of the 1930's was coming to a close. Then there were the hopes that were associated with the nascent Soviet experiment that, it was not unreasonable to believe, might offer an alternative to centuries of poverty and degradation and which, moreover, offered an alternative to a decadent and apparently faltering West which was in the throes, it appeared, of an unsolvable economic crisis.

It did not take a socialist or a Marxist to believe, in the 1930's, that the Western model of capitalist democracy was hopelessly flawed and unjust. There was the additional dilemma that there was no historical experience to draw upon, no one had ever succeeded before in coming so close to 'Utopia', let alone constructing its edifice. The architecture of Utopia would be piecemeal and according to circumstances, even the grandest plans needed detailed engineering; and there would have to be compromises in a country as underdeveloped as the Soviet Union – and with its expanse! Finally there was the question of ideals. The devastation of World War II and unmitigated Depression was no recommendation for the extant Western model. Hidden beneath the ideals was the much grimmer prospect of the necessity of finding an alternative to perpetual wars. The lionization of Stalin was encapsulated in hope, however naive was its final denouement

Not everyone in the West celebrated the arrival of Utopia in the Soviet Union. The literature of renunciation began in the early 1940's. The titles of the following list were indicative of the sea change of mood, though the revelations should have been more than a little embarrassing for true believers and fellow travelers. Typical of the literature were the following: Anton Ciliga, *The Russian Enigma,* London,1940; Walter Krivitsky, *I Was Stalin's Agent*, London, 1940; Louis Fischer, *Men in Power*, London, 1941; D. J. Dallin and B. I. Nicolaevsky, *Forced Labor in the Soviet Union,* London, 1948; Freda Utley, *Lost Illusion*, London, 1949; Eleonor Lipper, *Eleven Years in Soviet Prison Camps,* London, 1951.[42] After 1956 the list grew exponentially.

What had produced such an avalanche of apostasies? Had the revelations of prison camps, deportations, torture and liquidations been concealed from the earnest minds of the West prior to this avalanche of criticism? George Orwell's summary of events, written in June 1938, suffered no illusions. Though Orwell remained a socialist he was no true believer in the system created by Stalin, therefore less likely to be a victim of self-deception or blind credulity:

> All real power is concentrated in the hands of two or three million people, the town proletariat, theoretically the heirs of the revolution, having been robbed of the elementary right to strike; more recently, by the introduction of the internal passport system, have been reduced to a status resembling serfdom. The GPU are everywhere, everyone lives in constant terror of denunciation. . . . There are periodical waves of terror, sometimes the 'liquidation' of kulaks or 'nepmen', sometimes some monstrous State trial at which people who have been in prison for months or years are suddenly dragged forth to make incredible confessions. . . . Meanwhile the invisible Stalin is worshipped in terms that would have made Nero blush.[43]

And several years later, in 1944, Orwell offered this summation: "The sin of nearly all left-wingers is that they have wanted to be anti-fascist without being anti-totalitarian."[44] It was not long before the dam broke as a passel of apostasies challenged the previous gospel. In *The God That Failed*, which appeared in 1950, six prominent Western writers, initially among the most enthusiastic communists and true believers when communism was still in 'embryonic' form, expressed their disenchantment with its later development. 'Illusion', 'fanaticism', and 'dictatorship' were the new keywords employed by Arthur Koestler, Ignazio Silone, Richard Wright, Andre Gide, Louis Fischer and Stephen Spender.[45] Koestler, who was a true believer in the 1930's, expressed how Stalinism inspired idealism and then disillusionment:

> The addiction to the Soviet myth is as tenacious and difficult to cure as any other addiction. After the Lost Weekend in Utopia the temptation is strong to have just one last drop, even if watered down and sold under a different label. And there is always a supply of new labels on the Cominform's black market in ideals. They deal in slogans as bootleggers deal in faked spirits; and the more

innocent the customer, the more easily he becomes a victim of the ideological hooch sold under the trademark of Peace, Democracy, Progress or what have you.[46]

Shortly afterwards, in 1951, Douglas Hyde joined the growing list of the disillusioned with the publication of his autobiography, *I Believed: The Autobiography of a Former British Communist,* which combined the art of the confessional with the more sober and dispassionate inquiry of the historian. Hyde's complaints prefigured the plaintive laments and the embittered denunciations that became routine among Western Party members after the Soviet invasion of Hungary in 1956: the authoritarianism of the Party; the continuation of Party domination by the Soviets; the dictatorial control of Eastern Europe by the Soviets; and the cynical lies that were commonplace within the Party. Hyde followed the logic of his arguments by departing from the British Communist Party, and the entire edifice of Marxism, by embracing Roman Catholicism.[47]

A different path was followed by E. P. Thompson, who distinguished an authentic tradition of Marxism from its 'contaminated' Stalinist version. Thompson found it necessary to abandon the British Communist Party when it became clear that the Party was not about to follow the 'authentic' tradition. In Thompson's criticisms the difference between the idealist and the ideologue crystallized. The British Communists proved unable to disassociate themselves from or to condemn the Soviet intervention in Hungary, producing the withering scorn of Thompson's rejoinder. Yet there was something far more insidious and lamentable that Thompson regretted, it was that Stalinism itself had been a kind of Utopia – it was part of the utopian habit that was something like the addiction reproved by Koestler. But it was an authoritarian utopianism that was not the antidote intended by Marxism, to which, in its pristine form, Thompson still tenaciously clung. Thompson's parting shot, regrettable as he may have found it, admirably encapsulated the difficulty with (communist) Utopia, and it revealed also the lingering attachment to Utopia that Thompson still harbored:

> Stalinism is socialist theory and practice which has lost the ingredient of humanity. The Stalinist mode of thought is not that of dialectical materialism, but mechanical idealism. Stalinism is Leninism turned into stone. Instead of commencing with facts, social reality, Stalinist theory starts with the idea, the text, the axiom: facts, institutions, people, must be brought to conform to the idea. . . . Stalinist analysis, at its most degenerate, becomes a scholastic exercise, the search for 'formulations' 'correct' in relation to text but not to life.[48]

Thompson's exit from the Party was not a solitary one. Numerous communist intellectuals could no longer tolerate being in the belly of the whale: John Saville, Doris Lessing, Ronald L. Meek, Rodney Hilton and Christopher Hill all weighed anchor, taking with their departure some of the best minds of their generation and dealing a mortal blow in Britain to the remnants of Stalinist authoritarian utopianism.

Despite the swarming vituperations against Stalinist Utopia, despite the insidious monster which 'really existing socialism' had become in its Stalinist incarnation, and despite the seeming impossibility of achieving an 'earthly paradise', the ideal of Utopia did not perish with the rejection of Stalinism and the discrediting of the Soviet regime.[49] Not even Orwell, who had good reason for joining the anti-utopian legions that were assembled at the gates of 'the god that failed', was prepared to join the ranks of the disaffected utopians. In a review written in 1946, he made clear what he took to be the vast distance between Stalinism and 'utopian socialism':

> The 'earthly paradise' has never been realized, but as an idea it never seems to perish, despite the ease with which it can be debunked by practical politicians of all colors. Underneath it lies the belief that human nature is fairly decent to start with, and is capable of indefinite development. This belief has been the main driving force of the Socialist movement, including the underground sects who prepared the way for the Russian revolution, and it could be claimed that the Utopians, at present a scattered minority, are the true upholders of Socialist tradition.[50]

The pleas of Orwell and Thompson for a human ingredient in socialism is what kept socialism alive as a Utopia even after the totalitarian excesses of Stalin. It was the humanist utopian Marx that Walter Benjamin and Ernst Bloch stressed in the interwar period. Afterwards, Herbert Marcuse and Andre Gorz took up the refrain, returning often to the utopian socialists that lived and worked prior to Marx. Yet again Orwell proved prescient, even after Stalin the idea of Utopia as socialist paradise would not be given up.

Chapter 3
China, Chairman Mao and Peasant Utopianism

In 1949 the worst fears of the West were coming true. When Mao Tse-tung successfully led a communist revolution in China that year, more than a fifth of the planet was under communist rule. The secular religion was becoming epidemic. To an increasingly paranoid and hidebound West, the Chinese revolution provided another wake-up call. The anti-Western revolution begun in Russia on behalf of Utopia was expanding.

Utopia, as Maoist incarnation, was a blend of ideological rectitude, utopian imagery and moral asceticism, all intended to help galvanize Chinese society for mass action and to help prepare for the future heaven. The symbolism was messianic. Mao Tse-tung would transform himself into a cultic deity to symbolize the unity and dynamism of the future Utopia. In Maoist hopes, Utopia was given a monumental task, it had to overcome the privileges of a parasitical mandarin class, unify and guide purposeful individual initiative, expunge all the barriers of class, status, and education, break down distinctions between the city and the country, between workers and intellectuals, between old and young, men and women.[1] This meant not only creating new symbols to give clarity and cohesion, and to establish the leadership of the Chinese Communist Party (CCP) but, where necessary, to 'reculturate' those who did not understand or who refused to accept the birth and the development of the new creed. And this suggested another direction to Utopia, perhaps a more ominous dimension precisely because it envisioned not only a radical transformation of society based on asceticism and self-denial, but because messianic expectations and reculturation meant the transformation of human nature itself according to the demanding standard of Utopia.

Mao Tse-tung was confronted by a formidable task from the beginning. He had to develop China and energize the disconsolate Chinese masses into a modern twentieth-century country that could claim parity with and even surpass the West, overcome the backwardness and divisiveness of the past and create a sense of national unity and transcendent purpose. For Chairman Mao, communism was a universal world view, the answer to and rejection of the rapacious, imperial West, a philosophy of national and personal emancipation, a promised end of history that would overcome the ravages, uncertainties and injustices of the past.

With revolutionary communism as final objective, with a homespun peasant populist philosophy that would lift China by the bootstraps, Mao aimed to steer China out of its slavish and ignominious past into a great leap forward. Utopia would supersede history, the suffering of the past would be rectified by a final revelation, the peasant would be remolded into Man until he had achieved the nobility for the Great Society that lay ahead. All of this would require an energizing, ennobling and unifying vision, a dazzling, illumined, beckoning picture of the Utopia that lay ahead, a theology that eclipsed centuries of invasion and domination by the despised West.

Thus, Mao Tse-tung promised a New Jerusalem, he uttered a vision for China which pronounced an 'end of history' and an end to inner and outer torment. Those who disagreed or who opposed the Maoist vision were dismissed as class enemies, unworthies who opposed the interests of the masses. For true-believers, it was obvious that the peasant masses would be the beneficiaries of Utopia. Holy writ had simply to be handed down to the hapless masses from the priesthood until the empty receptacles – better blank and empty said Mao – were filled to the brim with Truth. Human beings would be fitted to the perfect symmetry of the future. Human nature would be recreated without the imperfections of original sin. This was the self-appointed task of Mao. He would scale the Olympian heights of Utopia while modernizing China, lift the Chinese peasant out of his slavish past, expel the foreigner while modernizing the nation. These were all formidable tasks, requiring selfless sacrifice, unremitting diligence and patience, austerity for a generation or more. All of this would require leadership, deference to master theoreticians and master builders, acceptance of a superior vision, coercion for those who resisted or who did not understand or share the same vision.

Reflecting the moral and political voluntarism that characterized his translation of Marx into the Chinese vernacular, Mao Tse-tung's revolutionary messianism revealed a penchant for seeing history as a moral struggle between the forces of good and evil. Maoist eschatology, through the promise of personal and national renewal and the expectation of a New Jerusalem, would help create and emancipate the Chinese nation.

In the end the dramaturgy presented by Chairman Mao embraced the Manichaen struggle between the communist apocalypse and the decadent materialism of the capitalist West. He would preside over a titanic struggle between rival and incompatible conceptions of the future, between the drive for Western hegemony and the assertion of Chinese autonomy. Communist paradise would rectify all past wrongs, thought Mao. He would engineer the new human beings that were to inhabit the noble kingdom of the future. Like a 'sun deity', he would rise in the East like a brilliant beam of light.

Utopia was paramount in the thinking of Mao Tse-tung almost from the beginning. It provided the historical context, political ideology and motive force to come to terms with the fluidity, randomness and brutishness of Chinese political life. For Mao, Utopia was an irresistible force. It offered the hope of overcoming the backwardness of a peasant nation which had been scourged by the aggrandizing West and brutalized by warlords who had endured and even thrived under Chiang Kai-shek's Nationalists, the Kuomintang. Coming from a peasant background, never overcoming a suspicion of intellectuals and of the Chinese mandarin class in particular, Mao harbored resentments that were indelible in much of the Chinese countryside. Endemic poverty, mass illiteracy, centuries of social resentment and clannishness, random violence often perpetrated by landlords and warlords and tolerated or encouraged by the Kuomintang, promised hopelessness, futility and passivity. It was difficult to imagine how, in this kaleidoscope of turmoil and helplessness, a people could be galvanized into a nation, let alone become a nation that had a unity of purpose and hoped to build a communist Utopia.

Yet, with Mao's faith in the peasant masses, convinced of his own messianic purpose, imbued with a sense of high historical hope, believing that personal and national destiny were interwoven, he prepared for the grand experiment. He began the construction of the future. As early as 1942, with the nation traumatized by war, Mao led what was called a Rectification Campaign, articulating a kind of peasant populism. He condemned the Chinese mandarin class, the intelligentsia that had served as the ruling bureaucracy, for its elitist dogmatism and formalism, its lack of humility and devotion to the Chinese people. He preached communist asceticism and repudiated self-indulgence and abstract dogmatism. To regard any ideas as religious dogma was hypocritical and unpragmatic. Those who did so were denounced in no uncertain terms: "Your dogma is less useful than shit,"[2] he pronounced, for unlike dogshit, dogma cannot fertilize fields.

Mao's anticipated universality in the glorious future had to wait, however. First there were the pragmatic needs of the present. During World War II the most urgent necessity was to expel the Japanese. There followed the civil war between the Chinese Communist Party (CCP) and the Kuomintang, which preoccupied Mao until 1949. Following the victory of the CCP against its Kuomintang rival in 1949, Mao conceded that the revolution had to be defended before paradise could be constructed. The CCP had to establish a political base, an effective national Party apparatus. It had to promote rapid industrialization to modernize China and to make it less vulnerable to Western capitalist nations. It had to create an industrial proletariat that would provide the cadres who would be loyal to State and Party. The Party had to remilitarize China to provide military cover against any possible incursion from the West – such as had happened to Russia after 1917. It had to develop a mass politics in the countryside to replace the traditional lethargy and passivity of the peasant with political devotion to the cause of the Party, and it would have to generate among the peasantry a utopian enthusiasm for the prospects of a communist heaven on earth.

In the immediate aftermath of communist victory in 1949, pragmatic necessity ruled in the building of the new China. Land-reform, backed by the army and the Party, meant the transference of land to the peasantry the better to eliminate the base of the Chinese gentry. Along the seaboard foreigners were expelled. Banks and factories that belonged to the Kuomintang and to foreign interests in the seaboard cities were nationalized, putting most large industry in China in the hands of the party-controlled state. Lesser industries were subjected to state regulation of wages and profits. Economic reconstruction, guided by the state, was left in large measure to the national and small business classes. As a result of all these measures normalcy returned, but China remained backward. Reform had created stability, but it was clearly only a beginning. The question was where to go from there?

In a nation like China, in which the peasantry constituted the vast majority of the population, it seemed paradoxical to make a revolution that espoused Marxist ideology as a panacea for the future. Marxism was a Western ideology, geared to Western political and economic institutions and practices. Marx himself only anticipated revolutions in countries that had experienced industrial capitalism and that had large urban working classes. Yet most of the leadership of the CCP, doctrinaire orthodox communists, believed that communism had to be built in the cities first. Communism would radiate from there to the rural peasant masses. The highly regimented and centralized Soviet example would be adopted as the paradigm for China.

As Mao understood it, this approach contained a number of paradoxes. In pre-industrial China, where capitalism existed in small enclaves at best, where there were only small pockets of urban industrial workers, many of whom would not support communism, orthodox Marxist ideology seemed inapplicable and inappropriate. There were other contradictions that Mao found hard to swallow as well. It was never clear to him how or why a populist insurgency could or would be served by an elite of urban intellectuals. He wondered how the interests of the peasant masses could be made compatible with the ostensible drive to urbanize and modernize China when presumably, as had happened in Russia, modernization would be at their expense? He asked how it was possible to encourage anti-imperialism (and even traditional Chinese xenophobia) while stressing the urgency of imitating and matching the detested West. The task of Mao was admittedly complex. He would have to set a peasant revolution into the cosmopolitan universals of Marxist-Leninist utopian ideals. He would have the Olympian task of rebuilding and unifying China while aiming at utopian transcendence, the daunting job of unifying theory and practice and adapting a Marxian worldview to conditions in China.

To accomplish all of this China would have to overcome its backwardness; it would have to modernize. Utopia would come next. But did this mean that for Mao utopian transcendence must be put in the service of economic mobilization, or that revolutionary messianism and peasant populism were only political ploys or ideological necessities? Did it mean, as Theodore H. Von Laue put it, that "Marxism-Leninism was but an improvised experimental ideology of mobilization for matching the Western model [and] Communism was but an adjustment to the pressures to the continuing world revolution of Westernization, a tool for catching up. . . ."[3]

Certainly it was possible to see Maoism and Chinese Communism as a nationalist counter-revolution against the West and Western imperialism, after all

Mao was the very incarnation of Chinese nationalism. But Mao retained a Marx-ist-Leninist gloss – adapted to China's national requirements – which did more than rationalize and justify the modernization of China. It was the theological, messianic elements of Maoism that guided Mao and that propelled China toward the Great Leap Forward in the late 1950's. Unlike China's Soviet counterpart which, after an initial revolutionary-messianic period, experienced a deradicali-zation and a substitutionism of pragmatic (often economic) goals, Maoist thought became more radicalized in the decade of the 1950's. Subsequently Mao abandoned the Soviet Communist road that he once had followed. By the mid-1950's his road to Utopia was to be built on the sturdy backs and 'blank' minds of the peasantry. The sturdy backs would rebuild the nation but the imagery of the future, stoked by Mao's pen and by his actions, would fill the blank minds.

The Mao-Tse-tung-thought that took shape in the 1950's was both concrete and utopian, pragmatic and millenarian, harshly realistic and poetically tran-scendent, cruel and idealistic, vindictive and conceived as 'just'. Chairman Mao, who consciously thought of himself as the head of a peasant populist movement, and whose nascent movement was nurtured by the Chinese rural population in the 1930's, came to fear and reject the city and urban culture. The city – which symbolized Western culture and dominance – had never been the focal point of Mao's celestial kingdom. Cities, Mao railed, were not only dens of iniquity that were antithetical to the kind of puritanical self-denial that was demanded by the revolution and the pristine Utopia of the future, they were also zones in which the imperial presence of the foreigners had dominated the Chinese landscape historically. The city was where the subjugation of China had always begun in the past; it was where the West met the East, to China's embarrassment and deg-radation. These unwarranted but irresistible incursions of the foreigner helped feed the fear and loathing that underscored much of Chinese xenophobia and rejection of the West.

As a populist philosophy, Maoism was in many respects pre-Marxist, point-ing toward its own idiosyncratic path. It emphasized the power of the individual to move history, the importance of the human will, the centrality of morality in the struggle between good and evil. Mao rejected the notion of objective and inviolable laws of history; history was not a science. Such beliefs had resonated among the utopian socialists before Marx, as well as in the utopian views of Marx, but they were also among the inherited values of Chinese civilization. Buoyed by tradition and inspired by Utopia, Mao pointed China toward a pure, pristine, egalitarian and ascetic future.

As early as 1927 Mao had argued, in the Hunan Report, that socialism would be easy to build in China because of the absence of both economic mod-ernization and 'bourgeois' ideology. The peasantry would be revolutionary be-cause it had not been contaminated by modern capitalism. Economic backward-ness was a virtue; it was better to be 'poor and blank'. Mao was convinced even in early formulations that the future of socialism did not depend on the devel-opment of material production nearly as much as on the development of moral virtue in the new men who were to populate the millennial order of the future. Revolutionary virtue, like the apocalyptic politics of Robespierre and the radical

Jacobins of the French Revolution, was to eclipse the past and inaugurate the new millennium. As it had done for Robespierre, virtue would abolish history; the new man would be reculturated by the trustees of the future Utopia.

Armed with such revolutionary virtue, the implacable Mao believed that anything was possible; mind could conquer matter, good could conquer evil. The universals to which Mao aspired required heroic sacrifice, but such sacrifices were part of the nobility of history. Thus the East Wind would prevail over the West Wind, he pronounced, but if the Western imperialists wanted a war Mao would delay the construction of paradise and fight the West to the finish. "We may lose more than 300 million people. So what? War is war. The years will pass and we'll get to work producing more babies than ever before."[4]

In 1951 Mao began a thought-reform – 'rectification' – campaign that was intended to reorient China toward his vision of the future, instill revolutionary enthusiasm in the nation and help maintain national discipline. Mao-Tse-tung-thought itself was held to be infallible, therefore a fit guide for the nation. In such precedent-setting times, with the past repudiated, authority broken and the monarchial system gone, in a world of flux and uncertainty in which immediate, forceful collective action was imperative, Mao sought to create a new world with more solid foundations. Now the nation had to be reeducated in the ways of a new kind of filial piety, in the ways of a new moral center, both of which were to be re-centered in a cult embodied by the person of Mao.

Beginning with the thirtieth anniversary of the CCP, 1 July 1951, Mao's principal texts were published in the press. Articles by leading ideologists began to appear, praising the greatness of Mao-Tse-tung-thought. On 23 October, 1951, Mao declared that "thought reform, and especially thought reform of all categories of intellectuals, is one of the most important preconditions for the thoroughgoing democratic transformation and progressive industrialization of our country."[5] The 'Three-Antis' campaign at the end of 1951, aimed at rooting out corruption, waste and bureaucracy, and the 'Five-Antis' campaign during the spring of 1952, which was intended to extend the first campaign, demonstrated more clearly how Mao intended to use thought reform on behalf of what he called democratic transformation. Democracy did not mean the search for truth through open debate, or the expression of diverse opinions in the search for consensus. In Mao's lexicon it meant the discovery, through 'dialectics', of Truth. Government officials and recalcitrant businessmen must be brought in tow; there was no place in China for the man who had his own conception of truth. The masses were a single collective, a single entity; they were a single personality embodying a single truth. People ought not run off in their own direction, they must not be in the habit of "forming mountaintops."[6] To prevent them from getting to mountaintops Mao introduced a national "Movement for the study of Mao Tse-tung's Thoughts." It was prudent to see the wisdom of Mao thought. Those who objected or who were recalcitrant in any way were 'remolded' in prison. To make them more lucid, they were often shackled in prison irons.[7]

Other mountaintops had to be removed as well. Though Mao had tolerated the 'enlightened gentry' and the 'prosperous peasant' in the early stages of the revolution, he soon moved with increasing savagery to liquidate these 'enemies of the people'. The Korean War provided a pretext for Mao to unleash the 'will' of the people, though much of the carnage had little to do with the threat of subversion, internal or external. On 21 February 1951 the CCP published "Regulations Regarding the Punishment of Counter-revolutionaries," specifying death sentences for a wide range of 'crimes'. The "Regulations" sanctioned vigilante justice in the countryside where peasant village leaders were already leading large public rallies which 'sentenced' gentry and 'rich peasants' for 'crimes' against the people. In the first half of 1951 as many as 800,000 'counter-revolutionary' cases were tried. Of these it is estimated that between two and three million were executed in a revolutionary *danse macabre*.[8]

Death, however, as Mao came to admit, made thought reform irrelevant. It was better to change minds than to sever heads. People were urged to "fight self," to "stick with the team," to "fight family authority," to oppose all private values and to embrace the Great Harmony. In practice this often meant public confessions followed by a period of contrition, or the public denunciation of one's father and the recognition of Mao the Father. Conversion to socialism meant life within the flock. Under the people's democratic dictatorship, Mao permitted the freedom of expression so long as it was not used for counter-revolutionary purposes.[9] But only Mao had a clear vision of what was counter-revolutionary and what was not.

As it turned out, only Mao could hear the hounds of heaven, others could not. Despite the eight 'Antis' the flock remained divided. Intellectuals remained indifferent to the Great Harmony, everywhere he looked Mao saw class divisions reappearing. Landlords and 'rich' peasants, he thought, were reintroducing capitalism. To correct this backsliding toward capitalism, Mao set his sights on a future of oneness. As architect of the future he adopted the first Five-Year Plan in 1953. Now rural collectivization would be pursued in earnest. By 1955, frustrated by the slow pace of collectivization, the decline of agricultural productivity and famine, Mao decided to accelerate the collectivization of farms and to nationalize all commerce and industry still in private hands. The future depended on winning the mind of the poor peasant who was "poor and blank", a perfect receptacle for the campaign for Utopia, a perfect vehicle in the war against the 'counter-revolutionaries'. Peasants, Mao argued, would heed the call to act in accordance with "the principles of voluntarism and mutual benefit, to organize agricultural producers' mutual-aid teams."[10] Peasants were urged to get on the road to socialism by using their mutual-aid teams to organize small agricultural producers' cooperatives. The uniting of these semi-socialist cooperatives into large rural cooperatives would help to steadily raise socialist consciousness among the peasantry through their personal experience. But the 'cooperative' movement, as part of the theater of Utopia, was anything but voluntary.[11]

The Five-Year Plan had some initial success. By the end of 1956 coal and steel production quadrupled, cement production doubled. Levies on industry in the form of taxes and profits accounted for more than seventy percent of government revenues. But these figures were deceptive; they concealed the costs of production. Worse, from Mao's viewpoint, nationalization and centralized planning were inflating bureaucracy in industry. Parallel party and industry staffs in each industrial unit were leading to a virtual explosion of managers. A state 'bureaucratic bourgeoisie' was emerging, not unlike the capitalist bourgeoisies of the West. Moreover, heavy reliance on Soviet experts only added to the servility of China and Chinese personnel. The Five-Year Plan was not creating a new China, it was recreating the old China. Material success was not enough: "Old ideas reflecting the old system remain in people's heads . . . we must change ideas . . . through socialist education. . . ."[12] The working class itself, said Mao, must produce the future managers, researchers and inventors, it must produce proletarian intellectuals who were "Red and Expert," who were dedicated communists and technically capable managers.

The Great Leap Forward

It was not enough to be technically proficient, the Chinese had to have the ideal of Utopia in their hearts, they had to exemplify the virtues of self-abnegation and neighborliness, they had to toil ceaselessly for the future. China was to be a Big Family, the relation of Mao and China one of emperor and subject. Socialism did not mean increased production, it meant universal sacrifice for the greater family; it was more than a question of making more steel. Mao wanted the hearts and minds of the Chinese. With their support he would find the right ideas to guide China into the future.

To encourage the discovery of the right ideas, Mao launched the 'let a hundred flowers bloom campaign' in 1956, ostensibly to expose the falsity of the old ideas of the past. What followed was a crescendo of opinion from Chinese intellectuals, much of it disappointing to Mao. Too much blooming forced him to abruptly cancel the hundred-flowers campaign. Professors who had bloomed, but who had expressed 'old ideas', found themselves cleaning lavatories and other menial tasks.[13]

In the background to all these campaigns was a growing gap between Mao's increasingly utopian aspirations and the more pragmatic objectives of the CCP. Mao assumed that the building of communism would be inclusive, cooperative, and egalitarian. The base for communism had to be the 'poor' peasantry because it had the 'correct' political consciousness, and still remembered and despised the pre-revolutionary regime. The CCP, on the contrary, believed that the building of communism must be a highly regimented and managed affair conducted by the upper part of the CCP hierarchy, which would stand above and guide the masses. Communism would be built in the cities and expand outwards into rural areas. It would be based on the industrial proletariat. The development of heavy industry remained the fundamental prerequisite, it was synonymous with the building of socialism.

From the beginning Mao had a peasant suspicion of urban culture and the mandarin mentality that had always prevailed in the city, and which had ruled the countryside from afar. Mao retained an antipathy for large-scale forms of economic and political administration and for bureaucracy in general. The oppressive bureaucratic structures that were being built by the Party and the Party's emphasis on heavy industry, the formation in urban areas of new political-administrative and technological-economic elites, was creating the over-development of urban areas at the expense of the rural cooperative movement. Mao saw all of this as an ideological deformity, a ritualization of socialist ideals, an abandonment of egalitarianism and the homespun rural values of "plain living and hard work" which, for him, had come to characterize the very essence of expectation.and hope.[14]

By 1956 Mao was increasingly separating himself from the views of the majority of the CCP. The Soviet model did not work, he argued; China was a rural peasant society. Mao impatiently yearned for the immediate realization of Utopia. It was time to create Man, if necessary by pure revolutionary zeal. The age of miracles was not over, it was time to abolish the past and inaugurate the new age. In September-October of 1957, almost by impulse, Mao prepared China for the Great Leap Forward, the leap beyond history. China would move directly to self-contained communes, each with its own industrial, agricultural and service sectors and its own defense militia. Here was the unity of thought and being, of hope and reality.

The Great Leap Forward was launched in 1958 at double-step speed. In January-February and again between August-December, some 700 million people, more than 90 percent of the population, were packed into People's Communes. The Communes were self-contained and self-administered in every way, from political, social, economic and administrative matters to educational, cultural and intellectual activities. Communal small-scale industries, especially steel production, the production of agricultural implements, coal mining to provide local fuel, the production of fertilizers, the encouragement of handicraft production for local consumption, were all organized at the communal level.[15]

All of this was a dramatic rupture with the past, as illustrated by Henan Province. Here 5,376 agricultural collectives were hammered into 208 large people's communes, each with an average of 8,000 households.[16] The communes were to maintain strict work discipline and were to practice an egalitarianism that harkened back to the English puritanical asceticism of the seventeenth-century. Hard work and self-denial, the sharing of sacrifice and reward in the commune, was the road to the future heaven.

By the end of 1958 the People's Communes were established throughout rural China. The communization of China, the pooling of all resources, the mobilization and sharing of labor, the development of light industry in rural areas for local markets, the creation of small-scale iron and steel furnaces, were under way. But Mao understood that to mobilize China for the prodigious tasks of reconstruction that lay ahead, he had to instill revolutionary enthusiasm in the peasantry. And he believed that the goals of communism could be internalized by the rural masses because they were more advanced in assimilating the spirit of communism than their better educated city brethren.[17]

Guided by the spirit of communism, Mao and the 'trustees of posterity' set about winning the revolutionary enthusiasm of the benighted "poor and blank" peasantry. Three years of hard work were to be succeeded by a thousand years of paradise. Mao's appeal was to the inherent goodness of the rural masses. The future Utopia did not depend as much on material satisfaction as it did on moral rectitude and social solidarity. Human will, not the objective laws of history, revolutionary spontaneity, not historical necessity, would create the Utopia which Mao envisioned. The antidote to bureaucratization, hierarchy, the stultification of ideals and the creation of new elites was the People's Commune.

Once in place the communes allowed no privilege for individuals or families. Production brigades numbering in the thousands maintained a severe work discipline. Men and women marched to work as though in a military parade, often accompanied by martial music. The fieldwork was organized as though the workers were working in a factory, the routinization and ritualizing of work was justified by the sacred duty of building the pristine symmetry of the egalitarian future. Everything was set into communal life; families ate in communal mess halls, children were put in communal nurseries and educated in common in communal schools. Family property was often communalized and the family household was replaced by the commune as the center of life. The narrow perspective of the peasant was supposed to be enlarged by this spartan routine of self-denial. Traditional attachments to family and self were to be replaced and transcended by the more expansive and universal attachments to commune, nation and even the entirety of humanity.[18] Mao's feverish hopes were based on the powers of the human spirit, whose locus was in the countryside where communism was to be born. History would be suspended, the past denied. This monumental experiment in salvationism needed only the engineer of utopian posterity. As in the Year I of the French Revolution, when utopian 'renewal' was ushered in by the Terror of Robespierre, so would Mao usher in the New Jerusalem and the renewal of China.

Thus, History itself was to be determined by enthusiasm, by the spirit of self-abnegation, chiliastic expectation, the will to revolutionary transcendence, the hope of achieving Utopia. A commentary on Mao-Tse-tung-thought in 1958 declared flatly that "many living examples show that there is only unproductive thought, there are no unproductive regions. There are only poor methods for cultivating the land, there is no such thing as poor land."[19] A jingle composed by the peasants of Hunan in 1958 captured the pristine, primitivist utopianism of Mao-Tse-tung-thought:

Setting up a people's commune is like going to heaven.
The achievements of a single night surpass those of several
Millennia.
The sharp knife severs the roots of private property
Opening a new historical era.[20]

From the beginning the Great Leap Forward had a pronounced utopian and even messianic element to it. The Great Leap Forward was intended to mark the transition from socialism, which 'officially' coincided with the completion of the rural collectives in 1958, to ecstasy. The General Will of the Chinese nation, mystically embodied and imminent in the authority of Maoist universalism, would now achieve its ultimate denouement, Absolute Justice. Instead of objective and scientific laws of history, as in Marxist-Leninist and Soviet rhetoric, Mao now offered pragmatic asceticism, mystical union and a leap into the utopian future. The sovereign power of the Chinese people was now replaced by the will of the guardian of posterity.

In practice, the Great Leap Forward abandoned the excessive concentration on industrialization which required capital assets that China did not possess. Mao had decided to concentrate on developing and industrializing rural areas because they concentrated its greatest asset, the size of its labor force. China would develop the countryside by unleashing its masses. China had the necessary resources, Mao surmised, if it relied on labor-intensive methods. Moreover, communist ideals could be pursued in the immediate present because they were sure to galvanize the peasant masses that possessed, in Mao's estimation, an inner communist consciousness. The development of a modern economy and the building of a society would occur simultaneously.

Communization, Mao hoped, was a prescription that would abolish distinctions between the city and the countryside, between intellectuals and manual workers and between workers and peasants. It would establish a universal brotherhood in which private and self-interest was effaced by a more expansive, transcendent communal interest. Eventually, Mao prophesied, the state would wither away. Would not the industrialization of the countryside, the combination of industrial and agricultural production, the combining of education and productive labor in various work-study schemes, the insistence that intellectuals and other brain workers participate in manual labor, would not such communal activities eliminate distinctions of privilege.[21] Such communalism was bound to instill an ethos of mutualism, establish the classless society of communism, foster universal happiness, and eliminate the need for state compulsion. But there still remained a wide gap between theory and practice, hope and reality, ideology and Utopia. The New Man tendered by Mao was bound to have a difficult gestation

Along with the actual blueprint for Utopia heralded in the Great Leap Forward went rhetoric, imagination and ideology. The new drama needed to be rationalized, it needed a creed to explain and justify the requirement for heroic sacrifice and detachment. For this Mao was up to the task. In Maoist dramaturgy, faith in Utopia became belief in the spiritual and moral transformation of people, especially the New Men who Mao saluted as the selfless reds and experts of the future. The road to Utopia became a religious pilgrimage, a sacred mission that had messianic dimensions, a convergence of liturgy and eschatology in Mao's monumental mission of transcendence. "If you are not completely reborn," he pronounced, "you cannot enter the door of Communism."[22] The objective shape of the world would be sacralized only after the revolutionizing, purification, and spiritualization of men. The Maoist good society of the future, therefore, depended foremost on the moral transformation of China. The spiritualized Utopia of the future required men and women who were indefatigable and selfless, who espoused the collective goals of communism, including revolutionary virtue, self-denial and total obedience. Communism was above all based on common spiritual bonds, but society had to maintain a constant vigil against 'incorrect thoughts'. The leap into the 'realm of freedom' required an act of pure faith. But it also required an enormous sacrifice: all dissent was bound to be taken as apostasy and sin.

The rural Utopia of the future, which was in many essentials an extension of the idealized peasant past and which extolled the peasant simplicity of folklore and legend, would quickly degenerate into organized slavishness and stultifying regimentation. Mandatory zealotry proved, in the end, no substitute for voluntary enthusiasm. Optimistic social engineering that attempted to perfect human nature by design was sure to forge the gulag of the future.

Maoist ideology, which was especially engineered for the Great Leap Forward, was an ideology of economic mobilization and development that consciously aimed to overcome Chinese backwardness. It was social engineering with universal, earth-shattering pretensions. Foremost, Mao was utopian prophet and visionary. Pragmatic social engineering and apocalyptic justice were linked, but in Mao's mind it was the latter which justified the former. Revolutionary utopian enthusiasm provided the incentive for the organized diligence of the present. Mao's 1945 speech on the ancient Chinese fable, "How Yu Kung Removed the Mountains," which was canonized in 1966 as part of the essence of Maoism, had made this explicit. The lesson drawn from the fable was that persistent, ceaseless work would lead to the promised land, diligence would be rewarded in the future.[23] The relation between obedience and salvation, hard work and future reward, self-denial and messianic expectation, the imperfect present and the perfected future, could hardly be missed in Mao's incantations. Maoist wisdom was theological, it promised fulfillment in the future, urged expiation in the present. It understood history as a dialectical interplay between good and evil, it invoked self-denial and personal asceticism in the present in preparation for the coming of the Final Kingdom. The apotheosis of Maoist thought itself, manufactured with enthusiasm by Mao, turned Mao thought into a venerated cultic object, making totalitarianism an even more likely result.

Mao insisted that communism could be achieved through the moral transformation of the Chinese people, through revolutionary will and the practice of self-abnegation and personal sacrifice. Communism did not have to await the fulfillment of the laws of history. The personal authority and will of Mao were substituted for the 'laws of history'. The kingdom of the future would be fulfilled despite the impoverishment of China, despite the absence of modernization (or perhaps because of its absence). It would be fulfilled because of the moral fervor and commitment of the Chinese people. Communism would not follow from a particular level of material development, or material enjoyment, but from the moral "New Men" who were a bridge to the future and who displayed a dedication based on self-denial, frugality, self-discipline, diligence and honesty, the virtues of the future kingdom. "We must all learn the spirit of absolute selflessness. . . . A man's ability may be great or small, but if he has this spirit, he is already noble-minded and pure, a man of moral integrity and above vulgar interests."[24]

Such values were recognizable in the West as the values of the Protestant Ethic, particularly Calvinist ideology. They were the ascetic values that contrib-

uted to the development of industrial capitalism in the West. In Calvinist ideology the practices of asceticism and self-denial were ethical commandments that
were intended to serve the greater glory of a transcendent God. Diligence, hard
work, self-denial were duties of mankind, a prerequisite if the Kingdom of God
were to be realized. Virtuous behavior was, therefore, not an end in and of itself,
but a means to a greater glory, it promised salvation and the realization of a transcendent kingdom. Maoism, too, envisioned a final kingdom which was to be
realized through the practice of ascetic virtue. Reaching the final goal required
high-purpose, Olympian commitment and, of course, selfless obedience. The
figure of Mao became a kind of apotheosis, a cultic deity who replaced the liturgy and attachments to tradition. Obedience became a special virtue equated
with the mission and purpose of service to the people. To rebel against such requirements was provocative and sinful. What was required was self-purification,
self-criticism and total subjection to the collective goal.[25]

Self-denial, asceticism, total obedience toward and heroic struggle for
higher goals, were admirable and exemplary. Yet what was notably absent in
Maoist thought was any sense of human freedom or the possibility of achieving
human potential. Even the 'red and expert' only internalized values prescribed
by Maoist ideology. The ascetic values promoted by Mao were the very same
values that Marx had associated with earlier Protestant culture and which were
the essence, in Marx's view, of a repressive capitalist culture, not the essence of
Man. Predictably, the Great Leap Forward ceased leaping not long after it began.

By the end of 1958 the prescribed Maoist system of values was in tatters,
the Great Leap Forward was failing to reverse or to correct the 'problems' of
collectivization. Nor had the Great Leap Forward earned the loyalty of the Chinese masses. The mass regimentation that had followed hard on 'revolutionary
spontaneity' only produced fatigue, resentment and even Maoist anxiety over
the possibility of realizing Utopia in the future. Reliance on local initiatives at
the expense of national coordination was producing failures of the backyard iron
and steel furnaces and faulty irrigation projects. The inability of local authorities
to manage large-scale undertakings, the lack of fiscal accountability, revealed
the shortcomings of the revolutionary communes and the difficulties realizing
communism. By 1960 there was widespread hunger, agricultural mechanization
was laggard, the peasant ranks of the Peoples Liberation Army were in revolt in
five provinces, and farmers were selling grain on the black market at exorbitant
prices, then engaging in orgies of consumption. The result was an end to Maoist
utopianism for a decade, the restoration of the village-based collective farms and
the resignation of Mao as Chairman of the People's Republic.[26]

Communist utopian radicalization had receded visibly when Mao openly
admitted to the failure of communization and to his own shortcomings in the
work of economic reconstruction and modernization. Even the utopian ideal was
tarnished. It had to be admitted that one of the chief reasons for the failure of the
People's Communes was the refusal of rich peasant villages to share their wealth
with poorer peasant villages after they had been forcibly integrated into the

Communes. Utopian rhetoric about a future classless society did not produce the kind of public altruism envisioned by Mao.

The Cultural Revolution

But the 'pursuit of the millennium' in China was not over. Another burst of utopian ferment, another pursuit of the classless, egalitarian 'good' society exercised China again in the 1960's. Mao never abandoned his faith in communism, but he no longer believed that the transition period toward it would be brief. By 1960 he agreed that the Great Leap Forward had to be dismantled, but he denied that it was the cause of all China's disasters. Utopian leaping had been disastrous, but the twin natural disasters of flooding and drought in 1960 would have compromised and reversed even the best of programs. Moreover, Mao blamed the CCP for much of the backsliding in China. His deepest scorn was reserved for the 'bourgeois' elements of the Party, functionaries like Liu Shaoqi, the new chairman of the People's Republic, and Deng Xiaoping (Liu's deputy), who relied on government regulation and on bureaucratic professionals who had little or no allegiance to the admittedly nebulous goals of Utopia.[27] The bloodless CCP lacked the kind of revolutionary enthusiasm and utopian idealism that Mao felt were necessary to lift China into the future.

Mao's utopian longings, his urges to combine brain and hand, his desire to remold the external world to the shape of his visions, were severely challenged by the failures of the Communes, but Mao did not abandon his utopian dreams during the dark days of 1959. "Even if there is a collapse," Mao mused, "that'll be all right. We'll rebuild. The worst that will happen is that the whole world will get a big laugh out of it." Defiantly, he added: "If you don't join me in carrying it [the Leap] through, I'll go on by myself, right to the point of being expelled by the Party – even then, I'll go and file a complaint with Marx."[28]

Soon Mao's desire to resurrect Utopia was fanned by the policies of Liu Shaoqi. Under Liu, increased production was stressed over social equality, bureaucratic authority and planning over communal autonomy, large-scale production, located mostly in urban areas, over small-scale production situated mostly in the countryside. Communes had to submit directly to the rule of Beijing. The urban unemployed was forced to return to the countryside. To motivate greater productivity, material incentives were introduced in agriculture and industry. The introduction of wage differentials in place of the utopian ideal of wage and income equality meant greater rewards for administrators, managers, professionals and technical experts, and reintroduced or reinforced the realities of class and class privilege which had been the onus of Maoist thought. More highly skilled industrial workers received greater compensation as well, replicating the income disparities of the West. In rural areas private farm plots were allowed again and were encouraged further by the expansion of private markets for the sale of produce. The government expanded its subsidies for large-scale industrial production, while minimizing support for less efficient small-scale rural production. Communist educators restored more rigorous, formal qualifications for advanced study, opening opportunities for the better prepared children of urban, professional and Mandarin families, but excluding students who were the children of the worker and peasant masses who, almost invariably, were not as well prepared for the university entrance examinations. Those who benefited from Liu's changes were, generally, those who already had privileges or were well situated to take advantage of them. Private farming, an expanded private market, the introduction of wage differentials, all reinforced by access to education for the already advantaged in Party and bureaucracy, together meant the return of a 'bourgeoisie' more akin to the Western model than to the official blandishments of Utopia. But if the Western 'bourgeoisie' derived its power and privileges from the ownership of property, the Chinese 'bourgeoisie' was based on its income, social status and access to higher education. The populist republic of Maoist utopian rhetoric was excluded by definition from the republic of the bureaucrats and engineers.

Mao's attempt to resurrect Utopia was based on his criticism of the new individualism and on the renewal of class privilege that was manifested in the Party. For popular support Mao appealed to the 'incorruptible' masses while skillfully tolerating, encouraging and engineering a Maoist cult that lifted his image above the humdrum routines of daily life. For practical measure Mao harnessed the grievances of the peasantry through the Socialist Education Movement, which he inaugurated in 1962. Through this forum he praised the ideals of socialist collectivism and egalitarianism and urged direct action by the people.

In doing so he bypassed the Party. Mao's ideas were supported by the People's Liberation Army as well, it was the Liberation Army's indoctrination campaign of the 1960's that lent credence and support to the development of the cult of Mao, promoting an uncritical acceptance of Maoist collectivist utopian ideals. Mao's strategy in this period was simple; galvanize the masses and renovate the egalitarian, chiliastic expectations generated earlier by the Great Leap Forward. During that earlier era Mao had bypassed the regular bureaucratic channels of State and Party, establishing a direct bond between himself and the peasant masses, and forging a link between his utopian expectations and the popular aspirations of Chinese peasants. Now Maoist thought was again promoted as the sacred liturgy of the utopian church.[29]

The campaign to promote Mao-thought in the 1960's, however, was patently fabricated. It depended largely on the People's Liberation Army (PLA), hardly an institution that had overcome bureaucracy or hierarchy, to promote Mao-thought and the millenarian ideals on which Mao-thought was based. In May 1964 the Political Department of the PLA published the first edition of *Quotations of Chairman Mao*. Over the next several years nearly one billion copies of the little red book, as it came to be called, were printed, along with another 150 million copies of *The Selected Works of Mao Tse-tung*. Mao's thought was so extravagantly praised and venerated that even Edgar Snow, no mean critic of Mao, questioned the wisdom of Mao's beatification. Snow had uneasy recollections of the similar worship of Joseph Stalin during World War II, suggesting an uncomfortable analogy and an ill omen for China's future.[30] But for Mao, who explained to Snow in 1965 that Khrushchev would not have fallen from power had he taken the effort to build up a cult around himself, the Mao cult alone could mobilize the masses, especially the more jubilant – and vulnerable – youth who would dare to rebel against the authority of Party and State. In the 'life and death' struggle that would follow there were only two choices. The restoration of the utopian mission, assisted by the renewal of the Mao cult, or the continuation of "bourgeois degeneration."[31]

Mao's frank appeal to youth was an admission of his fear that revolutionary idealism had been dulled by Party ritual, doctrine and bureaucratization. He targeted the Party and 'Mandarin' intellectuals for ritual cleansing. Admonishing youth against the tendency toward Mandarin exclusiveness and Confucian scholasticism, in 1964 Mao urged his youthful acolytes to avoid excessive reliance on books. "At present there is too much studying going on, and this is exceedingly harmful . . . the present method of education ruins talent and ruins youth. I do not approve of reading so many books."[32] Intellectuals were chided for lapsing into Mandarin habits and were advised to pack themselves off to villages and factories, to contribute directly to the building of communism. Mao's urgings were fraught with messianic overtones that had earlier characterized the Great Leap Forward. In the sweep of intellectuals into factory and collectives, he surmised, city and countryside would be bonded into a classless unity, into an unprivileged, egalitarian Utopia. The alienation and isolation of the West would be avoided through the unity of intellectuals and the multitudes. Knowledge based on books was to be avoided because it only reaffirmed Mandarin ways and it was based on knowledge of the past, not constructive visions of the future. Thought which departed from Mao's cautionary wisdom was revisionist heresy, it had to be excised, and its bearer had to be re-educated.

How intellectuals and the multitudes were to be unified in a great new Utopia soon became clear. The new road to Utopia, the Cultural Revolution, was now unsheathed. In February 1966, Mao established the Cultural Revolution Directorate. He called on youth to heed his visions and to remove the cancer of revisionism and privilege in China. On 20 March he invoked the spirit of youth to clean the Augean stables of the nation: "We need determined people who are young, have little education, a firm attitude and the political experience to take over the work."[33]

The war against the intellectuals soon gathered momentum. On 16 May Mao's wife, Chiang Ching, now officially in charge of the Cultural Revolution, issued the marching orders of the revolutionary movement. She attacked the 'scholar tyrants' who used 'abstruse' language to silence the class struggle and to keep politics out of academia. She knew how to counter this abuse: "Chairman Mao often says there is no construction without destruction. Destruction means criticism and repudiation – it means revolution."[34] Two days later Lin Piao made a speech to the Politburo in which he analyzed the history of *coups d'etat*. Force and propaganda were irresistible, "seizure of political power depends upon gun-barrels and inkwells. . . . Political power is the power to oppress others."[35] In the second half of May the Cultural Revolution began in earnest with the appearance of Red Guards, the storm-troopers of the revolution, and wall-posters.

The Red Guards, the youth brigades, first appeared on 29 May. They were from the middle school, aged twelve to fourteen. Their first act was to attack Tsinghua University. Gathering momentum, the Red Guards were soon joined by children from younger and older age groups, by students and even by members of CCP Youth Leagues, who revolted against the official leadership and took to the streets in gangs. As China's educational system ground to a halt in the early summer of 1966, faculty members fled in terror, hoping to escape capture and 're-education'.

The campaign against intellectuals received the full blessing and encouragement of Mao. Targets of the rampaging juveniles included reminders of anything Western, anything that exhibited signs of individuality or creativity. Individuality and creativity were signs of decadence, marks of distinction or wealth, not to be tolerated in an egalitarian society. Books or art works, the work of intellectuals, were randomly destroyed. Tea shops, private restaurants and theaters were all closed. Shops were prevented from selling cosmetics, slit skirts and sunglasses. The National Gallery of Arts was closed, libraries were emptied and shut. Large bonfires were built to consume the hated objects. The Party finally capitulated to the fury of the Red Guards. Responding to the victims who sought protection, the advice of the Central Committee of the CCP was to let the masses liberate themselves, "trust the masses, rely on them and respect their initiative. . . . Let the masses educate themselves . . . no measure should be taken against universities, colleges, middle and primary schools"[36]

Indeed, how well the masses educated themselves! The rampages of the Red Guards, urged on by poster incantations like "Smash his dog's head," produced 400,000 murder victims. Chiang Ching led the charge against the world of culture. She denounced capitalism because it destroyed art, then proceeded to denounce jazz, Impressionism, Symbolism, abstract art, Fauvism, and Modernism because they were decadent, obscene and corrupted the mind of youth. Red Guard squadrons under the command of Chiang Ching seized radio and television stations, newspapers and magazines, cameras and films. On 12 December 1966 many 'public enemies, including a horde of film and theater directors who had offended Chiang Ching, were paraded in front of 10,000 people at the Workers' Stadium with wooden placards around their necks.[37] There seemed to be no limits to the new Puritan revolt, no end to its anti-intellectualism. Though still vaguely millenarian there was no clear sense of what would replace the order that was being vilified and smashed.

The singular lexicon of Utopia was chilling as well as chiliastic. Sin would be expunged by ablution or coercion. The CCP itself was forced to bow to the new furies early in Mao's campaign. There can be no "peaceful transition," cried one Red Guard in May. "We are going to strike you down to the dust and keep you there," he admonished the 'counterrevolutionaries'.[38] Mao, after swimming in the Yangtze River, condescended to the Party's Central Committee: "All conventions must be smashed. The current great cultural-revolution is an earth-shaking event. Can we or do we dare undergo the test of socialism?"[39] Urging youth to become the soldiers of Utopia, Mao's rhetoric became even more incendiary. He summoned his soldiers to "bombard the headquarters" of the enemies of socialism while he dismissed Liu Shaoqi, illegally, as head of state.[40] By August, Mao's victory over the Party was total and unconditional. Although the Party still admonished workers not to expect the fulfillment of the revolution, adding that the development of production was still paramount, it urged peasants, workers, Party cadres and intellectuals to accept Mao-Tse-tung-thought as their guide. Less than a fortnight later, the Great Proletarian Cultural Revolution was officially consecrated in Beijing on Tien'anmen Square near the Gate of Heavenly Peace. Theodore Von Laue has captured the mythic and epic dimensions of the moment, which was attended by more than a million members of the Red Guard, many of them waving copies of Mao's *Quotations* and shouting passages of Mao-Tse-tung-thought, reaffirming the magnetism and the transforming power of Mao's renewed cult:

> As the sun rose in the East, Mao, clad in a soldier's fatigues stepped out onto the gallery of the famous gate. . . . Before him stood a youthful force setting out for revolution to the tune of "The East is Red," their battle hymn. No other country could mount the impressive displays of massed humanity organized during the cultural revolution; every human atom seemed fused with all the other human atoms in an exalted common dedication to Chairman Mao.[41]

Mao was conscious of the transforming power of Utopia. In his *Quotations* he anticipated not only the new order in China by "the beginning of the 21st century," but he spoke of the socialist countries as "an entirely new type in which the exploiting classes have been overthrown and the working people are in power."[42] Ignoring China's break with the Soviet Union in the spring of 1966, Mao looked forward to the new fraternal order in which "the principle of integrating internationalism with patriotism" is practiced in the relations between the socialist countries.[43] Utopia was consecrated as universal, cosmopolitan, transforming, happily blending with the new patriotism in which the cultic transfiguration of Mao substituted his person for both state and deity. Regimented revolutionary change was reinforced by the myth of collective community, enforced substitutionism was buttressed by mystical unity. Fantasy and ideology converged in the advent of Utopia.

Thus did Mao in his "life and death" struggle against "bourgeois restoration" create a powerful myth in which history blended with prophecy, in which libidinal satisfaction was transformed into a kind of mystical unity, all merged at the prophetic summit in the reconfiguration of the person of Mao. As utopian prophet and infallible leader Mao's political, ideological and 'religious' authority was not only unchallengeable, he represented a historic crusade of epic proportion that guided history to its inevitable and 'just' denouement. Mao embodied destiny, justice, history, he was mystically linked to the Chinese people, he was myth crystallized as infallible pope of the nascent church. The authority of Mao was not only supreme, his thoughts and powers were held to be supernatural and magical. They were not merely beyond challenge, they were believed to be transcendent. The utopian social order that was in progress was linked with the cosmic order. As the ancient Chinese emperors had once been identified as the "Sons of Heaven," linking the social and cosmic orders through their purity and virtue, so now the revered, though manipulated, image of Mao became an icon that represented "Heaven." The apotheosis of Mao became so complete, and his manipulated infallibility so established, at least among the Red Guards and youth acolytes, that it was impossible to challenge the new universal wisdom. Opponents who saw "Heaven" as a fanatical religious commonwealth in which no dissent would be tolerated, in which there could be no appeal against the godhead, were best advised to remain silent.

Western Fellow Travelers

The power of myth, the compelling need for and fantasizing of Utopia, was as addictive in the West as it was in China and the East. Utopia offered more than the hope of a bountiful future; it was a transcendent vision of unity, the end of personal alienation and isolation. It was the restoration of community, the recovery of Eden. It offered biblical simplicity, a vision of a Golden Age, but at the end of history, in fulfillment of a higher and even sublime transcendence. Western intellectuals, suffering from the travails of endemic war in the twentieth-century, or the apparent indifference and anarchy of their own societies, were especially susceptible to the blandishments of Utopia. They made endless pilgrimages to China in search of a fantasized society of compassion and harmony.

American intellectuals, caught in the vice of the war in Indochina, were especially likely to experience disillusionment with their country and, as in the 1930's, looked for political and spiritual alternatives. Many Americans sought to correct views of China that they considered false. Such views were shrouded in 'ignorance' of China and of communism, they argued, and were 'distorted' by American involvement in the war in Vietnam and by the Cold War in general. Intellectuals who were disenchanted with American politics and institutions in the 1960's found it difficult to criticize other societies, especially Third World countries that they thought were the innocent victims of the West. Moreover, disillusionment with endemic war and crass materialism in the United States produced the need for myth and transcendence, and led to a noble attempt to discover direction, purpose and meaning in the utopian communist experiment in China.

The rush of Western intellectuals to China, especially American intellectuals after the travel ban to China was lifted in 1972, was based on the desire to rediscover the utopian virtue that had long faded in the Soviet Union. Charles Frolic, who later became an apostate to the holy cause in the late 1970's, when he compared China's Great Leap Forward and Cultural Revolution to the Stalinist Russia of the 1930's, offered a retrospective explanation for the romanticized expiation that had captured his imagination during the earlier part of the decade:

In the 'developed' West, the idea of an emerging Chinese model appealed to many of us for a variety of reasons. The occupation of Czechoslovakia had just taken place. . . . We were, therefore, more willing to listen to the Chinese and to be more sympathetic to their cause if only because they were so aggressively anti-Soviet. Second, China was exotic to most of us, a repository of the wonderful secrets of the mysterious East. So why not accept the proposition that this strange culture may actually have found a superior way to modernize? Third, commitment to the new China was a form of expiation for some Westerners who felt that China had been wronged and exploited in its encounters with the West. . . . Fourth, for many intellectuals struggling to cope with the moral crisis of the sixties the Chinese model was a beacon of salvation showing that there still was hope for mankind. . . . Finally, for radicals throughout the world, the Chinese example was one last try for utopia, a more plausible socialist synthesis than anything tried in the past.[44]

Of course there was hardly universal acceptance among Western scholars and intellectuals of the Maoist experimentation with Utopia, even in the sixties and early seventies. Alberto Moravia's *Red Book and the Great Wall* (1968) noted the lack of free expression in the arts and literature. Numerous accounts by political tourists, among them French writers Robert Guillain, Jacques Marcuse, Jules Roy, American sociologist Herbert Passin and Swiss correspondent Lorenz Stucki, all noted that the Chinese techniques of 'hospitality' and the 'grand tour' had prevented them from learning much of China, except for the propaganda to which they were exposed.[45] But, generally, critical views of China did not prevail against the more auspicious droppings of fellow travelers like Staughton Lynd and Tom Hayden who, after traveling to the 'other side' to personally witness the Cultural Revolution, noted the difference between the purposeless chaos of the West and the purposeful conviction of China. "The sense of a different world is immediate."[46]

The epic and even ecstatic embracing of that "different world" had a messianic, missionary and apocalyptic tone about it. Hewlett Johnson, who thought that the apocalypse had arrived earlier in the Soviet Union, now welcomed it in China in tones that seemed to welcome the end of history (how often has this been proclaimed?). The comparison between Christian heaven and Utopia seemed inescapable to Johnson, who had argued earlier that the best values of Christianity had been realized in the Soviet Union during the thirties: "China . . . is performing an essentially religious act, entirely parallel with [the] Christian abhorrence of covetousness . . . freeing men from the bondage of the acquisitive instinct and paving the way for a new organization of life on a higher level of existence."[47] The habit of Chinese self-criticism reminded Johnson of Christian expiation, it was "reminiscent of the primitive Christian professions of a humble and contrite heart, and . . . of the communal forgiveness of the early Christian communities . . . an outlook [which] gives promise of unimaginable moral strength."[48]

The joining of morality and politics, of self-denial and dutiful obedience, of ascetic self-devotion and social obligation, was given messianic overtones by Westerners eager to discover harmonious alternatives to the dissipated energies and self-seeking individualism of the West. Mission, purpose, unity, hope, virtue, idealism, altruism, vitality, exemplary, buoyant, ascetic, were words that gushed to the lips of Westerners praising Maoist China against the hedonism of a West obsessed with sex, pornography, possessions and careerism. Some members of the Committee of Concerned Asian Scholars were convinced that the Chinese did not mind long separations from their families because they put work and duty to country ahead of personal satisfaction and domestic happiness. Simone de Beauvoir noted simply: "Far and away from being in contradiction, personal aspirations and duty to the country jibe."[49]

How she could be so certain was unclear, but examples in which Westerners linked the Maoist social order to a cosmic order, in which there was a kind of fusion between the "Sons of Heaven" and the "Mao-Sun," abounded in the West. The quest for Utopia, a preeminent Western ideal that had traversed from Christian to secular Utopia, remained a potent addiction, and even helped give shape to the understanding of, and the hope for, a secular earthly paradise. The desire to transcend the moral relativism and ethical uncertainty that had permeated Western secular society, at least since the nineteenth-century, gave shape, direction and meaning to the way that numerous intellectuals celebrated Mao's Utopia. Even a noted and judicious scholar like the American Sinologist John Fairbank, hardly a true believer, saw history as a moral crusade, a cosmic dramaturgy, in which a Maoist Utopia would instill social harmony and unity of purpose: "Under Mao the Chinese Revolution has become not only an advance in the industrial arts . . . but also a far-reaching moral crusade to change the very human Chinese personality in the direction of self-sacrifice and serving others."[50] China was a perfect unity of politics and morality, so much so that it was governed "by exemplary moral men, not laws."[51]

Fairbank's celebration of China as humanity's future was not unique. British social scientist Peter Worsley and fellow traveler Jan Myrdal, whose father was the celebrated Swedish sociologist Gunnar Myrdal, both remarked that 'Mao-Sun' was not just about material improvement or political reform but was also about the fundamental transvaluation of human nature. Worsley, in particular, used apocalyptic language to describe the 'new man' that was being manufactured in the utopian laboratories of China. Too Worsley it seemed that history moved through the struggle of the sacred and the profane, two poles symbolized by the redemptive cosmic Utopia of China and the decadent, materialist West. He fairly guffawed at "the Chinese attempt to transform human values and personal relationships at the level of everyday human life," and at the ability of the Maoists "to challenge assumptions that certain modes of behavior are naturally 'entailed' under conditions of industrial or city life . . . that some form of class system . . . is inevitable . . . that the attractiveness of material gratifications must, in the end, reassert itself."[52] It was not just the conditions of life that were being altered and improved in China, Utopia was being chiseled, like a massive statuary, by "the resocialization of people in new positive, humanistic social values" in ways that Worsley assumed were necessarily benign and prepossessing for the Chinese, the presumed benefactors of "resocialization."[53] The advent of Utopia was heralded as a type of "socialism that is not just about forms of ownership: it is about participation, democracy and altruism: a human texture of life."[54]

The will to believe was so powerful among intoxicated Westerners that the real China, and history itself, became invisible. Disenchantment with the perva-

sive inequalities in the West, the desire to reignite the idealism and utopian enthusiasm that had perished with the Soviet failure, the hope that equality, fraternity and social justice were still attainable, helped contribute to the irrepressible
desire among Western intellectuals to discover nobility in the Maoist resurrection of Utopia.

The intense hatred of bureaucracy among Western intellectuals in the
1960's led to a rejection of all that they associated with it: hierarchy, inequality,
depersonalization, routinization, all qualities that they associated with the mass
societies in the West. By contrast, many of those same intellectuals were more
receptive to the egalitarian appeals and propaganda of China. Italian journalist
Mary Macchiocchi discovered no bureaucratic or hierarchic mentality in
China.[55] Even deference to superiors had been replaced by the ubiquitous 'com-
rade'. Status distinctions were eradicated at the workplace, gone were the distinctions between management and labor. Even artistic activity had been democratized; everybody was encouraged to express themselves artistically. Felix
Greene, an English writer, observed a veritable "intellectual renaissance . . . [a]
cultural explosion."[56] So far as American economist John Kenneth Galbraith
could discern, the Chinese Communist ruling class was the least ostentatious in
history, though he failed to question the existence of a ruling class in Utopia.
Galbraith discovered little difference between rich and poor. He noted a virtual
equality of income between workers, scientists, engineers, plant managers and
local officials, although there was information even during Mao's lifetime that
conflicted with such an auspicious account.[57]

More dispassionate observers reported on the warts that were visible to the
naked eye. American social scientist Martin Whyte noted thirty ranks among
officials and employees in the state bureaucracy, with a pay differential that was
about 28:1 between the highest and lowest ranks. Technicians were on a different scale, which also contained severe inequalities.[58] Donald Zagoria observed
pervasive inequalities between rural communes located close to cities and communes in remote areas, between rich and poor brigades, and substantial differences between urban and rural incomes.[59] Edgar Snow, though a partisan of the
regime and a personal friend of Mao, disclosed that military pay differentials
ranged from a parsimonious $2.50 per month for a private to the magnanimous
sum of $360-400 for marshals.[60] Despite such disclosures there was a predispo-
sition among numerous fellow travelers to believe that equality prevailed in
China. Limited access to information, the pervasive belief that the absence of
political liberty was compensated by rapid material gains and the fervid hope of
finding an alternative to the fatuous materialism and moral uncertainty of the
West, all played a role in helping to maintain 'true belief' in the future heaven of
China.

Westerners who were disenchanted with the travails of modernity and who
had witnessed the corrosive effects of industrialization and 'modernization', as
well as the decline and dissipation of organic community in the West, were predisposed to welcome communism in China. Communism represented, they believed, rapid material improvement, but it promised an eschatological community as well. It even anticipated the end of human alienation and projected a final

redemptive community at the end of history. It projected community and the end of privation simultaneously. For American sociologist Peter Berger, who was not a fellow traveler or a true believer, socialism was a secularized eschatology that incorporated "a new rational order, the abolition of want and social inequality, and the complete liberation of the individual. Socialism . . . promises all the blessings of modernity and the liquidation of its costs . . . including . . . the cost of alienation."[61]

Maoist utopianism was not just an experiment that aimed at ending the accumulated penury and misery of centuries. It also symbolized, in Mao's eyes, the hope of a final redemptive act in which rural serenity blended with renewed human community. Mao's version of a messianic and redemptive community borrowed from the folkloric traditions of China. Maoism contained elements of traditional peasant wisdom. It fused peasant populism, drawing on the legacy of the Taiping rebellion in the nineteenth-century, and the Fourth of May movement after World War I.

By the second half of 1967, however, it was increasingly difficult to maintain illusions about Maoism, even for the most optimistic utopians or fellow travelers. Cruelty, despair, penury, inequality had not disappeared from China. Utopia appeared less credible and less desirable. Red Guards fought with conservative army groups in July 1967. For a while it appeared that China was on the verge of civil war. Red Guard violence reached a new pitch by the fall of 1967, urged on by Mao's call for destruction before construction. As the number of Red Guard victims rose into the tens of thousands Mao admitted that he had not anticipated the turn toward violence. "We were not mentally prepared for new problems."[62] Caught in a vortex of events beyond his control, Mao vacillated between revolutionary radicalism and the need for order. But revolutionary enthusiasm had created a momentum of its own, it had aimed its arrows against the new 'capitalist roaders', the 'bourgeoisie' ensconced in Party, government and society. And in aiming at these targets it had eroded the kind of individual and collective discipline needed to build a new polity. Maoist-inspired protest undermined all authority, from Confucian teachings to state and parental authority.[63] The intoxication of building paradise had only unleashed a new edition of Red Terror. Even Mao had to admit that the experiment in millenarianism had failed.

By 1970 the Cultural Revolution was finished as an experiment in the future. Political messianism gave way to the pragmatism of rapid industrialization and modernization. Parity with the West, rather than utopian grandeur, became the touchstone of the CCP and the post-Mao leadership. The cadres of leadership were now the de-radicalized professional bureaucrats, a new ruling class with little sympathy for the utopian ideals and fantasies of the revolutionary period. Now Utopia would be metastasized, the Chinese revolution would no longer look forward to future grandeur, only, as in Lenin's formulation, to electrification and modernization. The monolithic state power established by Mao would make the task of national regimentation manageable. It would not take long before China would return to some of the old benchmarks of Chinese civilization – even Confucianism was being resurrected by the late eighties to help codify discipline and establish order and unity. In place of utopian enthusiasm there was blatant regimentation, not the hope or the myth of universal cosmopolitanism but uninspired, pragmatic national self-interest. The lineaments of totalitarianism remained, but without the myth that was supposed to legitimize it.

Unquestionably Maoist millenarianism had a widespread appeal for the Chinese peasantry. Yet the appeal of Chinese communism to the peasantry originally had little to do with communist ideology. It derived much more from peasant hunger for land, resentment of Western imperialism and the belief that the communists were the only force able to resist the Japanese.[64] In China, much more than in the Soviet Union, communism and nationalism converged due to the intemperance of decadent rulers like Chiang Kai-shek, the brutality of invaders such as the Japanese, the forced unequal treaties imposed by the 'liberal' Western 'open door' policy, and the long history of indigenous Chinese political and cultural traditions – including the Boxer rebellion of 1900 – which aimed to expel the Russians from Manchuria. In addition there was the Fourth of May rebellion against the Kuomintang in 1919, an event which precipitated the formation of the CCP. All of these factors framed the foundation for the policy and the directions of the CCP.[65] But what turned Maoist communism into a volatile, populist revolutionary movement with global and historical aspirations, was its prophetic and messianic character, its notions of historical endism and the promise of human fulfillment in a not too distant secular paradise. Paradoxically, this helped enhance the power of the Party, not only because it alone had the power of prophecy, especially as personified by Mao, but also because it aspired to and was accepted as a vehicle of deliverance – embodied by the cultic reverence of Mao.

The appeal of Utopia was a mixture of prophesied transcendence, classless egalitarian unity and global cosmopolitanism; it also symbolized an ideological dramaturgy based on resistance to and hatred of (Western) incursions and domination. But the failures of the Great Leap Forward and the Cultural Revolution meant the abandonment of Utopia and the irrelevance of Marxism-Leninism, or Maoism, as a legitimizing political ideology. Henceforth, China abandoned ideology in favor of a more pragmatic and frankly authoritarian approach to modernization. China began to compete with other nations on the basis of economics rather than ideology. The new Mandarins of the Chinese Communist stewardship, as early as the 1980's, behaved more like Western technocrats than Marxists, more like nationalists than utopian-inspired Communists.

Chairman Mao was a nationalist, Marxist and utopian communist. He was committed to building a strong China that could compete with the West. Too accomplish that he hoped to build an egalitarian China based on cooperative, non-market economics. The ideological framework was Marxist, though a Marxism adapted to the needs of Chinese peasant culture. Maoism was an idiosyncratic blend of voluntarism and egalitarianism, mystically blended into a historical dialectic promising infinite fulfillment. That the two notions contradicted each other seems obvious in retrospect. Mao was never able to force the Chinese peasantry to be happy. Mandarin authoritarianism and the reculturation of the Chinese countryside implied that Utopia had to be driven home from the top down. But the Chinese peasant could never be blank and red, could never accept Mao's blend of authoritarianism and egalitarianism. Not only did each not quite fit the other, but the nobility of the goal could never be squared with the delayed timetable for achieving the goal. Moreover, Mao's task of retrofitting the Chinese peasantry with a cooperative culture of utopian ideals and harnessing that to double-step industrialization was bound to come to grief amidst a generation neither tutored in Marxist ideology nor likely to accept sacrifices that would only benefit future generations. Ultimately, Mao resorted to nationalism and pragmatism; the problem of lifting China up by its bootstraps in one generation after centuries of backwardness, poverty and isolation could not be overcome by utopian dreaming and mass reculturation, however noble the goal.

Maoism was a monumental experiment applied in a backward, peasant country. It was nothing less than an attempt at reculturating the peasant masses by imposing cooperative and utopian ideals, abolishing the degrading past of imperialist subjection and turning China into a utopian garden. That Mao's utopian experiment ultimately failed, however, was due as much to the economic backwardness of China and its almost total isolation from the West – and its long road toward liberal humanism – as to the structure of Utopia itself.

Part II
Marxism, Humanism and the Revolt against History

Marx's utopian ideals were never followed or applied by Lenin or Mao. In the West, however, the utopian Marx was taken up by a number of writers, including Walter Benjamin, Ernst Bloch, Herbert Marcuse and Andre Gorz. These writers were impressed by the utopian elements of Marx's ideas which they thought completed many of the major themes of Western Civilization: the liberal humanism that came forth from the Enlightenment; the biblical and epical notions of human liberty that came forth from the Jewish prophetic tradition and that were utopian to the core; the idea of human emancipation within human history that was associated, especially by Bloch, with early Christianity; and the human ingredient in history that presupposed an end to human alienation in life and work, an element that especially pervaded the work of Marcuse and Gorz.

Chapter 4
Walter Benjamin: Between Mysticism and Marxism

Walter Benjamin was fated to fall between two different and often opposed worlds. He was a Jew who rejected Zionism, a Marxist who embraced mysticism, a German who loved France, a materialist who thought reality could only be discovered through dream, a lover of classical theater and literature who saw great value in mass culture, a man of the twentieth who consciously exiled himself to the nineteenth-century, a resident of Berlin who wrote extensively about Paris.

Marxist, exile and Jew, Benjamin's life was as much a contradiction as the ironies that he detailed in his literary work and in the historical anomalies and oddities that he collected in his monumental tome, *The Arcades Project*. He was a Marxist who was thoroughly utopian and who believed in the primacy of consciousness. He was a materialist who looked for the face of God in the Jewish Kabbala, a Jew who preferred exile in Paris to Jerusalem, a historian who thought the truth of mankind could only be discovered in the journey through its collective unconscious dreams. Above all, he was a literary critic who was a utopian hoping to discover the significance of mankind's dreams and hopes in the surviving detritus, the footprints that humanity had left behind in the rubble of history. Jew, German, mystic, utopian, Marxist and critic, Benjamin hoped to unravel the chaos he found around him, the disaster called the twentieth-century. He hoped to do this by putting details of the past under a microscope, the better to find traces of the present, the better to shock the contemporary world by showing its discontinuities with the past. Not unlike his contemporary and friend, Ernst Bloch, whom he often quoted, Benjamin was a denizen of the nineteenth-century not only because of its more classical lines and cosmic harmonies, but because he was convinced the nineteenth saw the catastrophe of the twentieth-century in advance. By disinterring an earlier wisdom, he thought it possible to gain an understanding of the world inherited from the past, especially when put in juxtaposition with the present and its mordant concerns with commodity life, personal consumption and its obsessive forgetting. Thus, it was no accident that Benjamin studied Paris of the nineteenth-century, after all that earlier Paris was also the capital of revolution and revolutionary justice, of dream and utopian possibility. If one were attentive, one could read or decipher in nineteenth-century Paris, in the footprints of the past, both the detritus and the leavings left behind in that century, and its anticipation of a classless utopian future.

From the 1920's onward Benjamin's self-conscious mission was not to study great men and celebrated events but to pick up the primal history of the nineteenth-century, the collective unconscious of the past gathered up in snippets of aphorisms, anecdotes and citations. For Benjamin this could only be done through cunning, not through conceptual analysis but through something like dream interpretation, for the "nineteenth-century was the collective dream which we, its heirs, were obliged to reenter."[1]

To read Benjamin is like entering a dream city made up of snippets of the past that he wished to reenter. His approach was to use montage, like an Eisenstein film or surrealistic fantasy or dadaism with its deliberate destruction of form in favor of exploring the unconscious by sifting through the leavings of history. Benjamin's aim was to blast the eternal present out of the continuum of so-called historical progress, to confront the present by challenging the notion of homogeneous temporality. He wanted to crack open 'natural teleology and the notion of a fixed destiny, to demonstrate that the contemporary obsession with science and the mastery of nature meant the obliteration of the past and its promise of messianic time. It was precisely messianic time, the notion that history had meaning and content and was moving toward an apocalyptic triumph, a Utopia still undisclosed, that Benjamin wished to dislodge from the bourgeois insistence on secular meaninglessness and the interminable continuum of profane time.[2]

For Benjamin, industrial capitalism, with its own logic of the commodification of life, had robbed the past of its meaning and mystery, converting all corners of life into commerce and the calculus of gain. The same spirit had impacted on all corners of life, including art, which had become more about public reception, decoration and monetary value than about magic and redemption. At the same time, Benjamin highlighted the *flaneur*, a lonely, melancholic figure, much like Benjamin himself, who stood in the margins of history and time, anonymous and invisible. The *flaneur* was a figure no doubt passed up by history. He was neither ready to abandon the dreams and narratives of the past, nor able to adapt to or to be welcomed by the brave new era of contemporary industrial capitalism and the machine age, the age, as Benjamin put it, of mechanical reproduction.

Dream and the Flaneur

In his essay "Hashish in Marseilles," written in 1928, Benjamin began by describing the effects of hashish. He depicted a continual alternation of dreaming and waking, a sudden rupture of all memory of past events, a break in the continuum of history and time.[3] The trance induced by drugs cut one off from everyday reality, simultaneously inducing ecstasy and revealing the sterility of given forms of reality. Thus, hashish, like dream, fragmented time, or rather ruptured it, allowing the intoxicated to insert himself into the past heretofore obliterated by layers of time and compressed and distorted by culture.[4]

But if time was discontinuous, if history was anything but progressive and cumulative, if experience was fragmented by the limits of individual consciousness, Benjamin thought that the historical past could still be resurrected from the black hole of memory. To accomplish this he envisioned history in terms of space, not time. Just as Ernst Bloch expanded time into asynchronous reality, so Benjamin condensed space, looking for spatial affinities in the streets of Berlin and Paris and across the vast panorama of history. At the same time he expanded space, finding similarities in the nuances and gestures that occupied it. Thus, he insisted on conflating the political, rational sense with the mystical meaning of experience. He immersed himself in "contemplation of the sidewalk before me . . . which . . . could have been, precisely as these very stones, the sidewalk of Paris. These stones were the bread of my imagination which was suddenly seized by a ravenous hunger to taste what is the same in all places and countries."[5]

For Benjamin, drug addiction, notably hashish, was as much metaphor as intoxicant, for it overcame "fearing future misfortune, future solitude."[6] Alienated by modernity, uprooted in time and space, the *flaneur*, like Benjamin, felt the need to overcome loneliness by experiencing the sameness in all nuances. Trance and dream induced by intoxicants dissolved the isolation of the bourgeois world, triumphed over the loneliness of the human being trapped in the quarters of his urbanscape, overcame alienation and the barriers of internal exile by somehow discovering the affinities of space. Thus, Benjamin deconstructed reality and took each gesture as a trace of the universal. Bourgeois reality gave way to hope through its trance-like dissolution. Melancholy for the loss of the past at last gave way to hope for the future.[7]

Benjamin explored the dream world further in his 1929 essay on surrealism. He thought surrealism conclusive because it integrated all the aspects of life that had become fragments without a whole, or things without a reality. Life was only worth living, he said, "where the threshold between waking and sleeping was worn away in everyone as by the steps of multitudinous images flooding back and forth, language only seemed itself where sound and image, image and sound interpenetrated with automatic precision."[8] In surrealism the dream broke through bourgeois reality in fragments of consciousness. Moreover, in surrealist deconstruction, language matched the world that it described and understood; life and the word described each other. By stripping away layers of time, but especially by exploring and comparing spatial continuities through montage, surrealists had discovered the authentic in the world of dream and had broken through the continuum of history.[9]

At the same time, Benjamin insisted that surrealist thought was concerned with experience and the concrete, not just abstract theory. Surrealists wanted to transform the world, not simply experience religious or drug induced ecstasy. Surrealists Arthur Rimbaud, Guillaume Apollinaire and Andre Breton were after profane illumination, not just ecstatic overcoming of the limits of self. They sought the transvaluation of the world through anthropological inspiration, through an imagination fed by ecstatic dream. For what were dream and the deconstruction of reality, if not a primordial philosophy of revolt?[10]

What, then, Benjamin wondered, had surrealist writers like Breton and Apollinaire brought to the world? The answer was precisely atmosphere, the tracings of what had been lost, or was being lost, the first notices of what was being born, the first photos, the new architecture, the whole atmosphere of what conveyed melancholy, and which was the basis of revolutionary nihilism. The French surrealists, Benjamin insisted, were the first to notice how destitution, social and architectonic, the poverty of interiors for example, led to rebellion against not only existence, but of that particular existence in decadent France.[11] The surrealist understanding of the world of things, therefore, was a political understanding. Surrealist art, inspired by the unconscious, was ready for the task of deconstructing the class-ridden reality that was emerging in the twentieth century.[12]

Benjamin and surrealism were brought together by a mutual attraction to philosophical 'idealism'. Surrealists believed there was a parallel world of concepts, as real as the world of objects, and that the concept world came forth from the world of dream. The machine itself realized the old fable: the concept came before the object. This became political because the idea of perfection had to exist as the world of dream first; only later could it exist in the world of objects as they came forth from the ecstasy of dream and fantasy. Dreaming exploded the emerging capitalist world with ecstatic preparations for the next.[13]

In Benjamin's estimation, the surrealist revolt wasn't only an attempt to rearrange the world; it wasn't primarily about institutions. It was a rebellion that denied the legitimacy of the moral cosmos itself, a secular attempt at the moral and spiritual regeneration of mankind. It was an attempt to reinvent the moral basis of the universe and creation. It was a passionate revolt against the Catholic Church and the God that the Church enshrined in the cosmos, including the legitimacy of divine judgment. Thus, the surrealists thought they could not only recreate the cosmos through the imagination, they sought also to create a kind of moral manifesto that would highlight the sins and hypocrisy of the bourgeois world around them, a world that paled when juxtaposed with the world generated by dream.[14]

Such ideas appealed to Benjamin, never a sycophant of any church. He could understand the rebellion of the surrealists against God and nature. It matched his own sense of alienation from the world he was inheriting, his own disbelief in the eternal optimism and *gemutlichkeit* of Weimar Germany, especially when juxtaposed against the iniquities and failures of liberal democracy that abounded in Germany after World War I.

In this connection, Benjamin quoted Fyodor Dostoevsky, referring especially to Stavrogin's confession in *The Possessed,* which Benjamin compared to Arthur Rimbaud's *Chants de Maldorer.* The conventional view was that goodness, regardless of human virtue, was inspired by God, whereas evil stemmed entirely from human spontaneity and defect of character. Stavrogin, however, considered vileness as preformed, as inspired by the same God who made the universe. It was a point that Benjamin could embrace: "Dostoevsky's God created not only heaven and earth and man and beast, but also baseness, vengeance, cruelty."[15] Benjamin was left with two choices. Accept defective human nature and the God who created vileness, as did Arthur Rimbaud, or acknowledge a silent universe and reinvent the moral cosmos, as did Benjamin.

Benjamin appreciated the dilemma faced by the surrealists, but he could not swallow surrealism whole without a bit of indigestion. After all, could hatred and revulsion be a manifesto of action, could pessimism be a ritual of belief in a better future? Could the rejection of the world and of human nature such as it was, along with the God that created it, be a clarion call for action? Could poetry be resolved as revolution? Could rejecting religion lead to anything more than romantic rebellion? Could moral revolt lead to freedom?[16] Benjamin's cautious reply was surprising. He admitted that the surrealists had a radical concept of total human liberty that was adequate to the dream of human emancipation. They were the "first to liquidate the sclerotic liberal-moral-humanistic ideal of freedom. . . ."[17] They believed that freedom had to be enjoyed without any pragmatic calculations. Yet he cautioned that the surrealists usually skirted the issue of how to transform revolt against everything bourgeois, against the entire world as they found it, into political revolution. They never understood how to turn moral revulsion and romantic rebellion, how to turn ecstasy and intoxication, how to transform metaphysical revolt into human emancipation.[18]

And yet Benjamin thought the surrealists had come closer than anyone, through montage and dream, through intoxication and metaphor, through imagination and symbol (signification), to freeing mankind from the burdens of the modern Fall. They were among the few to reject the yoke of modern servitude, the oppressive class society and its denial of dream that Benjamin detailed in nineteenth-century Paris and twentieth-century Berlin.[19] Benjamin thought the surrealists had come ever closer to true communism when they called for the transvaluation of attitudes and values, and signified the value of dream in the revolutionizing of the world that they had inherited and despised. He understood their stance of radical pessimism toward the world, their deep mistrust of literature, freedom and the fate of European humanity, their lack of faith in the reconciliation "between classes, between nations, between individuals."[20] He approved the surrealist 'manifesto' that called for "expelling moral metaphor from politics."[21]

Benjamin approved the surrealists because they alone had made the dream revolutionary. They had assumed the double task of overthrowing the intellectual dominance of the bourgeoisie and making contact with the proletariat. The surrealists at least moved beyond contemplation to intoxication, envisioned turning life and work into pleasure, mocked the staid composure and smug demeanor of the bourgeois. They recognized the revolutionary stance of pessimism and the need for the systematic remaking of the world, beginning with the destruction of optimistic imagery and the entire system of iconic and symbolic affirmation. They understood that the bourgeois world was antithetical to human freedom and that the imagery they, the surrealists, exploded in their art was the first act of human emancipation, the first act in the deconstruction of the world and its reconstruction as Utopia.

In *One Way Street*, written in 1928, Benjamin summed up the significance of the diurnal (and nocturnal) dream, attempting to mine links between the unconscious and conscious mind. Dreams, he claimed, subverted the world as it existed, a world that was destroying what Benjamin took to be authentic, and therefore worth preserving. The dream was revolutionary; it exposed the perversity of the bourgeois world, so busy interring the past and everything human. It helped to restore, however fragmentary, the ruins of the past. And it was precisely these fragments of the unconscious that somehow related to and helped restore the primordial world of concepts from which artists drew their imaginative work. The dream was the door to the unconscious. It was also the linkage to truth before the contamination and compression of memory, before commercial propaganda and nationalistic ideology, so characteristic of Benjamin's world, had managed to sever humanity from its roots.[22]

Memory and Society

In "Berlin Chronicle," written by Benjamin in 1932 while in exile in Ibiza, Spain, he underscored the linkage between memory and truth, the connection between recollection and knowledge, the organic unity between the smallest detail or microcosm and the entire cosmos:

> He who has once begun to open the fan of memory never comes to the end of its segments; no image satisfies him, for he has seen that it can be unfolded, and only in its folds does the truth reside; that image, that taste, that touch for whose sake all this has been unfurled and dissected; and now remembrance advances from small to smallest details, from the smallest to the infinitesimal, while that which it encounters in these microcosms grows ever mightier.[23]

The modern world, Benjamin often complained, compressed, transformed, distorted and often obliterated memory by transforming the past, and the memory which might have recollected it, into images of the contemporary world's making. The result was that the modern era had no true memory of its own past, nor knowledge of the authentic experiences of that past. Humanity could therefore not see itself in its history, nor could it remember the dream in the past of its future. It had lost its ability to see, and replaced that right and ability with images, representations and significations conjured by mythmakers of the contemporary world. Thus, the bourgeoisie had created its own dream, its own intoxication with the phantasmagoria of objects and trinkets of the bourgeois world, which it then represented as both the dream of the past, and as the fulfillment of that dream in the present.

Benjamin believed that contemporary representations of the world saw the world in a fundamentally wrong way. In the modern world thought was displaced by propaganda (advertising), understanding ceded the way to sensation, and experience was replaced by simulation, sensation and sublimation. Moreover, images were subject to the manipulation and control of the image-makers who were selling both products and the system that made them. Benjamin concluded that only through the restoration and reclaiming of memory, only through the reconstruction of experience in memory, only through the recovery of the aura or context behind the image, could humanity reclaim its own history and memory, and in doing so emancipate itself.

"Berlin Chronicle" was not a simple exercise in the recollection of a Berlin childhood, but a way of understanding the present through a remembrance of things past. Through remembrance, Benjamin sought to escape the image-makers of contemporary Berlin; he could recover the Berlin of his experience, not the city of glitter and manufactured cant.

What was the truth of Benjamin's Berlin? It was a city composed of neighborhoods crisscrossed by the frontiers of social class. Benjamin felt closed in by his childhood, a prisoner of his middle-class existence. He felt himself entombed in the district "where the class that had pronounced him one of its numbers resided in a posture of self-satisfaction and resentment that turned it into something like a ghetto. . . ."[24] As for the poor, for rich children of Benjamin's generation the poor "lived at the back of beyond."[25] They, too, like Benjamin, were at the threshold – "far removed from the process of production and the exploitation not yet abstracted from it."[26] One could cross the border into this world of destitution, said Benjamin, but only as a *flaneur*, as one who was fascinated by the world which for the bourgeoisie had disappeared, or was invisible. Yet it was in his role of *flaneur* that Benjamin saw the very public humiliations endured by the poor for which his own class, and indeed his family, had no eyes.

Thus, Benjamin noted the experiences of his youth, experiences that were largely unmediated as he crossed into the "nothingness" beyond his own social borders. It was here that traces were left on the city, here that humanity had left its imprints, such as the man in the sandwich board who was ignored by the bourgeois passsersby and left to suffer his humiliations alone. It was here that trace and memory could be dug out of the continuum of history, that mankind could discover signposts in its hopeful journey toward redemption.[27] Through traces one could excavate reminiscences that were both "fleeting and eternal."[28] Reminiscences, moreover, that one had to disinter from the immediacy of experience before one could dispel the mystification of contemporary imagery.

Ever the *flaneur*, Benjamin saw himself as a bundle of impressions that congregated anonymously in his mind, a roving space without a fixed identity of his own, a man walking through the alleys in which he was able to detect a trace of himself, seizing moments where his own life had paused.[29] As *flaneur*, Benjamin seized on the connection between trace and memory, between experience and identity, between autobiography and history. Were not all these interconnections also pauses, ways of filling gaps that had been forgotten, misconstrued or falsified by the modern class-biased world?

Thus, the Berlin that Benjamin got to know was the Berlin of the "theater of purchases, on which occasions it first became apparent how my father's money could cut a path for us between the shop counters and assistants and mirrors, and the appraising eyes of our mother. In the ignominy of a new suit we stood there. . . ."[30] Benjamin remembered the purchase of commodities in the emporia of

Berlin as a burden on his conscience. He felt shame when his family purchased luxury goods, humiliation before the idols bearing the names of Mannheimer, Herzog and Israel, disgust with the whole iconic world in which beauties were so desirable and sumptuous and at the same time carried the burden of the past becoming the present. Yet here was a Benjamin who was rescued by the flashing images of the past, precisely because he relished the burden of guilt in the memory of his privilege. It was possible after all to disinter truth from the rubble of history, to remember and feel experience that did not have to be inferred, to 'see' pictures that did not suffer from the dislocation of images.[31]

To probe the role of memory and the unconscious further Benjamin made an intellectual journey to France where he discovered Marcel Proust. Proust was vastly admired by Benjamin because, like the latter, he was determined to disinter the past, to shatter the oppressive continuity of time, to destroy homogeneous temporality. And like Benjamin, Proust looked for the entire cosmos in each detail of the French 'aristocratic' bourgeoisie, of which Proust, himself, was a member. Like Benjamin, Proust understood the destructive power of laughter and irony:

> Proust's style is comedy, not humor. His laughter does not toss the world up but flings it down-at the risk that it will be smashed to pieces, which will then make him burst into tears. And unity of family and personality, of sexual morality and professional honor, are indeed smashed to bits. The pretensions of the bourgeoisie are shattered by laughter.[32]

Benjamin heartily approved Proust's anatomy of the bourgeoisie. Proust's method, he noted, was to focus on what the bourgeoisie had to say, and what it had to say was precisely chatter. It had nothing to say. It had only chatter to fill its time because it had been assimilated by the aristocracy and embraced the language and affectation of that aristocracy.[33]

Proust understood the code language of the 'aristocracy', insisted Benjamin, he understood the barriers between classes that could be encoded and mystified in language. For Proust, the upper ten thousand were a clan of criminals, "a band of conspirators [excluding] from their world everything that has a part in production or at least demands that this part be gracefully and bashfully concealed behind the kind of manner that is sported by the polished professionals of consumption."[34]

Benjamin, like Proust, understood the process of mystification, the violence of representation done to the past, especially by the vestiges of 'aristocracy'. Proust had described the process in a pungent way. So much so that it reeked of a "class which is everywhere pledged to camouflage its material basis and for this very reason is attached to a feudalism which has no intrinsic economic significance but is all the more serviceable as a mask of the upper middle class."[35] Proust, said Benjamin, was ahead of his class, his literary service served to rip off the mask and the veil, to de-glamorize what the aristocracy painstakingly concealed by its chatter. It was a task, moreover, that Proust could only accomplish through memory, through a recollection that tore off the mask.[36]

For Benjamin the question became what kind of memory was at issue? The answer was involuntary memory, a kind of recollection that for Benjamin was at the core of experience. Involuntary memory was in fact the essence of the human being, it was the filter in which experience took shape, was formed and became the experienced. Thus, Proust, with Benjamin looking over his shoulder, returned to his childhood past, to his world, to discover his roots and inception, and in so doing he recreated the world that had by his time been forgotten. Ironically, the world Proust resurrected, as Benjamin knew only too well, was the world Proust wanted to annihilate. But in so doing, Benjamin admonished, Proust had to reinvent and then annihilate himself. For the unmasking of his world must also unmask him to himself. And yet Proust was condemned to report what he saw, driven by involuntary memory, for anything less was also a kind of self-destruction, an annihilation of lived experience, a death of the ego passionately involved in the reconstruction of its own remembrance.[37]

For Benjamin the result of the search of involuntary memory was germane. For to pare back all the layers of history was to reveal what so many generations had painstakingly concealed even from themselves. At last the true anatomy of society and history came forth as a kind of human revelation. Proust, unlocking the unconscious, finally discovered himself, in fact reduced the whole universe to himself in his total self-absorption. And yet, in self-discovery, by concentrating the past into a single fresh instant, Proust liberated and rejuvenated the energies of that past from the frozen eternity of history. And here was Proust's greatest discovery, and perhaps Benjamin's as well. For it was precisely in the instant of self-recognition that Proust broke through the dream into awakening, it was precisely at the point of greatest self-discovery that he found the true convolutions of the self. And it was at this flashing point of history that Proust revealed the nature of his class, his band of conspirators and criminals, the uncharming 'bourgeois aristocracy', as no longer impenetrable and elusive. In unmasking himself, Proust at last managed to unmask the class for which he had so much contempt.[38] And so Benjamin made his point. Remembrance, whether in art or life, whether expressing contempt or rapture, was revolutionary, at once pointing the way toward the past and the future.

Dream, Art and Revolution

Benjamin believed that in the modern era of class relations, history was like the unconscious actions of the dreaming individual, without consciousness, purpose or direction. Thus, the nineteenth-century contained not only a world of things and a way of life, and a literature to go with it, but an image making imagination of a collective unconscious operating within the concrete world. Benjamin believed further, as Rolf Tiedemann has pointed out, that the "architectonic constructions such as the arcades owed their existence to and served the industrial order of production, while at the same time containing within themselves something unfulfilled, never to be fulfilled within the confines of capitalism—in this case, the glass architecture of the future. . . ."[39]

Benjamin thought each epoch had a side turned toward dream, the child's side. He scrutinized this side to "liberate the enormous energies of history . . . that are slumbering in the 'once upon a time' of classical historical narrative."[40] Here Benjamin revealed the dramatic influence of Freud and psychoanalysis on him. For just as the individual awakened to his oppressive reality, by using psychoanalysis to unlock the unconscious, so could society unlock the key to its reality through the process of transforming the dream into awakening.[41] To break through dream was to find the secret affinities hidden in the self, to discover one's rootedness in the collective. This was the importance of narcotic intoxication, or the dream, for both allowed the individual to overcome the isolation and anomie of the industrial bourgeois era and to perceive his natural affinities with humanity.[42]

In this Benjamin was influenced by Freud. He wished to 'see' the past, to understand its dreams, visions and hopes for itself. By seeing the past as it saw itself in dream, not through an image created by the present, Benjamin hoped to break through the mythmaking images of the present to the wishful images of the future as discovered by the past.

Benjamin's task, therefore, was twofold. First, he endeavored to use dreams as vehicles of understanding, whether conscious or unconscious, that provided windows to the past. Moreover, dreams were a-synchronous, they were not bound by space or time. The dream could therefore express spatial affinities, it could be forward looking as well as backward looking. It could express spatial correspondences while dispelling the seeming continuities and inevitability of conventional historical narrative. The dream was a kind of protest against the reality of the present, a present which had learned to translate concepts of the past into images that could be manipulated and sold, thereby turning ideas into images and images into propaganda. Secondly, by accomplishing the first task, Benjamin hoped that it might be possible to translate the dream the past had for itself into reality, for reality could never be contained in the dream itself.

Thus, Benjamin wished to bring the past into the present, rather than to drive the present into the past. In *The Arcades,* he assembled a mass of anecdotes, aphorisms, epithets, tales, jokes, memoirs, histories, a mass that is of mini-narratives and stitched them into a narrative of nineteenth-century Paris. To wander through these narratives is to wander through a dreamland which was not fully conscious, but which was striving forward toward its own dream in its imagined future. Benjamin had a point to make here. He noted that the future hoped for and dreamed about in the nineteenth-century did not coincide with the reality of Benjamin's own contemporary world. On the other hand, Benjamin thought that the narratives of art and literature, still alive as specific dreams and images of the past, could reflect the truth about the present.[43] This was possible because Benjamin's era still had social relations and moral values that were comparable to those of the nineteenth century; there were spatial affinities that made comparisons possible.

Thus, it was more critical than ever to let the past tell its own tales, reveal its own dreams and present its own images, the better to understand the truths about the images of the present. Benjamin noted that "the anecdote brings things near to us spatially, lets them enter our life."[44] It was the opposite of empathy that made things abstract. "The true method of making things present is: to represent them in our space (not to represent ourselves in their space). Only anecdotes can do this for us. Thus represented, the things allow no mediating construction from out of 'large contexts'.[45] In considering the Cathedral of Chartres, the point was not to empathize with the builders or their priests. The point was not to displace our being into theirs, but "to receive them into our space."[46] This was what the historian had to do through dream interpretation, Benjamin thought. The historian must not enter the past, the dead past, but had to make it alive by making the past enter him.[47] The historian had to penetrate the veil of capitalist mythology, to excavate the foundations, to discover the unmediated violence and biased jurisprudence on which contemporary capitalism was based.

Benjamin did not see himself as a historian, at least in the conventional sense, but as a collector. The collector combated the veil of capitalist mythology by divesting things of their commodified character. He set things into their real context, wrenching them out of linear history and into spatial affinities brought into relation by juxtaposition and montage. Only by allowing the fables, stories, moral tales and anecdotes of the past, whether in narrative form or plastic expression, to 'tell' their own feelings and thoughts through the collector, could they escape the mediations of the present.[48] Benjamin put it succinctly in his own dialectical fashion: "Every epoch, in fact, not only dreams the one to follow, but, in dreaming, precipitates its awakening. It bears an end within itself. . . ."[49]

Benjamin did not intend that any of this should be abstract or pure speculation. Much of his mature thought, including *The Arcades Project*, developed after Mussolini came to power in Italy, and evolved further after Hitler came to power in Germany in January, 1933. Benjamin's entire *oeuvre* could be seen as an antidote to Italian Fascism and National Socialism. Or as an attempt to understand and put in historical context how the obscurantism of his era, and its bourgeois system of symbolic misrepresentation of the dreams of an earlier period, had been transformed into a nightmare of epic proportion. For there were always fundamental questions that Benjamin felt compelled to answer: how and why did liberal democracy collapse into fascist dictatorship, how was industrial capitalism transformed into fascist nationalism? To understand all this, Benjamin needed to do nothing less than to decode the past, read the signposts of history, interpret the dreams.

In a lecture finished April 27, 1934, to be delivered at the Institute for the Study of Fascism (but never delivered), Benjamin defined the role of the intellectual, and by implication the artist.[50] The intellectual, he insisted, should serve a political function in society, he must be not only opposed to capital, sharing attitudes that are critical of society, but he must see himself consciously in his art and thought as a producer of relations. That is, he must anticipate Utopia. In this thought, Benjamin echoed Bertolt Brecht, the activist, Marxist playwright. The intellectual ought not to put himself above the proletariat, as its benefactor, but ought to place his art and thought squarely in its service.

Thus Benjamin, following Brecht, asserted that art must not express individual experience, but should concern the use and transformation of institutions and society. The intellectual had to do more than reflect the society in which he wrote, thought and created art. Dadaism, for example, was a movement that did in fact 'reflect' reality by including in montage detritus from the real world. But by taking cigarette butts and the blood of a murderer, Benjamin thought it also transformed the grotesque into a form of 'pleasure' to be consumed.[51]

Benjamin was also a close student of the impact of technology on art, he was painfully aware of its implications for art in the age of mechanical reproduction. Examples were everywhere in which art was adulterated, or used as propaganda, using the new technologies. Hitler, through Leni Riefensthal, repeatedly demonstrated the possible uses of film for both demonization and exaltation; art as persuasion, could be used as mass propaganda. Photography, which had the potential to overcome the gap between image and reality, nevertheless restored to "mass consumption, by fashionable adaptation, subjects that had earlier withdrawn themselves from it."[52] Too often, said Benjamin, the photographer or filmmaker used the apparatus in a way that took poverty and transformed it into consumption and entertainment. Benjamin railed against the new technology of cinema and photography for failing to overcome the gap between the written word and the image that, he claimed, ought to be the function of photography to abolish. He was critical of the photographer who could transform the world into an object of contemplation, taking it as a given which could be enjoyed.[53] At the same time he understood the revolutionary potential of the new arts, especially cinema and photography. They had the power to restore the aura of the image; they had the authority to make concrete the space of the past. Above all they had the ability to shock the viewer by revealing the grotesque and the unflattering in the sharp angles of shadow and relief. They had the power to show the world how it had been, and how it could be.

On the other hand, Benjamin returned to the art of Brecht precisely because it did not depend on technology or apparatus. He found in Brecht's theater an art that was not concerned with plot, or with action or with the technology of theater. Brecht returned theater to its most primitive state. He did not employ plots so much as situations, the better to invite critical thought. He constantly jarred his narratives with songs and interruptions, dispelling the illusions of continuity by offering montage and reflection.[54] He made theater irreducible because it put man at the center. And he made it revolutionary, Benjamin concluded, because it "was less concerned with filling the public with feelings, even seditious ones, than with alienating it in an enduring manner, through thinking, from the conditions in which it lives."[55]

In "The Work of Art in the Age of Mechanical Reproduction," which first appeared in 1936, Benjamin returned to his study of the relationships between art, society and revolution, and the implications for the production of art in an age of mechanical reproduction.[56] He found that the unique aspect of art was being destroyed in the modern world because art was now subject to mechanical reproduction, its images were no longer tied either to the art itself or to its original aura or context. In the process of being reproducible, the process of (re)production actually detached the work of art from its meaning, its inspiration and the entire world in which it was given birth. Content was transformed into image. Art, in other words was turned into an object and commodified, it became a pleasure to be consumed, it became purely functional. Art, said Benjamin, was now about ornament, not content. By wrenching art from its context, it ceased being critical and became decorative. Mechanical reproduction completed the liberation of art from meaning.[57] Moreover, in film making as in photography, equipment, or the apparatus, altered the very nature of perception itself. The apparatus became reality. The form determined the content.[58] In the modern bourgeois world, art became advertising, or even worse, propaganda. Art now became dangerous because it was metamorphosed into politics, and a particularly insidious form of politics at that in the Germany of the 1930's.

Benjamin responded to the many abuses of art, its annihilation as critique in the age of fascism, its total surrender of its original ritual content, the manipulation of its images to obtain and retain power. The politicizing of art was made possible because of the new technologies that allowed the mass production, manipulation and dissemination of images. It was made inevitable because of the very structure of new arts like cinema and photography that depended on the machine and the ability to mass-produce imagery. The new arts made manipulation much easier because of the enormous power of the moving image; or the suggestive power of photography. In either case the image became the center of power, the locus of control, a proclamation of what the world was like or was supposed to be. Indeed, the world itself. The conclusion seemed to be one of extreme pessimism. Art had ceased to be a narrative of liberation, it had ceased to be a dream of possibility, it was subject to political abuse, its images were manipulated and commercialized, it had been reduced to propaganda, the artist had disappeared from his art.

This was not the endpoint for Benjamin, however. Art, including art produced in the age of mechanical reproduction, could invoke several kinds of politics. Its imagery could shock in more than one direction. Benjamin again used dadaism as an example. Dadaism was an art form that deliberately distracted the viewer and proclaimed the utter uselessness of art. In so doing, Benjamin proffered, it insisted on the uselessness of bourgeois society and the lack of any meaning or utility of bourgeois reality. It assailed the spectator with his useless life, attacked the pretension of art in suggesting the beautiful. In this expression, suggested Benjamin, dadaism projected shock, the shock of outrage.[59]

Benjamin's argument now turned full circle. He insisted that film did the same. Unlike standard pictorial art such as painting, film replaced the viewer's placid contemplation with the dynamics of the moving image. The spectator could no longer freely associate and dominate the visual because the images of film moved too rapidly to be contemplated. Film shocked the spectator, and in so doing it heightened his presence of mind through the shock.[60] Thus, Benjamin didn't dismiss film because it suspended critical thought. On the contrary, film was revolutionary because it transformed the method and canon of seeing. It opened the perception of art to the masses, putting the public in the position of critic. It made public discourse possible.[61] It also made the seemingly unapproachable, approachable, not by restoring the original aura, or the authentic beginnings, or the source of artistic truth, but by demonstrating the relativity of perception, by displaying the otherwise invisible. Film, and photography, could demystify by making entire worlds transparent that otherwise were removed from the public eye. It could demystify by removing distance, revealing the hidden, portraying the possible, remembering the forgotten.

History and Utopia

What film could not deliver, however, poetry could. In Charles Baudelaire, Benjamin found a kindred spirit. Both men 'lived' outside history, both hoped to reside in the eternal. Both referred to modernity as transitory, to history as contingent, to progress as illusion. Both were enemies of the entire bourgeois world and the spirit of capitalism that characterized the modern world. Both thought that art was half-based on the fugitive and temporary, but both recognized the other half of art as eternal and immutable. And it was here that Benjamin most clearly discovered his sense of the utopian.[62]

It was as a mystic and utopian that Benjamin ventured into the past. It was there that he found the "affirmation of a mysterious presence at the back of things, as in the depths of the soul—the presence of Eternity [as well as the] need to break out of the confines of one's life through the immense prolongation of ancestral memory and of former lives."[63] Through dream and the unconscious one discovered one's ancestry. The dream was the preserve of truth, the place where one broke out of the continuum of history to the eternal. The dream was the place of art, Baudelaire perhaps its greatest practitioner. Baudelaire, Benjamin insisted, expressed in the most concrete and yet explosive manner a shock to the bourgeoisie. By discovering the truth in his dream vision, by uniting the disparate things of the world in his dream, he made sense of the senseless.[64] And in making sense of the world, in forcing the world to see itself as it really was, Baudelaire caught a glimpse of Utopia.

"On Some Motifs in Baudelaire," which Benjamin wrote in 1939, a year before his tragic death, he made some of his most explicit comments about his visions of Utopia. He referred to Baudelaire's efforts to capture the gaze "which pulls the poet after his dream."[65] The gaze, looking into the distance, restored the object, allowed it to reacquire its aura. The gaze interrupted the course of the world by fixing its stare on the past.[66]

Benjamin, therefore, did not set his gaze on the future. Utopia was not inevitable. Benjamin, a critic of Bolshevism and the Russian revolution, thought that Robespierre and Lenin had erred by forcing Utopia on history. He preferred Marx's assertions that the future could not be foreseen, or even defined. Benjamin's own goal was to snatch humanity from the catastrophe that awaited it around every bend.[67] He firmly believed that the catastrophe that awaited humanity was precisely the world of the bourgeois that had already arrived, the world that had led directly to fascism. This was the world of mass production and class warfare, the world that had in effect destroyed the aura, the world that had sacrificed nature for the unique, that worshiped the new at the expense of the sacred.[68]

A specific utopian dream vision that inspired Benjamin was that of the utopian socialist Charles Fourier. In looking backwards, Benjamin anticipated both Ernst Bloch and Herbert Marcuse, both of whom admired Fourier. It was Fourier who had anticipated the dream vision of Baudelaire, who had done the most to preserve the aura. Fourier brought work and play together, he recognized that when work was indistinguishable from play, the utopian vision on earth had arrived. Benjamin, living in an age with a much more advanced technology, lived in an era in which he thought Fourier's dream could be achieved, releasing mankind from the bondage of work. The fact that such a dream had not been achieved, argued Benjamin, was because the aura of the past that contained the possibility of a utopian future had largely disappeared from the vision of the present.[69] Hence, the restorative and revolutionary powers of the metaphysical revolt of Baudelaire.

Baudelaire inspired Benjamin. He awakened him to his own aura. Benjamin turned toward his dream vision and discovered that the arcades of the nineteenth-century represented the side of man turned toward dreams. Wandering through the passages of the arcades, mankind turned toward awakening. To explore the arcades was to experience "a not yet conscious knowledge of what has been: its advancement has the structure of awakening."[70] Knowledge, the discovery of Utopia, was awakening to what had passed. It was awareness that one could discover truth only in one's dream work by rescuing the dead from the past. All development was dialectical reversal in which history presented itself "as the art of experiencing the present as waking world, a world to which that dream we name the past refers in truth."[71] Awakening meant passing through and carrying out *"what has been* in remembering the dream."[72] Utopia meant awakening to the dream inside of humanity. Abetted by the dream visions of art, mankind could remember and recover the aura of things before humankind was displaced from its own history by commodity fetishism, or was turned into a seething conformist mass by the false mythology of fascism.

Benjamin was pessimistic about Marx's notion of historical progress and the dialectical unfolding of industrial capitalism into communism. The fact that National Socialism followed the era of capital and the liberal democracy of the Weimar Republic was hardly a confirmation of the predictive powers of Marx, who thought the advent of communism all but inevitable.

Moreover, the end of the *Arcades Project* was written under the impact of the 1939 Non-Aggression Pact. This pact was shattering to Benjamin, as it was to virtually all on the left, because it brought Stalin and Hitler into an alliance. It meant the definitive betrayal of communism. After this pact, one could have no illusions. At the same time Benjamin was able to write that the "classless society is not the ultimate goal of progress in history, but its rupture, so often attempted and finally brought about."[73] Humanity's dreams, by being made conscious, made it possible to possess reality. Humanity's dream images, however, did not belong to history as such, but to messianic time in which the dream was preserved as awakening reality. The duty of the historian was to recognize the image of the past not recognized by others in the present.[74]

Hence Benjamin's "gaze" fastened on what was unseen in the present, in order to disinter the object from its own disappearance in the past. Through the gaze, as Benjamin wrote in his "Theses on the Philosophy of History," a "redeemed mankind receives the fullness of the past — which is to say, only for a redeemed mankind has its past become citable in all its moments."[75] Mankind, however, was responsible for its own redemption, for awakening to the past in order to see itself in the present. Only through its gaze could the past be seized "as an image which flashes up at the instant when it can be recognized and is never seen again."[76]

For Benjamin, the danger of being swallowed by the present, especially a present so crass, was to risk being destroyed by man's own creations, to accept one's self-destruction. The greatest danger to humanity was to lose its memory. Historical understanding, however, did not mean recognizing the past as it really was, in the fashion of Leopold von Ranke. It meant seizing "hold of a memory as it flashes up at a moment of danger . . . historical materialism wishes to retain that image of the past which unexpectedly appears to man singled out by history at a moment of danger."[77] And the present was clearly a danger, for it robbed humanity of its memory, and it did so in a particularly invidious way. Echoing Marx's bellowing criticisms of the nineteenth-century bourgeoisie as a class that revolutionized all aspects of life in the name of the cash nexus, Benjamin excoriated the twentieth-century bourgeoisie. As a result of the modern capitalist ethic, he believed that tradition was giving way to conformity, information was overwhelming wisdom, and experience was being misinterpreted by ideology. The result was catastrophic. Man was removed from his own history, alienated from himself, seduced by a technology that could satiate desire, overwhelmed by the mechanical reproduction of images which were devoid of content.[78]

Despite these lamentations, Benjamin remained hopeful, even while in flight from the Nazis. The "Theses" were fraught with Benjamin's notion of messianic time, the possibility of breaking through profane time into the sacred, into the eternity of Utopia with all its visions of human perfection. He remained confident that critical thought could revive the tensions, expose the dangers and contradictions, shock the present by rediscovering the dreams of the past. He embraced historical materialism as the surest approach to messianic time, the eternal present. But unlike Marx's historical materialism, Benjamin's search for the eternal present took him to the detritus of the past, and the shock that past might represent for the present.[79]

Benjamin was in many respects a most unlikely Marxist. Yet he repeated many of the themes of Marx's utopianism. He was deeply distraught over the proletarianization and barbarization of mankind, which he linked to modern industrial capitalism. He blamed capitalist social relationships for robbing humanity of its dreams. He was a natural rebel against a society that had destroyed the harmonies that he sniffed in the airs of the past. Like Marx, he was a prophet of utopian possibilities, if one could only remove the layers of time that had erased humanity's memory of its own essence, or recombine the fragments before they were exploded by history. He thought it possible that mankind could overcome its alienation from itself and nature, could solve the riddle of history by breaking through to the eternal. That this could be done he had no doubt. For the eternal was inside mankind itself, within its collective consciousness, and especially within the symbolic expressions of art and philosophy, of theater and architecture, where mankind had always dreamed of a future without alienation.

Chapter 5
Ernst Bloch: Between Jesus and Marx

For many Western intellectuals World War I eroded forever the Enlightenment belief in the perfectibility of human society. History was no longer the story of endless progress while liberal democracy seemed a hopelessly inadequate panacea for the festering wounds of humanity. Western civilization itself seemed pointless, vapid and degenerate to a generation coming of age amidst the moldering ruins of the Great War. As a member of that generation, Ernst Bloch would soon become the self-conscious prophet of the philosophy of hope. Engaged in a Promethean effort to overcome the egoistic materialism of the Western world, he sought to discover absolute values while living in a century that embraced relativism and that often relapsed into barbarism.

Thus, Bloch emerged as exemplar and philosopher, in E. J. Hobsbawm's words, "of the Coleridgean era who . . . turned revolutionary: a natural rebel against mechanical rationalism" and a denizen in that rarified atmosphere of "cosmic harmonies, vital principles [and] living organisms."[1] Bloch was not easily seduced, as were many of his countrymen, by the modern demiurges that produced National Socialism in Germany. As a Jew he resented the folkish and racist elements that were integral to Nazism, as a rationalist he feared its lethal mix of mysticism and politics, and as a socialist Bloch was immune to the appeals of German nationalism.[2]

In 1918, Bloch recognized, in *The Spirit of Utopia*, Marx's great achievement in service to the cause of socialism. *The Spirit of Utopia*, however, was anything but orthodox Marxism. It set forth Bloch's idiosyncratic version of a future utopian socialism as a fusion of Christian mysticism, Jewish messianism, revolutionary theology and 'true' communism, the latter more in the sense of messianic, moralized communism than of Marx's scientific socialism.[3] These were the ingredients, Bloch believed, that prefigured, complemented and conferred legitimacy on socialism itself.[4]

By 1923, when Bloch published the second edition of *The Spirit of Utopia*, he characterized his classless Utopia in non-collectivist language that recalled the idealistic young Marx of the *Paris Manuscripts* rather than the Bolshevik experiment of Lenin. Bloch reminded his readers that man did not live by bread alone. Marx, he said, had omitted the "new man, the leap, the power of love and of light, morality itself [none of which had] been allotted the desirable degree of autonomy in the definitive social order."[5] Marx's scientific socialism might have defined the external world, but it failed to address the internal condition of humankind, its spiritual and moral malaise that required a veritable cultural revolution. Man would have to redefine himself in the space that was not determined by economics. Bloch stressed the linkage between cultural revolution, moral rebirth and utopian socialism. He concluded by lavishing praise on the "utopian superiority of Weitling's, Baader's [and] Tolstoy's utopianly superior world of love . . . the new force of the human encounter in Dostoevsky [and] the adventism of heretical history."[6]

Even after Bloch enthusiastically embraced Marx in the mid-1920's, this was a Marx that he could append to his own belief that mankind had striven eternally toward hope. History was driven, Bloch thought, by man dreaming of a better future; a future, moreover, that was prefigured, consciously or unconsciously, in the artistic and literary imagination. Bloch dismissed Marx's obsession with economics as fetishistic. He wondered why "the man who expelled any element of fetishism from the process of production, who banished all dreams, effective utopias, and religiously garbed teleologies from history, [why had that same man then treated the productive forces] in the same overconstitutive, pantheistic and mythicizing way?"[7]

Thus, where Marx dispassionately sought the historical laws of the 'dismal science' to explain the movements of history, Bloch passionately discovered 'traces' of a corpuscular utopian future. Instead of Marx's locus of class and class consciousness, Bloch's animus was mystical love as the foundation of the final realm of freedom. For Bloch the engine of history was the principle of hope, his central philosophical cachet by the 1920's, which inspired humanity to transform the present into the utopianized future. People, not outward things, made history; externals were merely suggestive, not creative. If Marx's determination applied to the economic future, to the necessary economic-institutional change, it failed to encompass "the new man, the leap, the power of love and light, and morality itself, [which] are not yet accorded the requisite independence in the definitive social order."[8]

Much of the rhetoric of the early Bloch was redolent with religious imagery, biblical symbols and messianic expectation, including a revolutionized and utopianized Christ. He was convinced, no later than 1923, that reason had to be abetted by hope and science had to be fulfilled by enthusiasm. Moreover, the secular paradise defined by Marx had to be rooted in mankind's primal religious instincts in which a wishful dreaming humanity could imagine the content of its utopian longing. In dismissing mankind's power of dreaming as illusion, in substituting the abstract laws of history for humanity's utopian instincts, Bloch thought Marx had missed a great opportunity. He had failed to acknowledge the inherent utopian tendency in history of human consciousness and longing.[9]

Bloch thought the deficiencies of Marxism obvious. Marx and his successors had failed to tap into the dream world, the world of wishful thinking that had long incubated as utopian longing and hopefulness. National Socialists and Italian Fascists had understood that fairy tales, folk songs, legends, poetry, art and literature, both high and popular culture, expressed the sentiments, beliefs, attitudes, desires and hopes of populations that were disoriented, marginalized and impoverished by the change, rootlessness and anomie of modern life. National Socialism and Italian Fascism both appealed to denizens of villages and towns through narratives of transcendence, hope and mythos. It was into these narratives that the National Socialists had fitted themselves, creating a mythology of belonging and a mystique rooted in blood and soil.

Thus, if Marx had erred by concentrating too exclusively on the objective structures of economics and history, Bloch amended Marx by focusing on human ideals, personal desires, the psychology of human hope, the religious impulse toward transcendence and the human impulse toward Utopia. Human volition, not objective law, was the engine of history. Human desire and dreams mattered; the mechanical rationalism that had failed to grab the popular imagination did not. Bloch believed that the eclipse of Utopia by 'science' had abridged human hope. It had created an apostrophized meta-history which seemed to exclude human intention, and which replaced the hoping individual with the abstract and amorphous social class.[10]

For Bloch, the point of departure for his studies in the 1930's became man with all his anxieties and hopes, man degraded and victim of his own opprobrious history, yet forward looking and capable of transcendence. Bloch's compendious work, *The Principle of Hope*, which resulted from a decade of labors during his exile in America – he composed the work between 1938-1947 and revised it in 1953 and 1959 – argued that history was replete with urges of transcendence. From archaic myth to Greek and Roman Antiquity, from the Hebrew prophets to the early Christian communism of the revolutionary Jesus, from the mysterious eschatology of Christ to the Final Kingdom of Joachim of Fiore, humankind sought liberation and Utopia. Moreover, Utopia was not only the quest for an ideal commonweal. It embraced the dream landscapes of urban architectural utopias, it anticipated images of perfect bodily health and the overcoming of death, it was a sublime world transformed by the humanization of technology. Utopia, far from having a permanently ethereal mystique consigned to the world of surrealist dream, far from being a repressed state of unrealizble and even dangerous fantasy – as Freud would have it – was a part of the latent content of human nature striving to realize its full humanity.[11] Utopia was realizable, Bloch insisted, it was part of the human essence to be hopeful, part of the mission of philosophy to unlock what had always been latent and hidden, part of man's striving to be unburdened and free.

Amidst the ruins of Europe and the destruction of the old world and its dreams of a secular paradise, seeing the displacement of his comfortable world of cosmic harmonies and vital principles by the destructive ultra-nationalist ideologies of the interwar period, Bloch labored to define his world of utopian dream. He saw his task as construing the meaning of human existence, of pushing man forward toward his essence, toward a human happiness and dignity that

he thought would only arrive with the creation of a classless society (communism).[12]
    Utopianism, therefore, performed a central role in history. It was the basis
of mankind's dreaming, and it was the goal of anticipatory illumination.
Through utopian dream the Not-Yet-Conscious became conscious. Moreover,
Bloch differed from Marx and virtually all Marxists in the nineteenth and twentieth-centuries; most of them denounced utopianism as illusory and based on
fantasy. But Bloch understood the emotive power of dream and fantasy, the passionate desires that were buried in illusion, hope and desire, the concealed aspirations that were hidden in fairy tales, popular songs, archaic legends and myths.
It was precisely this emotive world of the Not-Yet-Conscious that Utopia helped
illumine and make conscious. Utopia, far from being no-place, outside of history
and non-temporal, was simply the place that was not yet, a place that mankind's
own dreaming helped imagine, drive toward and create. Utopian thinking could
be abstract thought that was premature. But utopianism could also be concretely
utopian; it could refer to a future moment objectively based on a revolutionary
class. Concrete Utopia was grounded in objective possibility. It was goal and
realization of that goal. As consciousness discovered Utopia, it became an intellectual and material force in the realization of the concrete.[13] Unlike Marx,
Bloch thought the animus of history, as well as its goal, was utopian dreaming
and longing, a hoping and striving humanity.

Little Daydreams

Part I of Bloch's work, *The Principle of Hope*, entitled "Little Daydreams," set
the foundation for Bloch's entire life's work as well as for this encyclopedic
work. He began by noting that man's existence was pervaded by daydreams of a
better life than that which historically had been given him.[14] Even in Hegel and
Kant all knowledge was merely memory. But hope looked toward the future,
resembled the new "Front," wanted to break out of history and sought a break
with the past. Without a philosophy and knowledge of hope, and a conscience of
the possible, mankind would be stuck in the past, it would have no knowledge at
all.[15]
    Bloch insisted that freedom movements were historically guided by utopian
hopes. Marxist philosophy, for example, envisioned the future, and through its
dream activated that future.[16] The theme of Bloch's entire work was to activate
dreams of a better life. It was this path that led from little waking dreams to
strong ones, from wavering to rigorous dreams, from shadowy hopes to earthly
realities.[17] Dreaming illumined the path, it enlarged the hope, it challenged the
given, it carried one toward a future unlike anything before, it defined an "anticipatory consciousness" based on hope, both emotional and cognitive.[18] Already Bloch distinguished between the pejorative sense of utopian longing that
was abstract and fanciful, and the concrete sense of Utopia that was based on
imagination and desire, but also on cognitive understanding and knowledge of

history. Thus desire and knowledge came together in the Novum, in anticipation of Utopia.

"Little daydreams" was not limited to the fantasies, daydreams, desires and hopes of the working classes. It was addressed to the petit bourgeois shopkeeper and the rural villager, the declasse professional and the village peasant. All these groups had suffered under Wilhelmine Germany and many had lost all worldly gains in the hyperinflation of the 1920's and during the Depression of the early thirties. As a result, much of the population, as Bloch knew, imagined, dreamed about and hoped for a fulfilling life which did not push them to the margins of anomie and despair.[19] Both the bourgeois and the non-bourgeois, he added, overhaul "the given world, both in actions and in dreams."[20]

Thus, Bloch believed that "little daydreams" envisioned a shift in values from happiness as comfort to revolutionary wishful dream because the happiness of one would no longer be measured against the misery of others. Our fellow men would no longer be seen as a barrier to our own freedom, but the means of achieving it. The freedom of acquisition would cede to the freedom from acquisition, and from this would come the vision dream of "achievable solidarity . . . with all men."[21]

Anticipatory Consciousness

Bloch believed that "Little Daydreams" developed into an anticipatory consciousness because dreams were forward looking and utopian, hopeful and revolutionary, part of the Novum that Bloch himself longed for in personal and historical transcendence.

On the other hand, Bloch rejected Freud's, as well as C.G. Jung's and Alfred Adler's views of psychoanalysis. Freudian psychoanalysis was solitary, encapsulated and subterranean. It ignored the world and concentrated on the inner self as though it had no connection to the real world. The unconscious in Freud was backward looking. The unconscious mind of Freud's psychoanalysis was *"never* a *Not-Yet-Conscious*, an element of progressions; it consists rather of regressions."[22] The process of making the unconscious conscious could only draw from what has been. Freud could only look backward, there was *"nothing new in the Freudian unconscious."*[23]

Little daydreams contained urges, longings, drives, cravings, wishes and desires that propelled human nature beyond itself and drove it into the future. Freud's ideas, to the contrary, were saturated with bourgeois ideas, full of the past to which all mankind would have to adjust. In Freud, human impulses were totally disembodied from the socio-historical world into which man was born and lived.

Freud's disciples came out no better. C. G. Jung was nothing more than a psychoanalyzing fascist who reduced the "unconscious entirely to the primeval. . . . . All wishful images . . . only suggest prehistory."[24] Thus, consciousness paled beside the colorful night of the unconscious surrounded by the images of the primeval. Jung was condemned as racist, stained by an irrational primevalism. In Jung there was nothing new, only primitivism.[25]

Psychoanalysis in general was stigmatized by Bloch; it had only spicy drives which it conceptually lifted out of the living body.[26] The body's socio-economic world was never discussed in psychoanalysis, a critical omission, suggested Bloch, since it even contradicted the psychoanalytic conception of drives. Hunger was the drive that was always left out of psychoanalytic theory. Freud and Jung completely missed this, though hunger was a part of the drive toward self-preservation, so fundamental that it could set all the other drives into motion.[27] The fact that Freud was not concerned with hunger, Bloch believed, demonstrated how bourgeois he and his patients were. Bloch referred to the money complex as the only real drive, the drive toward self-preservation.[28]

Bloch warned against attempting to recover primal man. Man was historical. He could become barbaric, but he could never become Neanderthal. There was no pristine nature to recover. Human nature was in process of development. It was not stuck in the capitalist phase of egotism that rewarded and stimulated selfishness. Bloch anticipated that self-preservation ultimately meant the appetite to achieve "more authentic states for our unfolding self, unfolding in and as solidarity."[29] As humanity moved beyond self-preservation, its dreams became explosive. It decided to abolish the conditions in which man was oppressed. The drive for satisfaction became a "drive which survives the available world in the imagination."[30] Out of the desire for self-preservation and to satisfy the elemental need for nourishment, man's imagination of a better world stimulated his wish fantasies. He looked forward toward changing himself and others. He developed a wishful element and this galvanized him toward the goal of a better life. Dreams signified what was lacking; they were signifiers of a better world and a hope that could not be extinguished.[31]

Thus, Bloch created a historical narrative rooted in human psychology that moved toward a goal in the future, grounded in the expanding horizons of a fundamental drive. Moreover, the daydream was different from the nocturnal dream: the former could not be repressed, filtered out or relegated to the unconscious, it expressed fully what man wished to become in an un-oppressed state. The diurnal dream drove forward toward the Not-Yet-Conscious, it suggested a state that had never been conscious or existed in the past but was itself "forward dawning, into the New."[32] Thus, desire, as drive, turned into wish, and wish, forward looking, gave hope and birth to the Not-Yet-Conscious as it embraced the possibilities of the future.

Bloch conceded to Freud that there were some vivid nocturnal dreams that were wish-fulfilling. But this was not the wish fulfillment of the diurnal dream. Rather these were the wishes that became phobias because they were repressed, caused anxiety and ultimately despair.[33] The nocturnal dream could cause phobias, but never grant hope. It could cause complexes, but never be utopian.

Bloch's daydream, therefore, painted a better world, especially when a daydream became the basis of a "cleverly informed plan."[34] The daydream was a stepping stone to world improvement. The daydream led to art, and at the same time art had a utopian prospect, it embraced "joy as the figure that is approaching."[35] Only the daydream had overt knowledge of the defects of the world, "with acknowledgment of how good it could be."[36] The daydream was therefore a journey to the end. It began like the night dream with wishes but carried "them radically to their conclusion . . . to the place of their fulfillment."[37]

Whereas Freud's work was saturated with the forgotten, the No-Longer-Conscious, Bloch fastened on the diurnal dream, the home of the Not-Yet-Conscious. The daydream remained open toward the future; it was preconscious of something new. The Not-Yet-Conscious was "thus solely the preconscious of what is to come, the psychological birthplace of the New."[38]

The New however did not emerge from a vacuum, it was not mere subjective creation or random dream, it was not pure inspiration, though it benefited from the genius who saw it on the horizon. The new, Bloch insisted, came from a meeting of a specific genius and the objective conditions of the possible, it had to be ripe so the 'new' could "break through out of mere incubation . . ."[39]

The objective conditions in this case were socio-economic, the emergence of a proletariat, but also of a dispirited middle class. The subjective case, said Bloch, was none other than the genius of Marx. It was Marx the idealist who now appeared in the pages of *The Principle of Hope*, as a utopianized Marx. Marx, argued Bloch, was able to put light on the emergence of historical possibility, and in turn it was Marx who was inspired by it. Marx was enthused with hope even as he offered hard-headed analysis about real possibility.[40] The genius of Marx stood at the helm, illuminating the landscape of the future, making the not-yet-conscious conscious.[41] "And so the point is reached," Bloch proclaimed, "where hope itself . . . appears . . . in a *conscious-known* way as *utopian function*."[42]

Bloch found anticipatory consciousness throughout history. Utopian anticipation was recognized in Greek myth, Christian Adventism, Enlightenment metaphysics. Bloch traced it in architecture, music and art. He recognized the spirit of Utopia in the Strasbourg cathedral, he saw it in Dante's *Divine Comedy*, and especially in the *Hymn of Joy* in Beethoven. It was in Beethoven especially that he discovered "the concept of utopia as that of comprehended hope. . . ."[43] Below Breughel's cloak of mere fantasy was another Utopia, the Land of Cockaigne, the land of perpetual Sundays. In myth there was the liberation of the virgin whom the dragon held captive, as in the story of Perseus and Andromeda. Bloch compared this narrative to "the kingdom of Antichrist before the beginning of the New Jerusalem."[44] Moreover, he singled out Beethoven's *Fidelio* as belonging to the highest utopian order in the trumpet signal of the last act, which heralded Leonora's rescue of Fidelio. In this act, Bloch likened the arrival of the minister to the divine intervention of the Messiah because he embodied "the archetype of the vengeful, redeeming apocalypse."[45] In the trumpet's annunciation Bloch saw the storming of the Bastille, "the continual background for the music of *Fidelio*."[46] Thus archaic myth stepped out of the astral background and entered revolutionary history, filled with contemporary content and foreshadowing the Adventism of Utopia.

In addition to dream, Bloch believed that anticipatory consciousness was buried deep inside folk tales, songs, aphorisms, fables and fairy tales as humanity's not-yet-conscious but deepest utopian longings. Moreover, by juxtaposing the fragments of experience that were lodged in the images and symbols of these forms of artistic expression and consciousness, Bloch sought to reutilize these fragments and to signify them in a way that shocked readers into awareness of their inner needs. In theory, the shock would help them break out of themselves, allowing them to communicate effectively and to seek collective action and goals. By estranging readers from traditional modes of understanding, by reutilizing imagery in explosive ways, Bloch hoped to endow imagery, as Jack Zipes has pointed out, with "the very anticipatory illumination he endeavored to trace and analyze in works of art and everyday cultural phenomena."[47] Philosophy, like literature and art, could then "raise the not-yet-conscious to a point where [it] could grasp the direction humankind would have to take to bring about the fulfillment of those needs, wants and wishes that he [Bloch] saw scattered in dreams and daydreams."[48]

Bloch was convinced that the essence of human nature was the impulse of hope. This impulse was primordial. The essence of mankind was to look forward toward what it could become in anticipatory consciousness, to anticipate what had not-yet-become in the present world but was already taking shape in psychical and artistic representation. He thought it necessary to ferret out the signs, symbols and signifiers, the not-yet-conscious in the presentiments of what individuals lacked, needed, wanted and hoped to find. The main sightings of such needs were in daydreams and art, which not only shed light on the darkness of immediate experience, but which provided glimmers in the not-yet-conscious of a possible and a better world, and in so doing helped to clarify what was being experienced in the present.[49]

Anticipatory illuminations were therefore glimmerings of Utopia. They were a linkage between hope and reality, between dream and the future, between artistic imagination and Utopia, a bridge between pre-conscious glimmerings and fully illuminated consciousness. In the *Principle of Hope*, this linkage became explicit and framed the core values and dreams of Bloch's own philosophy. Here the truth of art had to do with "the available depictability of beautiful illusion."[50] Art as Utopia was the illusion of the real possible, an illusion manifested by the layers of reality in which it was partially concealed. But artistic illusion was more than illusion, it contained images that hinted at a possible future, images of anticipatory illuminations still concealed from the conscious mind. Anticipatory illumination became attainable "precisely because art drives its material to an end, in characters, situations, plots, landscapes, and brings them to a stated resolution in suffering, happiness and meaning."[51] Through art anticipatory illusion was attainable as something much more than dream.

For Bloch the acts of writing, reading, painting, composing were all acts in forming and recomposing the world. These acts left behind specific traces of intended meaning that served as illuminations of ultimate human purposes. The aim of philosophy was to read these illumined paths toward the future and to anticipate, collaboratively, the invariable direction toward a society without oppression.[52] In Bloch's sense, we all participated in the elaborate search for meaning in life, dreaming of a more authentic existence and a classless society. We were all responsible for the deciphering of signs that we had to weave into narratives that embodied anticipatory illuminations. All of us were detectives in the unraveling of experience and its re-formation as the thread that led from illusion to anticipation, from despair to hope. Bloch's universe, therefore, hinted at enigmatic signs waiting to be deciphered, he looked back upon a world and a history that needed to be read in order to be completed. As Fredric Jameson has noted, Bloch saw the world as an immense storehouse of enigmatic signs waiting to be translated. The task of the philosopher was to pierce the incognito of every lived moment.[53]

Outlines of a Better World: Religion and Utopia

Outlines of a better world was a compendium of explicitly conscious depictions of a better world, which Bloch discovered in the social architecture and geography of Utopia. He depicted medical, architectural, technological, geographical, social and literary utopias, projecting an alternative utopian future. Simultaneously, he believed that all utopian longings were bound to the times that wished and projected them, all had their timetables. Thus, a Utopia might anticipate a final communist happiness, but frame it in the imminence of the near future. St. Augustine was influenced by the incipient feudal economy, Thomas More by free trading capital, Campanella by the early form of manufacture under absolutism, Saint Simon by the new industry. Politically, More could not see past the coming of parliamentary democracy. Campanella could not anticipate transcending absolutism, hence the authoritarianism of his Utopia which demanded absolute order and the planning of every detail. Yet, all these utopias were transparent and aimed at heaven on earth.[54] Utopias varied, yet what remained unchanged was the will toward the utopian, the will to find the Novum, the will toward human freedom and bliss.

The conscious imagining of Utopia, however much a castle in the sky, was, in Bloch's estimation, an imagined trumpet that signified what was to come, a kind of annunciation: Moses liberating the Jews, or Jesus and the eschatological Sermon on the Mount. Outlines of a better world had an eternal pull because "the pull toward what is lacking never ends."[55]

For Bloch, this pull embraced religion; religion, not the church, was the essence of utopianism. In like manner, Bloch's Marx was now biblical, messianic and Adventist. Marx was a veritable prophet of paradise thundering prophecies in the New Canaan of profane history. Thus, Jewish messianism and Christian eschatology provided scaffolding for the eternal human yearning for transcendence, both were visions of Utopia on earth. In language that was itself eschatological, Bloch looked toward the unburdened future by finding traces of that future in the past. Each trace, however bound by its timetable, was at once a revelation and a conscious dawning of a better future. Each trace shed a light on the night of immediate experience.

Thus, Bloch's narrative was biblical in form and content; it was a veritable re-interpretation of the Bible and its utopianism in imagery, imagination and hope. Moses appeared as the savior of a nation, killed an overseer and was forced to flee from Egypt. The God that he imagined when abroad was not the God of masters but of free Bedouins. Yahweh represented a threat to the Pharaoh; Yahweh was the God of liberation, the God who led Moses out of Egypt.[56] Moreover, the Bible preserved the memory of nomadic, half-primitive communism. God's will, said Bloch, was to create a community without division of labor and private property.[57] The prophets continued this tradition, Bloch insisted, despite the period of Canaan and Judges, when private property and classes appeared along with deprivation and servitude and even the selling of debtors into slavery abroad. In the midst of exploitation, the prophets drew up the idea of judgment and anticipated the tones of an early social Utopia, giving a kind of proof that there was continuity between the present and the semi-communist Bedouin past. There also remained a connection with the Rechabites, a tribe in the south that had remained aloof from the "opulence and money economy of Canaan."[58] This tribe remained faithful to the desert god. Opposed to Solomon, who introduced classes and opulence for the few, were also the Nazarites, a group that abstained from signs of wealth. Their Yahweh was a stranger to private property, Bloch noted, and was also the god of the poor. Samson, Samuel and Elijah were all Nazarites, but so was John the Baptist.[59] All were enemies of the Golden Calf and of the opulent Church that followed Canaanite Baal.[60]

Thus, Bloch, himself in the prophetic-revolutionary tradition, saw a straight line from the primitive communism of the Nazarites to the prophets railing against wealth and tyranny, and from there to the "early Christian communism founded on love."[61] It was this tradition and belief that appeared in the prophetic anticipations of a harmonious kingdom of social justice "which was not just a legend."[62] And when the Hebrews strayed from this tradition and their Yahweh became a god of luxury, who indeed conquered the god Baal, and the Hebrews were divided by their own wealth, the prophets again set things aright. The prophet Amos had his Yahweh reclaim the future for the righteous by claiming to be a humble cowherd. Moreover, Amos's Yahweh announced that he would set a fire upon Judah that would devour the palaces of Jerusalem because they had sold the righteous for silver and had turned aside the ways of the meek.[63]

In Isaiah, Bloch found a genesis from biblical communism to the advent of utopian communism at the end of history and time. For Isaiah had proclaimed all who were thirsty would be brought to the waters, he that had no money would buy and eat, he would buy "wine and milk without money and without price."[64] And indeed a Utopia emerged in the words of Isaiah and the younger Micah. Thus, from Isaiah 2, 4 and Micah 4, 3 Bloch cited the following:

> For from Zion shall go forth the law, and the word of the Lord from Jerusalem. And he shall judge among the nations, and shall rebuke many people: and they shall beat their swords into plowshares and their spears into pruning hooks: nation shall not lift up sword against nation, neither shall they learn war any more. But they shall sit every man under his vine and under his fig tree; and none shall make them afraid."[65]

It was the content of the biblical Utopia, according to Bloch, that had informed every social Utopia since, including that of Zion.[66] This was the light of the night, and in Isaiah there remained yet more. For in Isaiah 54,14 it was said: "In righteousness shalt thou be established; thou shall be far from oppression; for thou shalt not fear; and from terror; for it shall not come near thee."[67]

It was in this social-revolutionary context that Bloch placed Jesus. When the Romans came they protected the rich against the rebellious peasants, and they protected the rich from the prophets whom they called agitators. Against the order of Roman rule and the privileged few, John the Baptist preached an end to the misery of the common people in Matthew 3, 10: "And now also the axe is laid under the root of the trees: therefore every tree which bringeth not forth good fruit is hewn down, and cast into the fire."[68] The coming of Jesus brought forth the same message, Bloch noted. Not that of the crucifixion which was a catastrophe, but the message that Jesus had come to put an end to suffering and to do it on earth. Jesus was the man to whom all change was entrusted, and yet proclaimed that his yoke was easy and his burden light.[69]

When Jesus told the Pharisees that the Kingdom of God is among you he meant that the kingdom was already alive and that this was the chosen kingdom already living in the disciples; it was a social, not an invisible kingdom. The world desired and discussed by Jesus was not the world to come after death, but the terrestrial world of Christian love, already represented by the early Christian community founded by Christ. In the biblical narrative, intoned Bloch, the kingdom of the other world became otherworldly only after the Cross and the crucifixion. And only after the Pilates and Neros converted to Christianity because the ruling class needed to defuse the communism of love by making it "as spiritual as possible."[70] But for Jesus the kingdom of the other world was to be brought to this world. Not by preaching peace, this world was after all the world of the devil, but by a universal upheaval that would make things aright.[71] The other world referred to by Jesus was also the world to come on earth. Isaiah had the same aspiration when he announced the coming of new heavens and a new earth. This was not, said Bloch, for Isaiah or Jesus, the other world of the angels after death, but the "equally terrestrial and super-terrestrial kingdom of love."[72] Bloch believed that Jesus saw himself in the messianic tradition. Jesus' depiction of himself as the Son of Man was labeled by Bloch as exaltation of the human and was distinct from the otherworldly Son of God. The Son of Man, Bloch argued, showed that the Messiah was no mere ambassador from Heaven. The Son of Man "is the highest title of all, and it means that man has become a figure of final, all conquering strength."[73]

Even Jesus' statement to render unto Caesar those things which are Caesar's and unto God those things that are God's was interpreted by Bloch in a revolutionary and apocalyptic fashion. Jesus was not just uttering a compromise; he had nothing but contempt for the state. If the Sermon on the Mount meant anything at all it meant the expectation of imminent catastrophe for both the temple and the state. Mark 13, the eschatological chapter, was a utopian tracing, according to Bloch, with messianic earthly tones. The catastrophe for the state was Jesus himself. The appeal in the Last Judgment would seem to suspend revolution and await a natural catastrophe, but always there was expectation of the coming new era. And indeed Jesus sensed that the catastrophe was already present, he no longer talked about loving one's enemies when it came to the Last Judgment. The new social community, the community of Christians, owed allegiance solely to Jesus. It existed through him and in him. Bloch cited John, who quoted Jesus saying that he was the vine and the disciples were the branches. And Matthew 25, 40: "Inasmuch as ye have done it unto one of the least of these my brethren, ye have done it unto me."[74]

In much of the Bible Bloch saw a blending of social revolution and messianic prophecy. Early Christians embraced Matthew as a social Utopia grounded in the communism of love. Matthew added a social mission for living humanity and a "mythically powerful person to watch over it."[75] Thus, overall, to the message that Jesus came to abolish death, the Christian community also came to oppose the powers of the existing world. Bloch did not naively believe that the message of Christianity was solely to create heaven on earth by removing the powers of the Romans, and by revolutionizing the state. But overall he did claim that the Bible had a social-apocalyptic-revolutionary message of imminence: the killing of the Egyptian overseer, the exodus, the "thundering prophets . . . the expulsion of the money-changers,"[76] the promises to the poor that their burden would be lightened all pointed in this direction.

Of course Bloch did not believe the Bible was simply a plan for a social Utopia. Christianity was never just an outcry against deprivation, it was a revolt against death and nothingness, it inserted "the Son of Man into both."[77] But the Bible pointed to an exodus toward a kingdom that flowed with milk and honey.[78] A kingdom, moreover, not regarded in the Bible as a "baptized Babel, not even . . . as a Church."[79]

Bloch saw St. Augustine's *City of God* as utopian also, despite Augustine's belief that grace was only for an elect and would only come at the end of time. Yet, Bloch insisted that Augustine celebrated the City of God as already present in the Church. In Augustine, Bloch noted, "the City of God marches ahead of man."[80] The community of perfection appeared as the fitting climax of history, not as in St. Paul in a transcendental version above and beyond history. The notion of the kingdom of God on earth was present throughout the Middle Ages and into the early modern era, so that the idea of brotherhood even outlasted "the theology of the Father."[81] In the modern era "human beings were henceforth utopianized as brothers"[82] even after the Father had 'disappeared'. Thus the message of Augustine survived throughout history as a message of brotherhood and fraternity, as a Utopia to be realized on earth.

Bloch also found the social-revolutionary utopianism of Jesus alive in the Christian apocalyptic messianism of Joachim of Fiore, who expounded his ideas around 1200. Joachim divided history into three stages. There was the Father of the Old Testament in which the law reigned supreme; the Son of the New Testament, in which love and the Church, divided into clerics and laity, reigned supreme. And there was the era to come, the era of the Holy Spirit, an era of illumination in which a kind of mystical democracy appeared, without need of masters and priests. An era, in other words, in which neither the state nor the

Church was needed.[83] The last stage was an age of spiritual perfection in which the spirit arrived as the final fulfillment of history, not as an exit from historical time into the eternal. Paradise would come as the historical future. The message was clearly social, apocalyptic and revolutionary. Joachim's chosen few, Bloch noted, were the poor who would go to paradise as living bodies and not just as spirits. There would be no social classes in the future society of the Third Testament. Instead, there would be an 'age of monks', a kind of monastic communism, an age of spiritual illumination, "without sundering, sin and the world that goes with it."[84] The theme in its entirety was one of spiritual and temporal liberation, an exodus from servitude, an escape from "the rule of clerics."[85] The kingdom of Christ was decidedly of this world. Misery was now expunged, ahead lay the millennium. Differences between rich and poor were abolished. The idea of fraternity was embraced. Moreover, the Joachimites urged tolerance towards Jews and heathens, unlike the Augustinians. Thus, the citizenship of the coming kingdom did not depend on baptism but in the perception of the "fraternal spirit in the inner word."[86] From here Bloch's narrative filled with tracings of Joachim. He saw his legacy in Thomas Munzer during the Peasant War of 1525, in the agrarian-communist Diggers a century later in England.[87] In the contemporary period, displaying the political naivete that would plague him for much of his life, he depicted the Soviet Union as the modern inheritor of Joachim's social hopefulness and revolutionary enthusiasm.[88]

Bloch believed that the real and authentic Christianity was the early Christianity of Christ, a Christianity whose tracings were to be found in the eschatological teachings of Joachim, Thomas Munzer and the Taborites, and later in the secular, socialist renderings of Charles Fourier and Marx. He faulted the Western Church for rejecting this tradition. It confined enthusiasm, after the Lateran Council of 1215, to apostles and ancient martyrs, depriving "Adventist beliefs of any kind of sanction."[89]

In contemporary history Bloch linked the Eastern Church, in an ironic twist, to the Adventism of Bolshevism. The Eastern Church taught a continuing presence of the Spirit outside the priestly Church amongst monks and laymen; and therefore the Eastern Church lacked the monopoly of administering the host and controlling the whole edifice of redemption. It was precisely this spirit that not only lived in Joachim but that made its way into Russian Christianity, Bloch argued. The Brotherhood of Adventist beliefs was celebrated by the sect of Chlysts which had a doctrine of Russian Christs, counting up to seven.[90] Moreover, Bloch continued, the Christo-romantic tradition sprung up on Bolshevist soil, in particular in the work of the chiliast Alexander Blok. In Blok's hymn, "March of the Twelve," which depicted a march of twelve Red Army soldiers, Christ preceded the revolution and led it, an act precisely in the tradition of the Eastern Church and its notion of the terrestrial presence of the Spirit.[91] Thus, in summary, Bloch traced the Spirit, a Spirit that began in Christ and continued into the final revolution-revelation as the coming of the kingdom on earth. A Spirit, moreover, that wound its way through the people and outside the priestly class and the authority of the Vatican, a Spirit that was millenarian and redemptive, revolutionary and chiliastic. Thus came the Holy Spirit bringing the social principles of early Christianity, of heretical Christianity and Adventist Utopia. Thus came Joachim's New Moral World, Christlikeness turned into society, "happiness, freedom, order . . . in its utopian application."[92]

It was not accidental or ironical that Bloch connected the fulminations of Joachim with those of Marx and Engels. After all, Marx and Engels were themselves in a tradition that was prophetic, messianic and chiliastic even as they rejected religion with their fullest spleen. Bloch believed profoundly that eschatological faith and earthly initiative went together.[93] Liberation theologians such as Gustavo Gutierrez have noted Bloch's creative syntheses of Christianity and radical social theory.[94] Bloch himself remarked that the analysis of alienation and the attempt to restore humanity to a non-alienated condition, which figured prominently in the early Marx, began with a critique of religion.[95] In this tradition, humanity projected into religion all hopes and aspirations that were blocked by society. Religion was, therefore, mystified consciousness, a disguised form in which humanity was speaking to itself.[96] It was in this sense that Bloch discovered and approved of Marx and Engels, denying the vulgar Marxist interpretation that Marx simply rejected religion tout court. A quote from the young Frederick Engels in 1842 summed it up: "The self-confidence of humanity, the new Grail around whose throne the nations jubilantly gather . . . This is our vocation: to become the Templars of this Grail, to gird our swords about our loins for its sake and cheerfully risk our lives in the last holy war, which will be followed by the millennium of freedom."[97]

Bloch discovered other connections between the Christian Final Kingdom and communist classless society. The inhabitants of Charles Fourier's socialist villages collectively owned the means of production; villages shared the burden of labor so that the land became a kind of socialist garden. Fourier saw this as a guarantee of freedom, said Bloch, but also as the victory of the basic passion, the Christian love of mankind, a society rooted in kindness and Christian love and not just moral duty or obligation as in the sense of the Old Testament. Fourier's future state flowed from the principles of Christianity'. Fourier's commune was a commune of "sheer Christian harmony."[98] Remove capitalism and one removed the last obstacle to mankind's life in Christian community, the obstacle of individualism and private property, the obstacle of greed and selfishness.[99]

Like Fourier, St. Simon did not anticipate an apocalypse, socialist or Christian. He was a thorough rationalist. He believed, Bloch noted, that socialism had to be organized by intellectual elites, savants who would guide humanity toward enlightenment and socialism. But Christian humanism still was fundamental and St. Simon believed in a kind of Christian humaneness. He therefore anticipated a socialism that did not do without Christianity, or at least the values of Christianity.[100]

Bloch also extolled the views of Wilhelm Weitling, though Weitling was scorned by Marx as a hopeless romantic utopian, because Weitling combined Adventist Christianity, a socialism of love, Jesus the carpenter, and a Baptist's reading of the Bible. Weitling the proletarian spoke from his own immediate suffering, said Bloch, and awaited the new messiah. Weitling's castle in the sky was humane, a gospel of the poor sinner, a castle in the air full of guarantees of harmony and freedom. In Weitling, Bloch saw a throwback to the dreams of the German Peasant War. Weitling longed for a giant union, a cooperative business order, classless society. Bloch saw real value in Weitling's unmistakable messianism because Weitling saw the Promised Land before Marx and Engels opened the "real entrances to it."[101]

Bloch's discussion of Marx followed similar themes. Messianism and utopianism converged in Marx. Marx, noted Bloch, was correct about the economic interest being a priority in dismantling previous society. But Marx was also aware of the need for utopian elements and the need for a definition of man as more than an economic being. To conquer the world of paradise one had to embrace Arcadia, there had to be a kind of chiliastic socialism of the heart. Nobody rushed to death on behalf of a "thoroughly organized production budget,"[102] said Bloch. Even the Bolshevik idea of Marxism, he added, contained the old Taborite-Joachite myth, though he explicitly denied that Marx's communism coincided with the Final Kingdom even in its radical Joachimite version.[103] Bloch thought Marx's vision was still the culmination and took its inspiration from the notion of the Golden Age, with the difference that Marx sought that Golden Age in the future, proof, said Bloch, that socialism was a Utopia as old as the history of the world.[104] And, one might add, that religion was its root.

Throughout "Outlines of a Better World," the narrative of Bloch is carried along by a language that is oracular. The orientation is always toward the possible, the concretely utopian, it is swept along by grand vistas: Christian love, advent of communism, Final Kingdom, Cross and end of suffering, righteous, prophetic, communism of love, Utopia and internationalism, the end of private property and the division of labor. Language becomes meta-historical, combining concept and narrative. Bloch, full of apocalyptic expectation, identifies eternal human purposes, anticipates the end of history. As in such meta-historical figures as Hegel, Marx, Jacob Burckhardt and Benedetto Croce, Bloch struggles to see history as a kind of grand narrative, as dramatic dialectic that could still, through the instilling of hope, achieve the final resolution, transform the world.

In Bloch's workings the messianic became a distillation of Jesus and Marx. Jesus himself was the kind of figure who embodied anticipatory illumination and earthly communism. He triumphed over evil and suffering. He signified the liberation of the poor in the earthly kingdom, the kingdom that he represented and intended to build in historical time. In this respect, Bloch believed that Marx embodied the genius that completed the eternal message and hope of Jesus. Messianism remained a language of hope, now in secular dross. It signified optimism, liberation, triumph, the end of history, salvation, the kingdom to come, good over evil, justice over injustice, the end of suffering.

Aesthetics and Utopia: Wishful Images of the Fulfilled Moment

In one of the most illuminating sections of *The Principle of Hope*, Bloch argued that wishful images of the fulfilled moment were nuggets of dream life that had always existed as traces of the fulfilled Utopia, culminating in the dream becoming reality. Wishful images of the fulfilled moment were the most sublime images of existence that humanity had been able to imagine.[105] They overcame the dualism of history, established a synthesis between the individual and the collective, between action and contemplation, solitude and friendship, body and soul. Fulfilled images were a way beyond class, beyond the alienated individual, they were a way toward *"solidarity which is rich in persons and extremely many voiced."*[106] Not Western democracy and its "standardization of the majority of yesterday,"[107] nor the liberal Western societies that arose in the aftermath of 1789 and 1848 with their felicitous inequalities, but a classless society, communal and equal.

It was in the cultural heritage from the past that Bloch found traces that led from the not-yet-conscious to the conscious, from anticipation to full illumination. The aesthetics of Utopia, the discovery of the sublime, its illumination in art and literature, in daydreams and religious yearning, in science and politics, meant that Bloch believed in the power of consciousness over the so-called logic of history, the power of signification over the laws of economics, the power of the imagination over the hypothetical laws of historicism. Aesthetic formations, by gathering glimpses of the beautiful, illuminated what was missing and might still be achieved, signifying hopes and horizons for individual and collective change.[108]

The most sublime images of the future Utopia were discovered by Bloch in music and art. Both were anticipatory and both were deeply subversive. Bloch saw a subversive element in music because of its utopianism and its evocation of the future in melodic-emotive terms. He believed that social and historical tendencies were reflected in sound material: "Handel's oratorios in their festive pride reflect rising imperialist England,"[109] England's global aspirations. But music was far more evocative than simply expressing reflections of classes and nations. It gave incomprehensible consolation even through the darkness, even through death, it contained a "surplus of hope-material,"[110] even at moments of overwhelming suffering and grief.

For Bloch, music could contain a messianic resonance. About Mozart, Bach and Beethoven, he asserted that their music anticipated a new social cosmos that was truly ascendant. Their language was apocalyptic, through it one passed into a cosmos of redemption. Mozart, Bach and Beethoven represented *"venturing beyond the limits in tone-spheres."*[111] Bloch believed that music revealed the essence of humanity and contained entirely, in tonal language, a new cosmos of morality and universality. Again Bloch reminded us of Beethoven's *Fidelio*: he referred to the trumpet call in the third overture of Leonora, "an overture which in reality is a utopian memory, a legend of fulfilled hope,"[112] a signal of the arrival of the messiah, of a coming freedom, of a world almost fulfilled. Through the language and imagery of chiliasm and messianism, of anticipation of the New Jerusalem, Bloch found music at the "frontiers of mankind . . . with new language and the call aura around captured intensity [which is still forming]."[113] Music brought forth Utopia. Music, in its sublimity, overcame the finiteness of the world by transcending time and space, by discovering the harmonic, by synthesizing the individual and the collective, solitude and joy, being alone and community.

If music conferred a sublime imagery of the future, religion, specifically Christianity, provided an imagery to contest what Bloch referred to as the cruelest form of anti-Utopianism, death.[114] Whereas Bloch had previously been concerned with the social-revolutionary project of Jesus, he now turned to the mystery of Christ and his triumph over mortality, through resurrection, ascension and the second coming (parousia). Bloch believed there was a shift in the Bible away from Jesus' radical project, so cruelly voided on the Cross. The shift ran counter to Jesus' personal revolution and toward the utopian use of the risen Christ by the Christian community, into the realm of wishful mysteries. The utopian Jesus became the utopianized Christ. Yet, despite this seeming transformation, Bloch saw continuity between the messianic Jesus, his social apocalyptic message of imminent catastrophe, and the utopian mysteries of the later books of the Bible. Bloch depicted Jesus' resurrection and ascension as an affirmation of human immortality. The greatest obstacle to humanity's utopian aspirations was overcome. For Bloch this was not the divine Christ being vindicated by his resurrection but the storming of heaven by humanity. It was Jesus, the Son of Man, at last transforming the City of God into the City of Man, merging earth into heaven.[115]

For Bloch, one of the major achievements of Joachim of Fiore was his recognition of the messianic-utopian message as it persisted in the transfiguration of Christ. In Joachim's Final Kingdom, the Kingdom of the Holy Spirit, a transfigured Christ overcame death and the Kingdom of God by returning to earth in the Second Coming. The Final Kingdom was terrestrial and triumphant. Messianism was conjoined with mystery, terrestrial and divine salvation merged in the divine and human in Christ.[116] Moreover, Bloch argued, in Joachim's Final Kingdom, the Christ who returned was not the Christ who appeared in the New Testament. The returned Christ was the comforter, the founder bearing the triumphant content of salvation, the revolutionary incorporating the future and the God of the past within himself.[117]

In the work of Joachim, Bloch traced the messianic Jesus, the Son of Man returning to his people, a human figure determined to save the degraded and to establish once and for all a just order of things on earth. The mysterious Christ joined the human Jesus in a final terrestrial incarnation, in a triumphant merging of the sacred and the profane as a final redemption of the human cosmos.[118]

Bloch's conclusion was that Christianity, as anticipatory illumination and as utopian vision, was profoundly necessary and revolutionary. Through Christianity, Bloch believed, God became the idea that mankind had of itself. Bloch completely rejected theism, however, because Christianity made it possible for man to complete his own history.[119] This could be fulfilled only with the "elimination of God himself . . ."[120] Bloch concluded that the narrative of Jesus, in both its messianic and mysterious aspects, dispelled all illusions that God controlled the way. "The religious kingdom-intention as such involves atheism, at least properly understood atheism."[121] Thus, the revolutionary Jesus and the transfigured Christ converged in man finding himself. Wishful thinking at last turned into self-realization.[122] And in a sense, mankind went through a long journey to discover itself in God, and to complete the journey of its hopes in its own utopianized history.

Of course, Bloch believed this transforming journey could only be completed through Marx, the ultimate utopian who combined analysis with enthusiasm, knowledge with justice. Through Marx the wishful image would be fulfilled, Marx was *"humanity actively comprehending itself."*[123] Marx addressed humanity by combining reason and hope, each could only blossom with the other.[124] It was Marx, said Bloch, more than any other, who made the Not-Yet-Conscious conscious, who combined the objective understanding of history with the subjective dreaming and hoping of humanity.[125] Whereas Bloch criticized Marx in his (Bloch's) earlier work as overly concerned with materialism and economics, the Marx of *The Principle of Hope* became a humanist. Hope alone inspired and consoled and provided an understanding of the world to which it could lead.[126] In Marx sobriety was only possible with enthusiasm. Marx was a prophet of the dream world of hoping humanity. Marxism was therefore the continuing fight against dehumanization, the fitting and only heir to the earlier utopian campaigns.[127] At the political level, Bloch continued, Marxism took over the campaign for humanization from the bourgeoisie. Marxism was the struggle against dehumanization. Authentic Marxism "will be nothing but the promotion of humanity."[128]

Marx's humanity, however, was an addressed humanity, an address "directed toward those alone who need it."[129] Marx's hostility was directed toward all those who dehumanized humanity. He urged revolution against those who, organized as a class, were causing the misery of all others. Humanization through revolution would at last shred the lingering cover of self-alienation.[130] Bloch, perhaps fitting Marx into his own schema for overcoming self-alienation, made Marx's humanism inclusive. By getting to the root of alienation in class society, the circle of humanity described by Marx was ever more expanding, reaching beyond the radically exploited *"toward all who suffer common deprivation under capitalism."*[131] Moreover, speaking in tones that were again apocalyptic and messianic, Bloch exhorted mankind to a social revolution that would finally remove "the covering of self-alienation from all mankind."[132]

In truly prophetic tones, Bloch unleashed a Marx in the tradition of the Hebrew prophets of the Bible. Marx himself became biblical and utopianized. In language that sounded arcane even in the Soviet world, Bloch admonished that Marxism was from the beginning "humanity in action, the realized human face."[133] Moreover, Bloch's Marx remained an idealist. Marx's work began with a passion to set things aright. The analytical Marx was enthused and activated by the dream of social paradise. Marx's letter to Ruge in 1843, in which he said that the world had 'long-possessed the dream' of the matter, 'of which it must only possess the consciousness of to possess it in reality', was a Marx that Bloch could build his house upon.[134] A Marx, in fact, who consciously brought the old work to completion and continued the utopian cultural heritage.[135] A Marx who rejected mechanical materialism, who envisaged "matter as being dynamically active in the direction of the future, to which the past itself refers."[136] Marxism, then, was about the transformation of the world, but it built on an inheritance that was based on the primal intention, the Golden Age. Marxism, rooted in cold analysis, took "the *fairytale* seriously, [took] the *dream of a Golden Age* practically."[137] Marxism and the inheritance of dream converged in the aspiration toward Utopia. In Marx, Bloch found the way illumined, and in himself he found a Marx completed by his own deepest urgings toward Utopia and a classless society.

The Politics of Utopia

In *The Principle of Hope*, Bloch saw Marxism leading to the realm of freedom, the "last chapter of the history of the world."[138] But in the same pages he argued that the Soviet Union contained a "free people on a free ground," a dictum that he retained in the 1959 edition.[139] In 1937 he had defended the Moscow Show Trials in a "Jubilee for Renegades." Of the victims of those trials, the so-called 'renegades', he noted that once they loved the Russian Revolution but "during the last two years they have lost their enthusiasm. They cannot get over the fact that this 20-year-old bolshevist child must rid itself of so many enemies, and that it discards them so ruthlessly."[140] In *Heritage of Our Times*, in roughly the same period, Bloch criticized vulgar Marxism, yet in the same volume he could say of the German Communist Party (KPD) that "what the party did before Hitler's victory was completely correct, it was simply what it did not do that was wrong."[141] This was an astonishing assertion, given Bloch's own criticism of the KPD for failing to identify and harvest the very dream world on which the entire system of Bloch's hopes and aspirations were based. It certainly cast doubt on the explanatory value of his entire analysis. Moreover, Bloch glossed over the Stalinist tactics of the KPD that weakened the ability of the German working class to resist Hitler and Nazism. The KPD was hardly correct in characterizing Social Democracy as Social Fascism or in its absurd and embittered campaigns against fellow leftists. The decision of the KPD to reject an alliance with the Social Democrats was the fatal turn that helped Hitler come to power. Yet Bloch himself believed that only the KPD and communists were progressive and utopian. He characterized alternative leftist politics as "social democratic dilution [and] Trotskyite obstructionism."[142]

A decade later Bloch was still an apostle of the Soviet Union, a true believer that Stalin was carrying the lantern on behalf of Marxism and utopianism. Thus, the Soviet Union had solved the question of women's rights since it had solved the question of workers' rights.[143] Bloch was so insistent in his defense of the Soviet Union and Stalin, which he saw as the best hope against the decadent and imperialist West, especially the United States, that he was shunned by the reconstructed Marxists of the Frankfurt Institute, especially its leader, Max Horkheimer.[144] Throughout the forties and fifties, Bloch maintained faith with Marx that the proletariat was the only universal class, the only class that stood against the tyranny of capitalism. In his inaugural lecture at the University of Leipzig, after Bloch moved to East Germany in 1949, he still believed that Marxism was the road to the realm of freedom. A Marxism, moreover, that was under the theoretical guidance of Lenin and Stalin, the political guidance of the party and the administrative guidance of central planning. "The always keen and well-thought-out, open and concrete wisdom of Lenin and Stalin watches over the path to the classless society."[145] At least until 1953, Bloch, who never seriously studied the history of the United States or the Soviet Union, saw the Soviet Union in the forefront of the struggle for communism, while he associated the United States with fascism and imperialism and called it a threat to world peace. He insisted that the police measures in East Germany and the restrictions on (in fact the absence of) freedom in the Soviet Union, were the result of the American development of nuclear weapons, the communist witch-hunts in the West and the onset of the Cold War.[146]

The architecture of Bloch's Utopia was to be built in the promised-land, therefore, under the guardianship of the party. The army of this struggle was to be the proletariat. Yet Bloch understood that he was caught up in his own contradictions. He knew quite well that the Soviet Union and the KPD in Germany were not the vehicles of his imagined Utopia. It was absurd to claim that the party was the guardian of Utopia, though this was precisely what Bloch had proclaimed in *The Principle of Hope*. Moreover, there was another glaring contradiction. Bloch had always defended democratic rights and grounded them in natural law. He repeated Rosa Luxemburg's belief that there could be no socialism without democracy, no democracy without socialism. Yet, it was obvious that the party in East Germany did not welcome the establishment of personal freedoms and democratic rights. After 1956, following Khrushchev's denunciations of Stalinism, Bloch saw a window of opportunity. He openly began to criticize the East German government and called for de-Stalinization in East Germany. The East German reply was personal denunciation of Bloch. Several years later the Berlin Wall was built. By 1961 Bloch was in the West, in West Germany, where he now began the last period of his utopian Marxism.[147]

Bloch now argued that despite the best intentions of Lenin, czarist socialism had triumphed in Russia. This was because of the "absence of long-standing forms of bourgeois freedom [with the result that the] dictatorship of the proletariat had to be established directly on the basis of . . . Czarism."[148] Elsewhere Bloch noted deficiencies in Marxism itself, notably the absence of Enlightenment liberalism in the work of Marx, a fatal absence that tended to reinforce the centralizing tendency of Stalin. Above all, Bloch now ruefully noted the absence, or neglect, of utopianism in the work of Marx, an omission that had prepared the way for scientific socialism and its rejection of democracy and de-emphasis of personal freedoms.[149]

None of this dimmed Bloch's belief in the need for and the justice of Utopia. If Marx had failed to stress human liberties, he was nevertheless utopian in his insistence that alienation could be overcome. Bloch repeatedly returned to Marx's epigraph on capitalist society, the necessity of eliminating all conditions that degraded and subjugated humanity.[150] In the West, he related the legacy of the industrial revolution to everything that was inhuman.[151] He blamed the profit motive for the "uglification" of the West (though now he admitted to the deformities of the East). He continued to complain about the destructiveness of capitalism and its machine goods that destroyed the old towns, robbing them of their beautiful houses and furniture, and the "imaginative silhouette of everything organically constructed."[152]

In the end it was Bloch's great achievement to understand that utopianism was a permanent feature of a hoping humanity. In daydreams, play and travel, dance and song, sport and leisure, music and art, church and theater, human beings would always aspire to fulfillment, would always be utopian.[153] Moreover, he left a huge legacy in which the present could always be critiqued by the perfection of an imaginary utopianized future.

Chapter 6
Herbert Marcuse: Between Marx and Freud

In so many ways Herbert Marcuse's work continued many of the themes of Ernst Bloch. But Marcuse's notion of utopian Marxism took a dramatic detour through Sigmund Freud's work, building bridges between Marx and Freud that neither would have dreamed of or approved. In *Eros and Civilization*, which appeared in 1955, Marcuse not only signaled the revival of utopian thought, he tried to put Freud's theory of instincts into a Marxist historical and sociological framework, abandoning Freud's negative meta-historical postulate about human nature in general. Thus, where Freud had assumed that human instincts had to be suppressed to prevent permanent chaos, what he called the reality principle, Marcuse characterized this as in fact the performance principle adapted to the needs of consumer (capitalist) society. Whereas Freud had argued that instinctual suppression of human instincts (id) had to override the infantile pleasure principle as the price of the survival of civilization, Marcuse concluded quite the opposite. The suppression of the human instincts had not curbed human aggression and civilized mankind. On the contrary, he argued, it had produced massive human neuroses by suppressing human pleasure in the name of the capitalist work discipline.[1]

Thus, Marcuse found that the reality principle had only increased the tendency of modern societies to be authoritarian, repressive and anti-liberatory; individuals had abandoned the pleasure principle and fantasy for societies that had in the meantime failed. It was true that the repression of human instincts had led to the conquest of nature, more needs were satisfied than ever before. But submission to the reality principle had only produced the mechanization and standardization of life. The new technical capacity had not been harnessed for human need. Writing in the context of the 1950's, Marcuse referred to the relapse into barbarism, concentration camps, mass extermination and pandemic war in the name of civilization. Science and its achievement, technology, had only assisted in producing chaos and human domination by providing the instruments of unfreedom. Man's libido and instincts were repressed and yet he was a mass murderer. The conclusion was obvious. Freud was mistaken in his assumption about the need to base civilization on repression. The repression of civilization had only led to war and domination.[2]

Utopia and the Principle of Happiness

Marcuse thought the performance principle might have been more necessary, or perhaps understandable, when Freud wrote in the early twentieth-century prior to the enormous development of technology and the progress of technics and civilization. The performance principle was based on scarcity, but industrial civilization had since learned to produce abundance and to relieve man of the need for repression. Moreover, once humankind was released from the necessity of alienated labor, it could be liberated from the dominance of the reality principle (the repression of instinct to meet need). Instinctual repression, therefore, was only necessary during an earlier stage of human and civilization growth. The possibility existed now for non-repressive development, for the full release of the energies of Eros, the maximizing of freedom and the unleashing of the pleasure principle.

Marcuse was convinced this did not signify a return to prehistoric savagery. Instinctual directions were not fixed eternally, they reflected changing historical needs. In the absence of a non-repressive reality principle, he believed the character of the libido would be transformed. Eros would not be dammed up in service to the demands of civilization. Once the body was not used only as an instrument of labor, it would be resexualized. "The repression involved in this spread of the libido would first manifest itself in a reactivation of all erotegenic zones and . . . in a decline of genital supremacy. The body in its entirety would become . . . an instrument of pleasure."[3]

Marcuse distinguished himself from one notable critic, Norman Brown, who counseled the orgasm as the route to the new freedom, implying the end of the monogamous family and linking sexual and personal liberation with the release of the libido. Marcuse denied Brown's argument. In the eroticizing of the entire personality, Marcuse envisioned the free play of individual needs and desires, human liberation from alienated labor, and the emergence of a realm of freedom (Eros) in which work and pleasure were no longer antithetical. Thus, work became play and leisure and not just relief from alienated labor. It became the sphere of all eroticized cultural and artistic activities. This was the realm of freedom, the reconciliation of reason and happiness. Even Thanatos, death, could be overcome, for there was no longer an instinctual urge toward death to avoid pain. Under the regime that ended repression, Eros could absorb the death instinct. Given the promise of Utopia, man no longer needed to surrender to death.[4]

Fantasy and Utopia

For Marcuse, the utopian link to the future was through fantasy. Fantasy had a progressive role to play in the liberation of humankind, it was the bridge between an irrational present capitalism based on the performance principle and repression, and the future state of communism. In communism, Marcuse was convinced, the performance principle, based on alienated labor, would be replaced by the unleashing of Eros, the conversion of work into pleasure and the freeing of man's instinctual energies. Freud, himself, had singled out fantasy as one realm of the human mind that retained great freedom, if not autonomy, from the reality principle. Fantasy could still operate at a conscious level; it was a conscious part of mind that could not be repressed to meet the standards of civilization or culture. Fantasy, therefore, as Freud had suggested, was subject only to the pleasure principle.[5]

Freud, however, thought of fantasy as largely useless, even dangerous, because it could lead to regression and the unleashing of instinctual savagery. The exercise of fantasy meant the suspension of the reality principle on which civilization was based. Fantasy could be pleasant, but it was the opposite of reality, it had to be suspended, repressed or regulated in the name of social harmony or sublimated into erotic activity. The function of Reason, therefore, was to overcome pleasure; the two principles contradicted each other. In Freud's estimation it was this conflict that caused neuroses in individuals. But the necessity of what he called Reason meant that repression was inevitable and socially desirable. Civilization was based on the suppression of instincts and the renunciation of pleasure, and this was the sine qua non of its ability to survive.[6] Moreover, in Freud's estimation, the notion of a future Golden Age was an illusion, unlikely in any case because coercion and the repression of human instincts were necessary in all civilizations.[7]

Marcuse, on the contrary, thought fantasy had a liberating role to play. He was convinced that fantasy linked "the deepest layers of the unconscious with the highest products of consciousness (art), the dream with the reality; it [preserved] the archetypes of the genus, the perpetual but repressed ideas of the collective and individual memory, the tabooed images of freedom."[8] Fantasy was constructive, hopeful and liberating, utopian because it "retained its image of the future and the structure and the tendencies of the psyche before its organization by . . . reality, prior to its becoming an individual set off against other individuals."[9]

In fantasy Marcuse saw remembrance "of the subhistorical past when the life of the individual was under the rule of the pleasure principle."[10] It was fantasy that envisioned the "reconciliation of the individual with the whole, of desire with realization, of happiness with reason."[11] Whereas harmony had been postponed into Utopia by the reality principle, "fantasy insists that it must and can become real, that behind the illusion lies *knowledge*."[12] Fantasy was therefore subjective, a kind of wish and at the same time not mere wish fulfillment, it was also objective because it was conscious. Fantasy, in Marcuse, had a revolutionary and explosive core because it helped recover the pleasure principal. It was the direct link to Eros and the id, the recovery of the authentic and human prior to the demands of repressive civilization. Fantasy was the eternal protest against the organization of life, man's memory of a Golden Age projected into the future as recovered Utopia.[13]

Marcuse saw art also as fantasy in protest against the organization of life. "The artistic imagination [shaped] the 'unconscious memory' of the liberation that failed. . . ."[14] Art was fantasy in representation, the negation of unfreedom. Art represented the image of man as free, it recovered the dream not only of freedom before repression, but of a return to freedom, a rediscovery of Eden and the memory of the unrepressed id. Echoing Ernst Bloch, Marcuse added that the opposition of fantasy to the reality principle was "more at home in such sub-real and surreal processes as dreaming, daydreaming, play and the 'stream of consciousness'."[15]

Memory and Utopia

It was through fantasy that memory was revived and restored. Imagination overcame forgetting and was the link to the subconscious. Freud had tried to understand the process of memory and the reasons for forgetting. He was convinced that forgetting was useful, it was a mechanism that helped repress the recollection of what was most unbearable. On the other hand, remembrance, by exposing the resulting neurosis, could assist one toward recovery. This was the very heart of psychoanalysis, for it presupposed that memory traces were not destroyed, they were 'imperishable. Moreover, Freud expanded the definition of memory traces, he speculated that his contemporaries could very well retain memory traces of earlier generations.[16]

Marcuse drew from Freud's ideas several revolutionary implications. Memory, remembrance, could rediscover the experience of freedom before it was repressed and forgotten by the demands of society and the performance principle. Memory could recollect that happiness had once existed, and therefore that it was possible to recover. It was "the flux of time," Marcuse remarked, that "helps men to forget what was and what can be: it makes them oblivious to the better past and the better future."[17] But mankind didn't forget because of the need to repress what was painful. Marcuse believed it was taught to forget, forgetting was the essence of the performance principle. Mankind acquired the notion that pleasure was short and that death was always hovering over it, humanity learned to abandon hope. Forgetting, therefore, had a social function; it sustained submissiveness and renunciation. "To forget is also to forgive what should not be forgiven if justice and freedom are to prevail."[18] To forget past suffering was to forgive it. "The restoration of remembrance to its rights [was a] vehicle of liberation."[19] Memory, Marcuse added, had always been cultivated in terms of Reason and obligation; it was one of the forms of bondage repression. Mankind was taught to remember duties, not pleasures, taboos but not desires. Memory was linked with bad conscience, guilt and sin. "Unhappiness and the threat of punishment, not happiness and the promise of freedom,"[20] were embedded in memory by civilization.

On this point, Marcuse echoed Walter Benjamin. For Benjamin, memory provided the key to the emancipation of individuals and humanity tout court. Memory advanced through details, down to the smallest details, the tiniest of memory traces until what had been unconscious suddenly became conscious in the boldest relief. Thus, Benjamin had believed that it was possible to uncover both repression and to overcome the layers of time in which memory and meaning were interred, until perception became conscious. It was precisely this kind of reasoning that resonated in the pages of Marcuse's *Eros and Civilization.*[21]

Memory, then, had a truth-value; its recovery was far more valuable than simply healing an individual neurosis. The value of memory was its ability to preserve promises that were "betrayed and even outlawed by the mature, civilized individual, but which had once been fulfilled in his dim past, and which are never entirely forgotten."[22] The orientation toward the past was therefore a "vehicle of future liberation."[23] Without the liberation of the repressed content of the memory, real freedom was unimaginable. From the myth of Orpheus to the novels of Proust, Marcuse noted, "happiness and freedom have been linked with the idea of the recapture of time: the *temps retrouve. . . .* But in so far as time retains its power over Eros, happiness is essentially a thing of the past. . . . Time loses its power when remembrance redeems the past."[24]

Memory, then, had a revolutionary function. It not only linked the origins of the repressed individual with the origins of repressive civilization, but it also preserved the "repressed ideas of the collective and individual memory [and] the archetypes of the genus."[25] Expanding on Freud, Marcuse argued that there was an archaic identity between the individual and the species that emerged in memory traces of the experiences of former generations. It was precisely this archaic heritage, not entirely buried by repression, Marcuse insisted, that bridged the gap "between individual and mass psychology."[26]

Marcuse took Freud's speculations about prehistoric society and grafted them onto his own concept of the explosive power and utopian content of memory, admitting that Freud's notions were a-historical and speculative. But he insisted that Freud's explanations about the origins of history and civilization had symbolic significance, and they fitted into Marcuse's own notion of the "archetypes of the genus" as well. In Freud's hypothetical depiction, the primal father, enjoying a monopoly of sexual pleasure, was overthrown in an act of parricide by his sons. But the newly liberated order soon gave way to the renewal of repression as a response to the emergence of guilt and also as a means to establish order to prevent future parricides. This beginning of civilization, Marcuse reasoned, "thus sustains the principal prohibitions, constraints and delays in gratification on which civilization depends."[27] But here Marcuse departed from Freud. For the new clan that promised liberty by removing the father and the taboos he had imposed, had now reintroduced a new repression, new taboos and the very denial of the liberty it had established in its own rebellion, all this on the basis of a monstrous crime.[28] The remembrance of gratification, of freedom, which was now instilled in collective consciousness, Marcuse concluded, persisted and reappeared throughout history as an indictment of repression.[29]

Freud's notion of the Oedipus Complex presented the same idea at the individual level. Oedipus symbolized an archetype, an archaic heritage, awakened by events parallel to ancient parricides. Marcuse followed a similar course, insisting that there were traces of the past in the individual subconscious mind, traces awakened by "concrete and tangible factors . . . every generation."[30] The individual had a memory inheritance in which the conflict between domination and gratification was made manifest by the memory of infantile gratification, a memory that could still tap into the psyche prior to its being structured by the performance principle.[31]

Marcuse also believed that religion had a role to play as a fantasy that persistently encountered Utopia. Christianity was a fantasy linked to a memory heritage of gratification prior to repression. Christianity fitted in well with Freud's archetype of the struggle between the father and the son; it was the ultimate challenge to the authority and patriarchy of the father. In Marcuse's estimation: "The life and death of Christ . . . appear as a struggle against the father – and as a triumph over the father. The message of the Son was the message of liberation: the overthrow of the Law (which is domination) by Agape (which is Eros)."[32] Jesus was therefore the heretical redeemer, the Messiah who came to liberate mankind. His subsequent transubstantiation, however, followed by deification, meant denial of the liberation of the flesh, a surrendering of the Gospel to the Law, "the father-rule restored and strengthened."[33]

Marcuse's point was that institutionalized Christianity, in the name of the Law and the Father, had a history of fighting heretical movements that wanted to reconstitute the principle of liberation. Organized Christianity had been used to apply the standards of repression throughout history. Yet as a principle it still retained what he called the so-called illusions of a paradise, and hence preserved the memory traces of freedom and Eros.[34]

Instinct, Fantasy and Rebellion

In *Eros and Civilization*, Marcuse believed that the truths kept alive in the imagination were not merely escapist affirmations but corresponded to a conceivable reality. Psychoanalytic theory granted him a scientific basis for believing that imagination and dream corresponded also to an experienced reality. In fantasy and imagination Marcuse thought he had discovered a window to the unconscious and to the archaic memory of the whole individual prior to the repressive layers of civilization. The instinctual self, through fantasy and dream and by entering into the unconscious, thus provided a glimpse into primal memory, and the specific memory of a satisfaction that culture could not grant.[35]

On the relation between instinct, freedom and memory, Marcuse made what might have been his most important contribution to social theory. He criticized Freud because he felt the latter had taken account of the need for repression but had ignored or denied the life of subjectivity, the independence of intuition and the instinctual life that could escape repression at particular historical moments. Thus, Freud had concentrated on history at the expense of nature (and a different moment of history as well), on intellect but not intuition and instinct. And it was precisely in this realm that Marcuse found the potential of human liberation. The instincts remained the incorruptible governors of the laws of gratification, and it was gratification, the demand for the realization of pleasure, precisely at the moment of history then reached, that Marcuse believed would break through the suppression that had once been demanded and then sustained by civilization.[36]

Marcuse's argument followed several strands. On the one hand he maintained that the instinctual world remained intact, mental processes such as reversal, reversion, sublimation, explicit repression were purely psychological categories, alterations in what was essentially an immutable, self-contained instinctual structure. But, while the instinctual structure remained intact, it was also necessary to expand it to include the socio-historical world into which the self was born.[37] Marcuse insisted that the "reality which shapes the instincts as well as their need and satisfaction is a socio-historical world."[38]

Thus, Marcuse was laying a foundation for explaining not only why the instincts had not led to liberated individuals and an unrepressed civilization, but also why they could, under emerging social and historical conditions, be the foundation of a radically transformed society. Where before instincts could be repressed by repressing need, the new society actually developed and promoted new needs that it could not satisfy at precisely the moment when there was no need for their repression.[39]

Marcuse thought he had found, deep in the unconscious, the instinct of rebellion, an instinct moreover which could lead to a liberation once known within the libido itself. Memory was the link to gratification during past stages of development. As such the past reclaimed the future. It generated the wish that paradise be recreated. And at the same time history generated new realities that made such a wish possible to fulfill.[40] Marcuse projected a psychological reformulation of the anticipatory memory that he had formulated as early as 1937. Memory projected into the future images of liberation drawn from the past; what was to be remembered and recollected were the archaic beginnings of the individual when Eros was still unchallenged and reigned supreme.[41]

It was Marcuse's grafting of Marxian and Freudian concepts and his own instinctual rebellion, that led him to call for resistance to society's expectations in every venue from the factory assembly line to the marriage bed to military service to raising the flag.[42] His notion of the performance principle enabled him to extend Marx's concept of alienation from the political economy of industrial society into the biological realm of the libido. Civilization, by imposing the performance principle, had created genital supremacy, detaching man's sexual being from his total human fulfillment by concentrating the libido in one part of the body. The performance principle trapped man in his own pleasure and limited his freedom, Eros, to the merely sexual or procreative. By limiting Eros to genital pleasure, the rest of the body was freed for use as an instrument of labor.[43] In this way happiness became private, fulfilled only in one's sexual life; Eros was no longer public, no longer extended into the world. The only way toward genuine freedom, Marcuse argued, was through a resexualization of the entire body. Only in this way could the tyranny of the merely genital or procreative be broken. Thus Marcuse not only extended Freud beyond what Freud had ever anticipated, he also transcended Marx in dealing only with instincts and their repression. At the same time it was impossible to place Marcuse's work in the context of psychoanalysis since he had not attempted to define the limits of the unconscious.[44]

In *Eros and Civilization,* Marcuse managed to discover revolutionary implications in Freud's pessimistic diagnoses about the predominance of sexuality, the centrality of the events of early childhood in determining the behavior of adult life, and the death instinct. Marcuse had come to believe, in the relatively quiescent 1950's, presciently as it turned out, that human fulfillment was possible and that mankind was not inherently destructive. Marcuse was convinced the way toward human fulfillment was through the erotocizing of the body, a condition that not only insisted on the realization of the pleasure principle, but which achieved its climax quite literally in the reclaiming of human happiness as the real goal of newly liberated mankind. It was the taming of humanity, its repression and therefore the repression of Eros that had diverted mankind from the noble pursuit of human happiness. It was civilization claiming that mankind had to be tamed that had caused neuroses and unfreedom. It was the thwarting of instinct that had caused immeasurable misery and cosmic injustice. It was the curbing of human freedom that had produced the twentieth-century, a totally advanced civilization in both productive power and destructiveness, as well as the ultimate repression of the human body and its pleasures.[45]

With these formulations, Marcuse looked forward toward an end of the pain and strife of history that had resulted from man's inability to overcome scarcity and pessimism. This was the Marcuse who became the darling of the 1960's, the philosopher who preached an end to human suffering and needless want. This was the prophet of *Eros and Civilization*, the man who anticipated the unleashing of the libido as Eros, the victory of optimism, the unfettering of the instinct of freedom, and the eroticizing of reality by turning life into pleasure. Thus Marcuse meant to unleash the libido as the first step in breaking the binds of repression, the first step toward eroticizing society and culture, the first step toward the beginning of non-repression in daily life.

One Dimensional Society

What transpired by the early Sixties was disappointing to Marcuse. He saw around him only the celebration of sexual permissiveness. He became known as the philosopher of the orgasm. He saw himself surrounded, not by the quest for liberation, but by the glorification of hedonism. In the raw pursuit of pleasure by the young generation, he saw a new road that would lead straight back to totalitarianism, a result of the conscious separation of the instinctual from the intellectual, the separation of pleasure from thought. He saw a modern form of alienation in which the individual was becoming enslaved by his own passions and the seemingly spontaneous creation of new needs. In the meantime the pursuit of unfettered pleasure meant the acceptance of repression in other spheres. This was especially true of the sphere of work inasmuch as mankind could now turn inward and revel in its own but very private pleasure, much like an addict who is content to transform the world that exists in his own head.[46] The 1962 Preface to *Eros and Civilization* amplified these themes, but Marcuse was even bleaker in *One Dimensional Man,* which appeared in 1964.

When Marcuse published *One Dimensional Man,* he was completing a circle that went from Marx to Freud and back to Marx. For the first time the revolutionary implications of Marcuse's thought were made explicit. Shorn of the clouded Hegelian vernacular, he targeted modern America. There was a profound pessimism in *One Dimensional Man.* Marcuse saw only mass conformity, stupefaction induced by private pleasures and a welfare system that softened the edges of remaining pockets of poverty and deprivation. In effect, Marcuse thought America was a becoming a one-dimensional society. He saw in the United States, the most advanced industrial society in the world, an industrial civilization that had reached a comfortable and "reasonable unfreedom," a society in which technology was triumphant [nuclear weapons] over critical thought.[47] In the Preface he deplored "the union of growing productivity and growing destruction; the brinkmanship of annihilation; the surrender of thought, hope and fear to the decisions of the powers that be [a reference to the possibility of nuclear annihilation and the suspension of criticism]; the preservation of misery in the face of unprecedented wealth . . ."[48] He depicted a one-dimensional society in which the Welfare and Warfare states existed in perfect harmony, in which the universal "flattening out" of values meant that citizens failed to notice the absence of any real choices.[49] In modern America Marcuse rued "the flattening out of the antagonism between culture and social reality" that resulted from the "obliteration of the oppositional, alien, and transcendent elements" of culture.[50] Everywhere thought and language had come to merely reflect the realities they described, they no longer aspired to transcend or transform.

Watching the war in Vietnam, which was just beginning to gather momentum, but which had gathered little opposition, Marcuse saw yet another instance of the flattening of choices and values. Moreover, Marcuse's earlier advice to eroticize life by turning work into pleasure, his utopianized urgings to transform society into Eros, seemed to be lost amidst a sea of private pleasures and harmless meditations. Zen, existentialism, the beat way of life, psychedelic drugs and unlimited erotic pleasure, were all becoming means of private accommodation that were indifferent to political or economic choices and were hardly a road toward Eros and the eroticizing of society.[51] Moreover, mindless pleasures not only weren't conducive to the creation of just societies, they were compatible with passivity, mass conformity and manipulation. A counter culture that rebelled by turning to drugs and hallucination was anything but liberating. Ironically, the society of abundance was quite seductive, but not necessarily because of some hidden persuaders. Even the working class had become bloated and affluent when Marcuse was writing in the 1960's. Marcuse could hardly think of it as having a radical mission or as an agency of socialism. Agency, it seemed, would only come about from outsiders and outcasts. But about this Marcuse remained skeptical. In the meantime the revolution of rising expectations for the good life, synonymous in the 1960's with white flight from the cities, concealed the Hobbesian world that was emerging. In this world, Marcuse observed, the weakest were driven even further into poverty while the newly affluent surrounded themselves in suburban ghettoes with the consumer goods that were their reward for accepting the status quo.[52]

Drawing on the work of contemporaries such as David Riesman's *Lonely Crowd* and William Whyte's *The Organization Man*, Marcuse drew a picture of American society drowned in passivity and conformity. Reflecting C. W. Mills' *Power Elite*, Marcuse believed that the leaders in industry, politics and the military had effectively neutralized the instinctual rebellion that he had earlier heralded in *Eros and Society*. The younger generation whose rebellion he had anticipated and urged, were instead being drawn toward mass conformity and were increasingly addicted to the private pleasures that the new elite could provide. The trade-off was therefore complete, even counter cultural ideas and expressions could be absorbed in a society that promoted self-indulgence and needless consumption in a sea of often useless and rapidly obsolescent gadgetry. The result was that increasing income was ceaselessly chasing new kinds of goods and services, while new gaps of income and wealth were constantly being created in the midst of plenty.[53] Marcuse's gloomy conclusion was that contemporary society was likely to remain one-dimensional:

> Social controls exact the overwhelming need for the production and consumption of waste; the need for stupefying work where it is no longer a real necessity; the need for modes of relaxation which soothe and prolong this stupefaction . . . a free press which censors itself, free choice between brands and gadgets.[54]

Thus, protest could be accommodated, integrated and made harmless by the dominant system over which the power elite presided. The mass consumer industry and mass media could either sate or convince and usually do both. Industrial society was becoming technological society and this, with its powers to integrate and sate through consumption or to persuade through advertisements using hidden persuaders or overt campaigns, had great potential for mind control. Marcuse went as far as to call such a tendency totalitarian, though he emphasized the aspect of psychological control rather than overt political repression:

> In the medium of technology, culture, politics and the economy emerge into an omnipresent system which swallows up or repulses all alternatives. The productivity and growth potential of this system stabilize the society and contain technical progress within the framework of domination. Technological rationality has become political rationality. . . . Technological rationality reveals its political character as it becomes the great vehicle of better domination, creating a truly totalitarian universe in which society and nature, mind and body are kept in a state of permanent mobilization for the defense of this universe.[55]

As a result of this line of thought, Marcuse completely lost faith in the working class as a vehicle of future freedom. It had ceased to be the class that Marx had anticipated and had been seduced by affluence and the influence of mass media. Instead of becoming a core of future socialism, the working class was now a cohesive element of society; its membership included the patriots and defenders of the nation and of the status quo. But if blue collar workers had disappointed him, Marcuse took sustenance from the populations that were permanently alienated, the exploited and the persecuted of color, the unemployed and the marginalized, the permanently powerless and skeptical. These were the groups that he looked toward at the end of *One Dimensional Man*:

> The substratum of the outcasts and outsiders, the exploited and persecuted of other races and colors, the unemployed and the unemployable. They exist outside the democratic process; their life is the most immediate and the real need for ending intolerable conditions and institutions. Thus their opposition is revolutionary even if their consciousness is not. . . . The critical theory of society possesses no concepts which could bridge the gap between the present and its future; holding no promise and showing no success, it remains negative. Thus it wants to remain loyal to those who, without hope, have given and give their life to the Great Refusal. It is only for the sake of those without hope that hope is given to us. (last sentence from Walter Benjamin).[56]

Toward Utopia

Despite Marcuse's disappointment and gloomy forecast, historical events in the Sixties soon energized the author of *Eros and Society* and *One Dimensional Man*. The heating up of the war in Vietnam produced an anti-war movement at precisely the same time that the Civil Rights movement was exercising blacks and liberal whites and the Berkeley Free Speech movement was politicizing university youth across much of the country. For the first time suburban whites, often enthused with radical ideologies like Marxism and Anarchism, were sitting in the same classroom with militant blacks who were trying to break out of urban ghettoes. The mixture was explosive. In addition, the affluent young were in full rebellion against the work ethic, puritanical attitudes toward sex and marriage and even the life styles and dress of their parents. The generation that came of age in the Sixties almost instinctively aimed at an easy transition into post-bourgeois society, a society which escaped the futility of useless and alienated work and rejected neo-imperialism and foreign adventures abroad.[57]

By the mid-Sixties, Marcuse was aware that his ideas were beginning to resonate with many members of the young generation. It was becoming clear that a portion of that generation had not incorporated the values and language of conventional politics and the propaganda machine, but were generating a language of their own that was in fact both critical and transcendent. Some youths at least were beginning to ask the questions that somehow escaped the net of one-dimensionality that Marcuse had feared and railed against just several years earlier.[58] Suddenly he began to sense the instinctual rebellion that he had theorized in *Eros and Civilization*, even though he also saw a young generation still passively absorbed in its own private pleasures.

As a result, Marcuse was swept along by the enthusiasm of the anti-Vietnam war movement and student radicalism. He was intimately involved with student resistance to the draft and was something of a guru to the New Left and the student movement at Berkeley. For their part, students were themselves coming under the influence of the ideas of *Eros and Civilization* and understood instinctively the notion of repression that Marcuse had been at pains to articulate. The synergy of enthusiasm expanded horizons. Students, inspired by *Eros and Civilization*, made connections between erotic and libidinal repression and powerlessness in politics. The message was both personal and political; take back your own lives by ending the repression of both, engage in eroticism and in extending personal pleasure, oppose the tyranny of the draft and the state. Personal liberation was the first step toward political empowerment, authentic feeling a necessary precondition for political transformation. Personal problems were not divorced from political questions; to demand personal freedom was to oppose the war in Vietnam and to define a commitment to history; to believe in universal freedom was to oppose the war and the draft that made the war possible.[59]

In fact, Marcuse and the student movement inspired each other. In 1967, in a lecture on "The End of Utopia," given at the Free University of Berlin, which was also a center of student radicalism, Marcuse's discussion actually meant the opposite of what his title suggested. Utopia had finished, but not because it was impractical or muddle headed or simply wrong. Utopia, far from being impossible, was now realizable; it had become something practical and no longer utopian and beyond historical possibility. "All the material and intellectual forces which could be put to work for the realization of a free society are at hand,"[60] he told his audience. Marcuse was becoming optimistic that the socio-historical barriers to achieving liberation were disappearing. He consciously rejected positivism and scientism, including Marxism, and stressed the "possibility that the path to socialism may proceed from science to utopia and not from utopia to science."[61] Despite the gathering momentum of the war in Vietnam, Marcuse saw a number of tendencies in history suggesting that the end of history and the coming of Utopia were at hand. Among the examples that he cited were the English pop movement, intellectuals and students as anti-capitalist (statist) forces; various liberation struggles in the Third World that were fighting in the spirit of Che Guevara and Franz Fanon; the moral-sexual rebellion which acted as a disintegrative force; the beatnik and hippie movements which expressed a qualitative movement toward socialist society and which also expressed the Great Refusal by definition. Marcuse looked back toward Fourier and the utopian communal socialism he had espoused. His verdict was that the path toward socialism could proceed from science to Utopia, from Marx to Fourier, from the laws of history to human desire and need.[62]

In the same year, 1967, Marcuse attended the Dialectics of Liberation conference at the Roundhouse in London where, holding a daffodil, he greeted the hippie youth in attendance. In Marcuse's address he stressed the role that the hippies were playing in the movement toward human liberation. Hippies, he told the audience, represented "the appearance of new instinctual needs and values [and embodied] a synthesis of sexual, moral and political rebellion" [that was a veritable] transvaluation of values."[63]

Marcuse picked up on the temperament of the moment. Indeed, the conference itself, with its blend of intellectuals and student activists, including Stokely Carmichael, Paul Goodman and R. D. Laing, seemed to be part of a movement that was just about to reach its climax in a literal explosion in the years 1967-1968. Widespread student revolts were occurring on a number of campuses at Western universities, the Black Power movement was becoming powerful enough to shake the authorities of the U. S., the renewal of feminism was challenging the defenders of traditional patriarchy, the New Left was regrouping around the *May Day Manifesto* of 1968, and even the communist world was being shaken by movements such as the Prague Spring of 1968.[64]

Marcuse, shoved prominently into the middle of the visceral revolution that seemed to be encircling the globe, was in the meantime extending the theoretical scaffolding he had begun in *Eros and Civilization*, emboldened by the instinctual heralding of Utopia toward which he hoped and believed history was heading. Just prior to the May events in Paris, he wrote his most utopian work to date, *An Essay on Liberation*, which had yet to appear when the student rebellion erupted in Paris in May 1968.

Marcuse's essay was infused with optimism and was inspired with more hope than in any previous period. He looked toward the young, the intelligentsia, leaders of the black ghettos, the underprivileged, peasants in the Third World and the industrial proletariat, all marginalized populations, as the hope of the future. This was precisely because their hopes and objectives could never be met or constrained by the societies in which they lived. Indeed, the Cuban revolution and the struggle in Vietnam demonstrated what could happen at the margins where the superpowers could not constrain the demands for justice and change.[65]

It was in this historical context that Marcuse insisted Utopia should no longer be seen as simply unreal or "no place."[66] Rather it had to be seen as "that which [was] blocked from coming about by the power of the established societies."[67] Here, Marcuse, the utopian optimist, invoked the biology of instinctual needs. In the Black Power, Student Free Speech, Anti-War, Civil Rights and Feminist movements he saw real qualitative change instinctually erupting in the needs of mankind, in human nature expressing and craving needs and satisfactions which were "even antagonistic to those prevalent in the exploitative societies. Such a change would constitute the instinctual basis for freedom that the long history of class society [had] blocked. Freedom is no longer adapting to competitive performances, not tolerating aggression and brutishness."[68] In this way, he believed, rebellion and the road to freedom took root in the very nature and biology of the person, although the trigger of rebellion was the historical event. Moreover, technical progress had reached a stage in which reality no longer needed to be defined by the debilitating competition for social survival and advancement.[69]

Marcuse now felt it possible to demonstrate that biology could be a force in human liberation, that human nature could define itself freely without sublimation, that the reclaiming of Eros could be a force in human emancipation and not simply a factor in sexual satisfaction. Real liberation was possible because instinctual needs, pleasures and the libido had come into conflict with the established norms and values of America. Thus, the war in Vietnam constituted a value system that was in direct contradiction with biology and the desire for self-preservation. It also posed a conflict in the moral sphere because religion and the proscription against killing and taking human life could not be reconciled with the organized brutality of war. Instinctual rebellion, by rousing fantasies envisioning political and social alternatives, by imagining societies in which happiness was based on the pleasure principle, posed a conflict ultimately between conscience and a duty prescribed by the state, between inner morality and state-defined patriotism. For Marcuse, the emergence of liberation movements in Vietnam and Cuba, and the assertion of alternative politics in America, posed a conflict also between libidinal satisfaction through the commodity, in which corporate capitalism created artificial needs, and true satisfaction expressed in needs that were self-determined.[70]

Art and the Aesthetics of Utopia

This was not the endpoint for Marcuse's argument. For to apply the pleasure principle to society meant to invoke a social aesthetics as well. For human beings to be happy they had to surround themselves with the beautiful. Marcuse believed that the biology of instinctual needs required a beautiful society. Such a society demanded the elimination of violence, a morality squared with culture, a blending of aesthetics and logic and of beauty and reason. The desired society was one in which the beautiful pertained to Eros and not Thanatos. "Beauty has the power to check aggression,"[71] noted Marcuse, the beautiful was kin to liberation. For it insisted on "the harmonious union of sensuousness, imagination and reason in the beautiful, as the Form in which and nature come into their own: fulfillment."[72] By applying aesthetics to politics, by affirming Eros in personal freedom, mankind could not only signal the end of violence, it could herald the coming of Utopia.

Thus, Marcuse was convinced that human freedom was a question of biology, a matter of unleashing the libidinal energy demanded by mankind's instinctual urges precisely when history made this possible. Previously, class society had shaped the imagination, but the diminishing of necessity had unleashed the instinctual energy that demanded a new social aesthetics. Aesthetics required that class society give way to a new order based on the beautiful in imagination.[73]

There was now no question that Marcuse understood the rebellions of the Sixties as forms of protest that could radically shake and even revolutionize society. He saw in the young intelligentsia, "the right and the truth of the imagination [becoming] the demands of political action. . . ."[74] He envisioned "surrealistic forms of protest and refusal"[75] becoming political. He saw a political protest that reached into aesthetics, invoking the sensuous power of the imagination. He saw a new consciousness and not just a new material reality. He was confident the time had come for thought to determine being. He criticized Marxists for refraining from imagining the future and for refusing to generate a language that anticipated it. He embraced the search for another language and a new way not only of imagining the world, but a new kind of discourse that imagined it. He believed a new semantic universe had already arrived in the language of the hippies and the French radicals in Paris. The hippies created a subculture and a language that fundamentally saw the world in a way determined by them, and consciously rejected the language of Newspeak and military speak, so common during the Cold War and the war in Vietnam. Peace, trip, and pot were symbolic of a counter order. As a semantic revolution they dissolved the images of governing institutions and recreated in their own images the makings of a powerfully transformed order. The language and the art (wall paintings and graffiti, later rap music) of black militants was another case in point. Creating images and language was a means of negating and sublimating the older semantic language that was as fixed as the order that produced it. The new language was a language of negation. Black music like jazz was a language of subversion. Everywhere Marcuse saw a counter-culture emerging out of the instinctual needs of the younger generation, out of the urgings of women long suffering from patriarchy, out of the hopes of marginalized blacks still excluded by explicit and implicit segregation.[76]

In May 1968, all the counter-cultural and opposition movements of the 1960's remarked by Marcuse crystallized in France. These events, embodied in the ideas and speeches of Daniel Cohn-Bendit, a kind of neo-anarchist who represented in himself the disintegrative tendencies noted so often by Marcuse, pointed toward the kind of utopianism that Marcuse had long anticipated. France, so often the home of revolution in the nineteenth-century, made yet another revolution, only a revolution of a different sort. Instead of attempting to seize the state, the French movement simply bypassed it. Parisian students, workers, farmers, artists and professionals seized control of their workplaces and schools and democratized them, and for a time paralyzed the authorities. Even de Gaulle was befuddled and failed to act quickly. Students ruled over Paris, self-management was engaged everywhere.[77]

Paris in 1968 mixed the ideas of utopianism and radicalism from all directions, but it surely embodied the utopianism that was so much a part of Marcuse's message. One could find the ideas of Freud, Charles Reich, surrealists Louis Aragon and Andre Breton, Salvador Dali, Mikhail Bakunin and Charles Fourier in the mix, all of them singled out for their profound understanding of revolutionary change, and all of them opposed to or unconvinced by scientific socialism. Only the utopian Marx of the Paris Commune and the Lenin of the early Soviets were resurrected. Liberation was now seen as personal and political. The old model of pure and simple political revolution, such as had occurred in 1789 and 1917, was seen as obsolete. Revolution had to be absolute and pervasive, daily life had to be transformed before there could be political transformation. The work and ideas of the International Situationists could be seen everywhere, their pamphlets, books, journals and graffiti proclaimed all power to the imagination and the dream that was real. Consciousness now came before being, the idea before reality. Revolutionary transformation was in the air, simply seize control over the conditions of life, self-management, auto-gestion was in the moment, the past no longer determined the present.[78]

The Art of Liberation

The events of May 1968 in Paris suggested to Marcuse that his hopes and theories were vindicated not only in the imagination, but also by contemporary historical events. The May events of Paris and their reverberations throughout the Western world sustained Marcuse and his faith in the explosive possibilities of liberation. He was active in the auditoriums from the outset of the revolutionary events. There was even a day called *journee marcusienne* at occupied Nanterre, during which he counseled the avoidance of violence. He also stressed that the idea of centralized mass-based revolution was obsolete. But in the context of the revolutionary morality that was emerging on the streets of Paris and in the halls of the university, he also advised that it was time to realize what before had only been utopian dreaming. The time for liberation was at hand. The concrete and the ideal were merging. Liberation, formerly sheltered in the ideals of philosophy and in forms of art, had entered history as concrete reality. Ernst Bloch welcomed Marcuse's speech in Korcula by proclaiming that Marcuse had truly arrived on time. In sum, Marcuse argued that the May movement had broken with the authoritarian structures of established society, but it had also broken with the authoritarianism of the established opposition, the Old Left and the Communist Party.[79]

Marcuse had always been attacked from the right because it resented his influence with youth. But from the summer of 1968 he was also attacked by the Old Left, Yuri Zhukov in *Pravda* in May, the Italian Communist Giorgio Amendola in June, American Gus Hall in July.[80]

Marcuse, however, celebrated the insurgents' newly found faith in the reason of the imagination. He thought it symbolized the rupture with the repressive continuum of needs that had been the chief obstacle to radical change in the age of one-dimensional affluence. In responding to the new dimensions of liberation, as he understood it, Marcuse used a narrative prose that heralded back to the early nineteenth-century language of romantic Germany, the heyday of Hegel and Schiller. But he also used the heretical language of medieval politics that had its own messianic tendencies toward transcendence. He referred to the striking students of Toulouse, then demanding the revival of the language of the troubadours, the Albigensians, a medieval heretical group known for its radical messianism and utopianizing of Jesus. Moreover, the graffiti of angry youth, Marcuse insisted, conjoined Karl Marx and Andre Breton. Hence, the symbolism of post-May events began to merge with the sensibilities of utopian symmetry and the language of liberation, though Marcuse still appreciated the lingering limits of the New Left's politics of private liberation and personal angst. Yet here was a promise, a rupture had surfaced in the cracks of established society; a potential alliance was emerging between the working class, the radical intelligentsia and radicalized students. A new aesthetic sensibility was merging into a new political possibility.[81]

What was the new sensibility and why was it politically important? For Marcuse, aesthetics carried a double connotation that referred to the foundations of art and the domain of the senses. The gratification of aesthetic needs would not be a private affair like a visitation to the art museum for the purpose of consuming art, or even attending the theater. The domain of art implied an aesthetically ordered social world, a society in which the imagination could shape both the mental and material worlds by measuring one against the other. The aesthetic became political precisely because it still created in the imagination the ideal order that could be translated into the real order of politics. It was in this sense that aesthetics, based on the ideal and yet suggesting a link to political reality, escaped the problem of modern society in which two dimensions were reduced to one-dimensionality. Art had the potential to be revolutionary precisely because it could find liberating possibilities in the universals that it discovered in the ideals of philosophy. Hence Marcuse went back to Plato and Schiller to discover the forms and norms that transcended the one-dimensional reality of the world.[82]

In the wake of the events of 1968 in Paris, Marcuse added a preface to his book on the art of liberation that showed a growing sense of optimism. On the one hand, he noted the global domination of multinational corporations and the Western states that sustained them, their economic and military hold in the four continents, their neocolonial empires, and, most important, their "unshaken capacity to subject the majority of the underlying population to their overwhelming productivity and force."[83] On the other hand, he was encouraged by the opposition to corporate domination. He saw a possible road to socialism in the "emergence of different goals and values, different aspirations in the men and women who resist and deny the massive exploitative power of corporate capitalism, even in its most comfortable and liberal realizations."[84] The Great Refusal took a variety of forms

Marcuse also took solace from the revolutions in Vietnam, Cuba and China, where he thought the struggle was also against the bureaucratic administration of socialism. "The guerilla forces in Latin America seem to be animated by that same subversive impulse: liberation."[85] Simultaneously, the United States showed strains and could not indefinitely deliver guns and butter, "napalm and color TV."[86] In France, the student movement had demonstrated not only an alternative society, but had captured for a short period "the libertarian power of the red and black flags."[87] Thus, contemporary events showed the limits of power and the possibilities of liberated societies which could break through the constraints of the past. Moreover, Marcuse noted the similarity between the ideas of the Parisian militants and his own ideas. The coincidence was striking:

The radical utopian character of their demands far surpasses the hypotheses of my essay; and, yet these demands were formulated in the course of action itself; they are expressions of concrete political practice. The militants have invalidated the concept of "utopia" – they have denounced a vicious ideology. No matter whether their action was a revolt or an abortive revolution, it is a turning point. In proclaiming the 'permanent challenge', the 'permanent education', the Great Refusal, they recognize the mark of social repression, even in the most sublime manifestations of traditional culture, even in the most spectacular manifestations of technical progress. They have again raised a specter of a revolution that subordinates technology and industry to higher standards of living and the solidarity of the human species, the abolition of poverty.[88]

The weaknesses of Marcuse's book, *An Essay on Liberation*, were evident. Among them was his theory of agency. Marginalized populations like blacks, hippies, students, women and Third Worlders often were not revolutionary, nor were they necessarily utopian. In any case, they were not inherently radical nor were they united as a group or class in opposition to capitalism, as Marcuse had hoped. Moreover, Marcuse's entire system rested on the assumption that the student generation of the Sixties was instinctually in rebellion against the empty materialism and exploitative values of capitalism. But instinctual rebellion against capitalism, if it could be called instinctual, hardly survived the 1960's. By the 1970's, the United States, to borrow from Marcuse's own terminology, was returning to the kind of one-dimensionality that Marcuse thought had been transcended by a generation of young students viscerally opposed to the war in Vietnam and in favor of the Civil Rights movement. The instinctual rebellion that Freud thought had to be repressed, and that Marcuse said must be unleashed, did not appear to be an integral part of human nature after all, and certainly not with respect to the rejection of capitalism.

Further, Marcuse consciously based some of his most important concepts on Freud's speculations, and time has not been kind to Freud. Freud's work no longer commands the heights of psychology, as it did when Marcuse was writing. Many of Freud's ideas are taken as a kind of psychic poetry, anything but the science that purported to revolutionize the understanding of the human mind. Moreover, Marcuse himself radicalized Freud in a way that Freud's thought simply would not be able to support. Freud was a social conservative. His fundamental belief in the necessity of social repression was simply incompatible with Marcuse's desire for the unleashing of Eros and the conversion of life into pleasure. Marcuse believed that alienated work was the result of capitalism. Freud thought alienation part of the human condition. Freud, unlike Marcuse, thought alienated labor the price we had to pay if civilization were to survive

In addition, Marcuse saw the Cultural Revolution in China as a foundation for the future liberation of the individual precisely at the point when Chinese utopianism was expiring in massive repression. He misread the same Cultural Revolution, seeing it as evidence of a worldwide movement toward liberation. He also understood Cuba as a revolution of hope, when even many on the left were not quite so sure.

On the other hand there were many strengths in Marcuse's thought. He saw the contradictions of America and the West, including neo-imperialism, the American war in Vietnam, American support for dictators worldwide, the vast disparities of wealth and power in America and globally. Marcuse also understood the eternal paradox inherent in the clash between the pursuit of pleasure and the need to build a stable civilization and civil society. Practically alone, even on the left, he tried to retain an element of play in life that he thought had been needlessly, indeed erroneously abandoned, while still sustaining a life of culture and the mind.[89]

It was this turn of mind that had brought Marcuse to the study of Freud, but all the concepts he discussed in his work on Freud were already present in his earlier Left Hegelian period. The linkage between fantasy, memory and Utopia, the notion of an almost primeval innocence of humankind before it was corrupted by social repression and civilization, the belief that contemporary industrial society had robbed culture of its humanity, were all part of Marcuse's thought from the beginning. Marcuse remained the philosopher of happiness, romantically insisting that humanity had a right to fulfillment, and that happiness, as an ideal norm, must always be the measure against which to judge modern industrial civilization. It is especially in this last sense that Marcuse's work endures.

Chapter 7
Andre Gorz: From Red to Green Utopia

In 1975, a decade and a half before the tumbling of the Berlin Wall, Andre Gorz, in *Ecology as Politics*, predicted the ideological bankruptcy of East and West, of 'really existing socialism' and Western liberal polity, of reflexive 'productivism' in both of its versions, orthodox Marxist-Leninist and Western liberal economics. From an avowedly utopian stance based on a model of 'rational' ecology, Gorz concluded that both East and West had produced systems that were neither economically sustainable, nor socially egalitarian, nor politically manageable, despite the abundance that had been created by the modern technological revolution. In Gorz's estimation, the logic of unlimited development, of inherent 'productivism', whether motivated by the planners of state socialism in the East or the promoters of private enterprise in the West, had led inevitably to environmental degradation, nullifying much of the economic progress that had resulted from technological advance.[1]

Ironically, Western capitalist democracies recognized, by the 1970's, that there could not be endless expansion without greater care for the environment, and that this entailed additional costs for environmental protection. But, as Gorz pointed out, these costs could be passed on to the consumer who would unwittingly end up subsidizing the degradation of the environment. This made it possible to soften, if not to ignore, ecological restraints, while the increased costs of protecting the environment, unmatched by any corresponding rise in productivity, were already producing economic stagnation that appeared to be permanent and structural. In the capitalist West, then, it was becoming increasingly possible to integrate ecological costs – even if it was at the expense of overall economic efficiency – while subverting or obscuring alternative social and ecological practices.

Ecology, then, could be used to inform alternative social practices and to subvert the ideology of illimitable growth, but it could as readily be used to reaffirm growth-oriented capitalism – or socialism – without restraint. Ecology could be either liberatory or repressive. Gorz found little comfort in Marxist-Leninist political economy on this point, because it was a mirror image of the Western faith in unrestrained economic development, though it remained a powerful analytical critique of Western market-driven capitalism. Gorz's democratic socialist solution, based on 'rational' ecological practice, might seem a bit antiquated to the post-Cold War generation, but to Gorz such a linkage was visionary, practical and necessary if environmental degradation and the production and consumption of socially unnecessary products were to be avoided in the future.[2]

Ecology as Politics

In *Ecology as Politics*, Gorz traveled the road from Red to Green Utopia. He denigrated the centralist, authoritarian utopias of the East as the perverse direct descendants of scientific socialism and Marxism-Leninism. He wondered how to preserve the libertarian-pluralist impulses of the liberal capitalist West, while criticizing its standard of profit above social utility and rational ecology. His proposed Utopia, sketched out in *Ecology as Politics*, demonstrated a healthy skepticism toward the so-called utopias of both East and West. The Eastern model, scientific socialism, or 'really existing socialism', by compelling 'expected' and 'required' behavior in Utopia, sacrificed human freedom and the reality of political liberty. The West, with its expectation that government should abdicate its power to protect and rationalize resources by resorting to the market to resolve all social and economic problems, canonized liberty at the expense of equality and community. The cardinal sin of the West, Gorz argued, was to confuse democracy with the free market and economic liberalism, although the market economy had often produced enormous gaps of income and wealth in the West that had persistently subverted democracy. As a result, Gorz questioned whether the free market and economic liberalism were even compatible with Western democracy.

But if central planning in an authoritarian society, and free market liberalism in an open society, produced social domination and privilege in both, how was it possible to produce a 'rational ecology' based on human need rather than the endless production of useless gadgets and planned obsolescence?

Gorz's answer was simple and complex. A 'rational ecology' implied alternative social practices based on voluntary association and human fulfillment rather than social domination. The demand and the need for Utopia followed from this premise. Social and political elites in the liberal democratic West had too often sacrificed political choice, convincing their publics to accept their decisions as 'technical necessity', while in the East political choice was buried in the many layers of bureaucratic deformities. Post-industrial technological society, therefore, transcended social and political types, whether East or West. In an ironic twist, Gorz saw little difference between really existing socialism and

Western democracy. Both had to be scrapped. The way toward the future uto-pian society implied a different kind of technology and a different use of that technology, and, therefore, a different kind of society. Gorz was explicit. "The institutions and structures of the state are to a large extent determined by the nature and weight of its technologies [so that] the struggle for different tech-nologies is essential for the struggle for a different society."[3]

The solution suggested by Gorz was to organize local and regional collec-tivities and "joint control [of producers and consumers] over products and pro-duction processes."[4] Communal cells, at the local and the regional level, would provide a basis for self-empowerment and would constitute the "permanent fo-cus of political action."[5] Utopian practices demanded a down-scaling of the level and application of technology; wasteful production would be ended, more dura-ble products would be created, new work patterns would be encouraged, natural agriculture would be adopted. Less energy-intensive technologies would sup-plant higher energy-consuming technologies like the automobile. The imagina-tion would be encouraged by banning television broadcasting on weekends, a propitious idea, though not easy to square with Gorz's desire to preserve a liber-tarian Utopia because it emitted a malodorous whiff of the Leninist notion of moral and political rectitude.[6]

But this was not Gorz's intention. He criticized those who thought Utopia could be realized by the socialist seizure of state power because that would not alter the system of domination or the relationship of human beings to each other and to nature. "Socialism [was] not immune to technofascism [not the least be-cause it historically had set out to] multiply the powers of the state without de-veloping simultaneously the autonomy of civil society."[7] Gorz's Utopia, then, would preserve the libertarian, democratic and pluralist tendencies that charac-terized Western civil society. Political despotism in the name of utopian longing was judged incompatible with the requirements of human emancipation.

Gorz's utopian ideals almost seemed an idiosyncratic, cranky blend of post-Marxist sophistication and a simple homilitic looking backward. In Utopia we shall all work less, we shall need less, we shall be freer because we shall not be enslaved by our desires, and we shall dispense with all the gadgetry of modern technology, none of which has increased human happiness. Gorz was not simply bemoaning the disappearance of rural pre-industrial life, or trumpeting the ba-nalities of modern cosmopolitanism. His argument was neither a craving for a Gothic Utopia of the vintage of a William Morris, nor a rejection tout court of modernity. No less than Ernst Bloch, he was no modern Luddite. But the need for ecological balance, for a restored symmetry between community and nature, and for the democratization of work, school and community, were no longer utopian idylls. They were the sine qua non of a necessary stewardship for the preservation of the globe as a livable planet. In asserting this, Gorz had moved beyond classical Marxism. The real animus for a stewardship of the planet was the total community, not the working-class. The entire community would stew-ard the control and use of resources. The real nexus of struggle was no longer the shop floor or the union shop, but the school and the neighborhood.

Moreover, Gorz's objective was the mutuality of decision-making rather than the privatization of power by a political elite, in both East and West.[8] Gorz's vision was not obscured by a feeling of plaintive melancholy for a past that was irrecoverably lost. The problem of modernity, Gorz surmised, in both East and West, was the loss of civil society over the control of ecological, social and economic choices. The problem was reminiscent of Orwell's incubus in which he saw technological advance coinciding with political authoritarianism, wider gaps in social inequality, and the super concentration of wealth. Gorz appreciated Orwell's point, which he took as a criticism of Western technocratic democracies. Western civil society had been increasingly diminished by the increasing power of the state, the growing omnipotence of the 'market' and the flattening of democratic choice. Hence, Gorz found himself struggling to stop the shrinking of social autonomy and the displacement of communal self-action by so-called technically proficient and scientifically 'neutral' managers. The restoration of civil society was paramount in reclaiming and rebuilding democracy and 'self-management'. Moreover, civil society offered the only refuge from the totalitarian classical Right and the orthodox authoritarian Left of post-Leninist vintage.[9] Gorz's Utopia, then, would be distinctly low-tech and communitarian. Yet there remained the old socialist gadfly of the 'transition' to the promised land: did the problem of transition reveal a congenital defect or a historical abnormality?

Even before Gorz explicitly bade adieu to the working class, his Eco-Marxist position led him to the precipice of abandoning workers as an instrument of transformation into a utopian future. The proletariat had ceased to be a universal class, not the least because, as Stanley Aronowitz put it, "the transformation by capital of science and technology as the main producing forces of society [had] multiplied human productive powers"[10] and had thereby satisfied the most primal needs and desires of a deproletarianized workforce. Aronowitz provided a cautionary tale, however. Along with the satisfaction of material and subliminal desires, the increased powers of production had been accompanied by an increasing domination for entirely irrational ends. Hence, the apparent illogic that the rapid increase in scientific and technological advance had been matched by the no less prodigious expansion of the means of destruction. The Reason of science did not necessarily lead to a technically assisted Utopia despite solving the basic needs of everyday life.[11]

Gorz knew that the expanded satisfactions of private life in the West had produced a quiescent working-class, but by the 1970's he believed that the degradation of environment, workplace and neighborhood meant that higher levels of consumption and a living wage were insufficient. People still required satisfaction and self-actualization in life and work, a satisfaction that Gorz believed would transcend and subvert prevailing social relations. It would do so, he was convinced, by raising qualitative demands for self-management in the work environment and over living space.[12] Historically, Gorz added, the increasing diversion of capital into technical innovation did not have satisfaction as its aim. Windmills, as the great historian Marc Bloch had shown, lost out only because the wind was everywhere and could not be monopolized. Technical progress, therefore, did not equate with social or human advance.

Farewell to the Working Class

In *Farewell to the Working Class*, Gorz explicitly contradicted the Marxist axiom that the future unalienated society was likely to be fashioned by a cohesive proletariat whose self-interest coincided with the establishment of a universal association of workers. The modern working classes, he argued, were unlikely to play a future liberating role because of their economic dislocation, social alienation and political fragmentation. Moreover, many skilled workers were neither predisposed to the liberation of time or the abolition of work, Gorz's two central concerns. Workers preferred the defense of jobs and craft skills against the encroachments of automation. For Gorz, on the contrary, the way to the future was the abolition of 'work' – the precondition for the liberation of time – because work in capitalist society was neither free nor an end in itself, while 'self-determined' activity was freely chosen and purposive.

In advanced Western capitalist society, Gorz pointed out in the late 1970's, the abolition of work was already being accomplished by the advance of technology and automation. Given the unwillingness and the inability to foreshorten the work-week – the advent of the global economy attested further to that unlikelihood – the result was a growing mass of disaffected and unemployed workers, a proletariat of temporary laborers at best. On the other hand, there remained an aristocracy of tenured, skilled workers, opposed to the abolition of work because automation signaled the end of both jobs and skills that had previously provided economic security, job satisfaction and even a degree of political unity among similarly secured workers. Based on this reality, Gorz concluded that "protecting jobs and skills, rather than seeking to control and benefit from the way in which work is abolished, will remain the major concern of traditional trade unionism."[13]

The way toward a liberated future, Gorz admonished, was no longer through those individuals who identified with their work or found it fulfilling, but through the growing multitudes "who see 'their' work as a tedious necessity in which it is impossible to be fully involved."[14] Gorz called these multitudes a "non-class of non-workers," the permanently alienated, dispirited and marginalized that resulted from an explosion of labor-unburdening technology:

> Its goal is the abolition of workers and work rather than their appropriation. And this prefigures the future world. The abolition of work can have no other social subject than this non-class. I do not infer from this that it is already capable of taking the process of abolishing work under its control and of producing a society based upon the liberation of time. All I am asserting is that such a society cannot be produced without, or in opposition, to this non-class, but only by it or with its support.[15]

Gorz's argument meant a definite break with classical Marxism. Marxists responded with a bundle of criticisms of Gorz's formulations. Why should an amalgam of 'non-workers' prefigure a future world without the distinctive alienation of work and life that characterized the contemporary capitalist world? The assertion that the abolition of work could have no other social subject than Gorz's 'non-class' was seen as doubtful because such a non-class was not interested in the quixotic pursuit of the liberation of time. It was difficult to foresee how such a non-class could achieve a class-consciousness that was the sine qua non for human liberation, just as it was impossible to imagine why an amalgamation of non-class individuals could transcend the reality of its social fragmentation.

Gorz had anticipated these objections. He denied that his non-class had a historical and social mission comparable to the mission that Marx had assigned to the proletariat. He argued that the Marxist notion of a revolutionary proletariat was perversely romantic and even theological because it perceived the working-class as a subject transcending its members. History became an autonomous process happening through the unwitting agency of working-class members accomplishing unconsciously the task of a higher historical consciousness.[16]

The non-class designated by Gorz, however, did not represent a 'social subject' in the classical sense. "It has no transcendent unity or mission, and hence no overall conception of history and society,"[17] This was because it was not a class and could not constitute itself as a class consciously or unconsciously. "It [was] not the harbinger of a new subject-society offering integration and salvation to its individual members."[18] The members of the 'non-class' represented a potential movement which was open-ended and undetermined. Gorz believed the movement embraced, by definition, libertarian values. It had a historical ethos that aimed at abolishing the self-alienation of meaningless work through freely-determined activity.[19] Gorz concluded that there were a number of political possibilities and directions that the movement could take, but he expected that it would have to combine spontaneity and organization in no especial prescriptive order.[20]

These were the conclusions that Gorz reached in 1980, more than a decade after the failure of the 1968 rebellion in France, a failed movement that had resounding implications for French intellectuals still frustrated by the inability of Marxism to provide a way toward human liberation. Traditional Marxism had projected an unalienated, harmonian future together with a comprehensive theory that provided a sense of historical continuity, a stratagem of action and a hypothetically unchallengeable moral authority, all based on the conviction that the proletariat was the universal class with a uniquely apocalyptic, historical mission. But it was precisely that moral vision and historical theory that were inadequate for his purposes.[21]

Gorz's 'farewell to the working class' was an acknowledgement of the superannuated arguments of classical Marxism. The belief that it was necessary to "seize power in order to build a new world" was obsolete.[22] Moreover, Utopia, Gorz admonished, could not be built by decree. Comprehensive visions of the future were too likely to be superimposed from above by totalitarian visionaries.' Bereft of the classical visions of liberation, without a comprehensive theory of history that was inclusive of a socialist eschatology, the incipient non-class was faced with the challenge of the silence of history. The future no longer spoke to the present, the past no longer informed the future. On the other hand, the decomposition of modern society and the acceleration of automation were increasingly creating a space in which individuals could escape the heteronomy of modern capitalist work relations. Gorz saw a space where "individual sovereignty beyond economic rationality and external restraint" could be recovered.[23] He kept faith with Marx's meaning after all, despite the earlier tag of 'theology' that he appended to Marx's ideas on the proletariat and history. Substantive, revolutionary change, would arise out of the actual experiences of people. Alienated individuals, by simply claiming their autonomy, could recover the space they had lost.

The Paths to Paradise

In *Paths to Paradise*, published in 1983, Gorz was convinced that a postmillennial order was coming that promised a total eclipse of Western style capitalism. He anticipated that "the present crisis [would] break the continuity of two centuries of history, [that had been] marked by the expansion of industrialism and the spread of commodity relations."[24] Earlier anticipations by the prophets of post-capitalist society, including Marx, had concluded that capital had produced a technology whose efficiency made possible the abolition of work and the abolition of a society based on 'disposable time' as the measure of wealth. Technology made possible an annunciation of the future, and the certain dissolution of the old industrial order.[25] Gorz concurred that the further development of technology in the West had created the possibility of a socialist and unburdened future:

> Times of crisis are also times of great freedom. Our world is out of joint; societies are disintegrating, our lifelong hopes and values are crumbling. The future ceases to be a continuation of past trends. The meaning of present development is confused; the meaning of history suspended. Because the curtain has fallen on the old order and no other order waits in the wings, we must improvise the future as never before.[26]

These were gloomy prophecies, as were the warnings that followed. "There can be no piecemeal solutions; the obstacles will only be overcome by overall restructuring, total transformation."[27] Gorz was not looking to kindle a kind of eco-despotism here – he had warned earlier readers against the perils of 'techno-fascism'. History still remained open-ended. But there were flashpoints accompanying the dissolution of the old order, and these did not promise automatically a primrose path to a final paradise.

However, Western capitalism had unleashed the liberatory potential of technology. Automation made it possible to meet basic needs and release human time for freely chosen activities. "Labor time can no longer be the measure of exchange value, nor exchange value the measure of economic value. Wages can no longer depend on the amount of work performed, nor the right to an income or having a job."[28] The technological revolution had revealed the decay of both capitalism and really existing socialism, for the accelerating growth of production was accompanied by the diminishing use of both capital and labor. Capital, which no longer served as the basis of accumulation when new investment displaced the ability to consume, would end ignominiously in its own 'consumption,' while the basic socialist principle, 'to each according to his labor' was just as obsolete in a system which no longer recognized labor as the creator of wealth. "Automation, therefore, takes us beyond capitalism and socialism."[29] Automation was the precondition of the abolition of work and a sine qua non of human liberation. For Gorz, this made it possible to recuperate the venerable idea of an independent social income, an idea which had been broached as early as the 1790's in England. Historically, the idea of a guaranteed social minimum income for all families had been supported even by some American conservatives – in the form of a negative income tax in the case of Milton Friedman – but with the proviso that such an income would replace the welfare system and its chronic bureaucratic deformities. The aim was to abolish a cumbersome and irrational system of overlapping bureaucratic layers, and to create a unitary system of administration.[30] "Thus, in its conservative variant, a guaranteed income has the essential aim not of eradicating poverty and unemployment, but of making them socially acceptable at the least cost to society."[31] On the other hand, the utopian visions entertained by Gorz anticipated an income guaranteed for life as "the social form which income takes" when automation had vastly reduced the obligation to work.[32] The function of a guaranteed income, then, unlike Friedman's scheme, was to provide a bridge into the post-capitalist era. Gorz concluded that the 'social income' should not be designated as a social wage but as a portion of society's total wealth – or total production – based on the principle, not of 'each according to his labor', but of 'each according to his needs'. Since all were still obliged to participate in the task of socially necessary work, however intermittent such a task might be in a post-automation age, it followed that everyone had the "right of access to the social wealth which they have combined to produce through their intermittent work."[33] Whereas the basic premise of industrial capitalism, its 'law of value', was that the wage was paid for labor, the social income no longer paid for "work and workers" but for "life and citizens."[34] Emancipation began not after industrial capitalism but within it, not by its supersession through a mystical transcendence but by a parallel growth inside it. Penultimately, the logic of capital abolished itself through the sheer obsolescence of a society that could no longer measure its success by its ability to exchange time for subsistence. The modern technological revolution at last made possible the dissolution of all lingering obedience to the domination of economic activity, even the desire to see in technology the next Utopia. And the reduction of the 'realm of necessity' made possible an expanded realm of autoproduction, an area of work that was not institutionalized, an area of autonomous work in which 'unnecessary goods' were made for "sheer pleasure" and for the sake of freely chosen "indulgence."[35]

What Gorz offered as an alternative was an egalitarian model in the best traditions of Utopia, a communal basis of living and working rooted in the voluntary association of workers, a union of local cooperatives based on a perpetually broadening nexus of mutually exchanged goods and services. One almost has the giddy sensation of a time traveler commingling with the Rochdale Pioneers. Monetary relations are abolished, exchange assumes a non-market form. And the old Marxist maxim becomes everyday reality: "From each according to his abilities, to each according to his needs."

This was a familiar refrain, even an admirable one, but Gorz's readers were still entitled to wonder how his utopian musings would be accomplished. Who would establish the new work relations, who would transform human nature in Gorz's republic of virtue in what appeared yet another Utopia of interminable organizers?

Gorz clearly rejected the Leninist model of the 'dictatorship of the proletariat' and so-called centralized planning; he embraced a libertarian Utopia that avoided the obsequious scrimmaging of 'really existing socialism'. His model and inspiration was France in 1968, when workers, students and visionaries, joined by large sections of the middle class, simply took over the streets and universities of France, combining both political and personal self-action and autonomy. As Marcuse had once urged his compatriots toward the Great Refusal, so Gorz came to believe that the great middle class simply had to reclaim its birthright. It was after all only a question of values and political will.

But by the 1980's, as Gorz tried to define a post-liberation Utopia, France, like all of Western Europe, had settled into a Technocracy in which a 'left-leaning' elite applied the standards of 'Reason' in administering France from above. The politics of 'left' and 'right' were consigned to oblivion; France was treated like a machine that only required technical tinkering by technicians who stood at the helm of power. Decisions once left to citizens were now consigned to a technically minded elite; political choices of the past became technical problems of the present. The space of politics and of active citizenship was shrunken by the technical complexities of modern life, and by the claims of an elite that said it alone understood and could resolve those complexities.

Thus, Gorz's dilemma persisted. Modern Western democracies had created technical cornucopias along with the formal establishment of liberty. But the market economies of the West, even in an age of abundance, had not created egalitarian societies, nor resolved lingering gaps in access to housing, education and medical care. Gaps of wealth persisted, and that meant gaps in the distribution of power as well as the persistence of social and power elites. These continuing social and political deformities meant an opening for Gorz's insistence on full personal and political autonomy as the only legitimate road toward ecological balance and social justice. Yet, by the 1990's, Gorz's agenda appeared more difficult to achieve than ever before. The disappearance of the Soviet Union, the collapse of Marxism as a global force that could challenge the corporate domination of global markets and resources, the evolution of China into a hybrid that combined 'dictatorship of the proletariat', Chinese nationalism and competitive capitalism, did not point toward the kind of green socialist democracy envisioned by Gorz. It remained to be seen whether the French model of 1968 was an historical anomaly or an event that could once again ignite and mobilize the desire for personal and political autonomy.

Chapter 8
Conclusion: What's Left?

Karl Marx may have been his own worst enemy when he derided utopian socialism and the utopian socialists as unrealistic dreamers, peddlers of a fantasized
future they didn't know how to reach. Yet both Marx and Engels, when they
were not engaged in bitter polemics against rival socialist (and non-socialist)
views of history and society, clearly anticipated and fantasized the future themselves. Marx, in particular, was not averse to imagining a post-historical communist society in which humankind was no longer alienated and divided against
itself. The society that Marx hoped for, dreamed of, fantasized about and
prophesized was a vision of a future in which there would be no human exploitation of other human beings. In Marx's estimation, the Industrial Revolution
would make this possible. Indeed, mankind's ability to produce all of its needs
and desires had already made exploitation obsolete. Marx dreamed of a society
in which human alienation would disappear and human aggression would be
replaced by social cooperation. The reality, for Marx, was that humanity, in an
age of industrial plenty, could make its own history as it freely chose. History no
longer had to be blind. On the contrary, the past was not oblivious because humanity could now anticipate its future. Mankind could be free precisely because
it could dream. The future communist paradise would come about because it
was needed and just, not because it was historically inevitable. The future was at
hand because it could be anticipated. Human happiness could at last be the
measure of human being.

Marx's utopian speculations were not limited to his earlier writings, his so-
called Hegelian phase. Rather he continued his utopian anticipations throughout
his life. Most notably his utopianism became even lyrical on many pages of the
Grundrisse, where he sketched the outlines of *Capital*.

If the utopianism of Marx sounds odd in the West today, it is partially because much of his utopian work was published late in the West, and because his
work became known mostly through the prism of his successors, in particular

Lenin, in whom utopianism was notably authoritarian. Yet, much of the fault lies with Marx himself because his polemical work denigrated the utopian socialists. When criticizing the utopians, Marx claimed he was interested only in disclosing the anatomy of the present, not fantasizing an unknown future. Utopianism, to Marx, was heresy. At the same time Marx believed, as would Lenin, that the laws of history could be understood, even if the future could not be anticipated or known. But for both Marx and Lenin this posed no problem. Whatever the future brought, it would issue out of the historical experience of the proletariat. This made the pursuit of the goal legitimate and even noble. When the time came, workers would know what was just.

The ambiguities of Marx made it possible for his successors to detract utopian thinking as delusionary, a useless exercise in fantasy. Karl Kautsky, as we have seen, preferred science to utopianism, he was unwilling to invent recipes for the future. Yet he refused to have a science without goals, while simultaneously insisting that goals could be chosen and understood only by the scientific keepers of posterity. This was the intelligentsia, whose role was to introduce both the goal and the science to its subalterns, the working-class, whose interests it would identify and represent. Thus, Kautsky reintroduced utopianism through the back door. At the same time he helped distort democracy and democratic socialism, perhaps forever, by deflating utopianism, and by insisting that an intelligentsia knew best the interests of the working-class for whom it would choose the goals and the means of achieving them.

Lenin also built on the ambiguities that he found in Marx. The result was an authoritarian utopianism not unlike the authoritarianism of Kautsky's approach. Except that Lenin employed the Party instead of the intelligentsia as his vehicle for leading the working class toward the future. There was in Lenin, also, a dictatorial tendency. He insisted there must be one and only one vision of the future, a vision that he would define and embody and then legitimize through the Party. Lenin, therefore, did not abandon goals. But they were to be chosen by a small revolutionary elite, a vanguard with infallible knowledge of the truth which would lead the working-class to the promised land.

Not surprisingly, Lenin found another of Marx's ambiguities to help him rationalize the unchallenged authority of the Party. He fastened onto Marx's notion of the dictatorship of the proletariat, an idea that seemed to him to fit well into the conditions of revolutionary Russia. An idea, moreover, that rationalized revolution and Lenin's seizure of absolute power. Marx had used the phrase during two periods of upheaval, the French Revolution of 1848 and the Paris Commune of 1871. On both occasions he intended 'dictatorship' as a temporary solution, much in the manner of the ancient Romans. Lenin, however, put no such strictures on his dictatorship. This was partly because of history and partly because of ideology. Backward, czarist Russia, with its polyglot of peoples and languages, its isolated enclaves of peasant peoples and their innumerable grudges against each other and the czars, its economic backwardness and legendary inefficiency, could only advance if organized with industrial precision by an enlightened and dedicated elite. Russia's tardy development required double-step industrialization, its appalling ignorance mandated a hardy and enlightened elite that could unify and guide the nation toward a chosen vision. Moreover, all this could be done only with noble goals that promised an egalitarian future. Such a future was worth fighting for; it was worth the many sacrifices that would have to be made before the installation of Utopia. Thus, Lenin's Marxism rationalized away both liberalism and democracy. Pluralist society would never work in Russia. Democracy would introduce too many visions, too many possible futures, too many utopian roads. It would sabotage the work of the Party, undermine the unity of purpose and introduce fractiousness, dividing the nation against itself.

Lenin's practical Marxist nationalism brought him to power, but in his pursuit of an egalitarian dream he uncoupled socialism and democracy in Russia from the first moment of the revolution, even before. And in denying that there was more than a single vision of the future, by denigrating Western notions of pluralism, Lenin effectively denied the cardinal principle of Western democracy, whether of the liberal or social variety. Namely, that individuals are the best judges of their own interests. Lenin's substitutionism may have helped him solve some of his strategic problems, how to attain and hold power in a country riddled with clannishness, petty jealousies and internecine rivalries that were capable of tearing the social fabric apart. It may have sustained him in ruling a country that had never experienced democratic pluralism. But it made some of his greatest socialist, anarchist and democratic rivals shudder at the prospect of establishing authoritarian or dictatorial politics, without at the same time attaining anything like Marx's post-alienated society. The warnings had been there from the beginning, from Marx himself to Kautsky to Rosa Luxemberg, the great leader of the German Communists. By setting up one part of society over another, by designating a revolutionary elite to define the needs and desires of the working masses whose best interests it proclaimed to know and represent, Lenin corrupted Utopia, perhaps forever.

Marxism-Leninism concentrated political power in the Bolshevik elite with disastrous results for the future of Utopia. Yet, in the more developed and democratic West, it was the utopian Marx that was discovered and rediscovered by a number of thinkers who labeled themselves as both Marxists and utopians. Walter Benjamin, Ernst Bloch, Herbert Marcuse and Andre Gorz differed in many respects. But they were united in valuing Marx as a preeminent utopian thinker while simultaneously esteeming the ideas of Charles Fourier and utopian socialism in general because of Utopia's commitment to the 'human ingredient'. It was Benjamin and Bloch, in particular, who drew the linkages between religion and Utopia, between the humane and widely shared impulse of hope that religion offered, and the same impulse that Utopia promised on earth. Bloch's linkage between Christian communalism and transcendence, and Marx's anticipated biblical communism, had immense prophetic power. Millennial expectation was not only present in both, it was the driving emotional force and the express connection, as Bloch understood it, between the historical Jesus and the utopian Marx. Utopia, as historian Krishan Kumar has noted, "is not religion, but without a religious underpinning, without the structure of belief and sentiment that religion incomparably provides, it is possible that Utopia is not capable of arousing a significant and heartfelt response, on anything like a mass scale."[1] For Bloch, too, religion was the unconscious background of Utopia, the essential if hidden essence.

Utopia, however, as a religious-secular ideology in the twentieth century, was never reassuring. It ended in the gulag in the Soviet Union. After 1948 one could add the odd concoction that became known in China as Maoism. Neither Stalin nor Mao achieved anything like Marx's, Benjamin's or Bloch's fantasized, post-alienated future. Thus, in the post-World War II era, many intellectuals in Eastern Europe abandoned the dream of communism because it had failed to be transcendent and hopeful. Utopia died in the wake of Stalinist murder and the Soviet bullying of Poland in 1956. The invasion of Czechoslovakia in 1968 was simply the last death rattle.

In Western Europe, Marxist Utopia fared little better. Despite the legions of the convinced and numerous fellow travelers that simply took up Maoism as the new great hope after the failure of Stalinism, many more simply dismissed it as ideology or worse. Utopia in its 'left' configuration had produced terror and genocide in Russia. Given time, China was sure to follow the same path. Intellectuals in Western Europe left their respective Communist Parties in droves after World War II, looking for more pragmatic approaches to politics and social justice. Given the vast technological changes and scientific advances that were made in the decades following the Second World War, not surprisingly, many embraced 'scientific' social planning as the road to the future. Post-war European technocrats dismissed Marxism, Fascism and all ideologies as the dead weight of the past, impossible dreaming and much worse. In this context, 'left' and 'right' no longer mattered, they had proved a dead road, the kind of politics that was now obsolete.

Earlier H. G. Wells, utopian, non-Marxist, historian and technocrat, had attempted to couple Science and Utopia, and had looked to the state as the place where they could merge in so-called scientific planning. That such a linkage might turn into a totalitarian nightmare, as George Orwell pointed out, did not occur to a writer like Wells who articulated his utopian ideals prior to Adolf Hitler and Joseph Stalin coming to power.

When Wells wrote his most seminal pieces – those very writings that Orwell claimed had more influence on the young generation than any other works in print in the English-speaking world – it was possible, perhaps even desirable to couple science with historical progress and economic planning. The debate over the utility of science and technology, the implications and the advisability of (central) economic planning became critical during the interwar period. Depression, the necessity of wartime planning during World War II, the need to plan domestic economic reconstruction after the war, and the hope that Europe could become more unified and less nationalistic, all pointed to the need for some kind of central planning. The conclusion seemed obvious. If Europe were to avoid war in the future, there had to be a much greater pooling of scientific and technical knowledge within separate nation-states and within Europe as a whole.

Thus, a new 'rationalism' emerged in the post-war era in Europe, especially in France. Progress was linked, not only to technical efficiency and technological advance, but also to the acceptance of the Wellsian premises about the scientific management of man and society. Technocracy emerged as a modern rationalist Utopia, a form of society in which a 'neutral' technical intelligentsia, a sophisticated group of experts who were not invested in a society by ownership, claimed to adopt norms that were theoretically guided only by the higher standards of Reason. The adoption, direction and application of new technologies, and the management of financial resources, were matters for neutral social engineers to decide. There was to be no more politics of left and right.

The new forms of Technocracy, the renewed faith in the powers of science and technology that emerged in the immediate postwar era (despite massive disillusionment), raised many of the old questions once raised by Orwell about Wells (and by Marx about capitalism and Marcuse about Soviet Communism). In what sense could or should society be managed 'from above'? Was it possible to apply the methods of science and the study of nature to the study and management of human beings in society, such as many of the new technocrats proposed? To what extent was democratic pluralism compatible with socially engineered technocracy? If decisions formerly amenable to popular pressures from below now became technical decisions only within the purview of experts, would not public scrutiny and popular accountability be compromised and lost in the face of the 'higher' rational knowledge of technically superior technocrats?[2] Was there a necessary (or plausible) linkage between social technocracy and human liberation, between decision making from the top-down and popular consensus?

Distinct from bureaucracies that characterized all states, Technocracy was assumed by its defenders to mean an elevated state of understanding put to use for the higher good, not simply the more elemental manipulation of physical forces and material things that characterized the nature and use of technology. One paladin of the new technocratic order was John Kenneth Galbraith. Galbraith offered an increasingly conventional description of what he understood as the new social phenomenon and why he thought that Reason had finally manifested itself in History. He celebrated technocratic triumphalism, not as the final triumph of human history or the endpoint of mankind's ideological evolution, but as a necessary, positive and perhaps decisive step in the saga of human evolution.[3]

To the generation of technocrats of the 1960's and 1970's, planning appeared, by definition, to be rational. Disinterested technocrats would reach conclusions based on the public commonweal. They would not be subject to the maelstrom of politics and ideology. The presumption was that a single, unitary vision could be established because post-modern society was becoming homogeneous, more uniformly middle-class. Such a vision clearly transcended classical liberalism. As Marxist philosopher and historian George Lichtheim put it, it was the "explicit aim of the planners to promote a social equilibrium no longer subject to the periodic crises which were part of the price paid by modern society for the institution of a market economy."[4] The ideological debate that had endured for more than a century between socialists and liberals, planners and libertarians, defenders of state intervention and stalwarts of a hypothetical market economy, was transcended by the new Utopia. As a social and economic system, Technocracy claimed legitimacy just because, on the basis of technical efficiency, it could meet the elemental material needs of the citizenry.

As for democracy, in the technocratic perspective it was reduced "to a choice between competing political elites having the same basic ends in view."[5] In technocratic logic, democratic choices in the modern 'post-industrial' era in which society had become relatively homogeneous, were choices between two elites, neither of which was likely to disavow the need for centralized planning, nor even to have radically different social objectives. In technocratic theory there were no more private or class interests, only a unitary, rational definition and attachment to the public good.

Almost unnoticed at the time, technocratic theory coincided with the success of Western industrial capitalism following World War II. It was this success that made it rough going for utopian thought, especially for Marxist inspired utopianism. Although Stalin and Khrushchev, and a host of Western Marxists, anticipated a final economic crisis in the West, Western capitalist countries experienced a boom after World War II that reduced the Depression to a fading memory. By the 1950's and 1960's there appeared affordable and decent housing, department stores that were stuffed with inexpensive mass-produced consumer goods and automobiles that were within the reach of the vast majority of Western populations. Economic growth in the United States, already robust in the 1950's, rose a staggering 52.8% in the 1960's. In the same decade median family income in the U. S. rose 39.7%.[6] In the decades following World War II, Western capitalist countries embraced the Welfare State, stabilizing their own social orders and issuing a direct challenge to socialism and Marxism.

Yet, despite the real gains of the West, there remained critics of the Welfare State who were immune to the blandishments of a hypothetically neutral and progressive technocratic Utopia. For them the advance of science and the so-called logic of the natural sciences were misnomers, so many symbolic myths that hid the real social conflicts and the realities of human and social domination that were embodied in scientific and technological decisions. How the logic of the natural sciences was applied, what direction it took, how technical resources were to be utilized and on whose behalf, were all highly charged political choices. Science and scientific progress, and especially the evolution of technology were neither neutral nor value-free.

One of the best known of the critics of Technocracy was Herbert Marcuse. Marcuse believed that the liberating force of technology had been transformed into exactly the opposite, "a fetter of liberation, the instrumentalization of man," repeating axiomatically some of the earlier Orwellian visions of a coming technological incubus presided over by Big Brother.[7] Marcuse predicted that the new technical efficiency, the ability to exploit technical and mental resources as never before, would increase the gap between those who understood and controlled the new knowledge and those who were excluded from or ignorant of it.[8]

The vehemence and passion of Marcuse's lamentations in the anti-authoritarian 1960's bore the traces of utopian reflections and personal anxieties that stemmed from and were still scarred by the memories and simulacra of the Nazi era from which Marcuse had fled, both ideologically and physically. Marcuse had witnessed the convergence of technological advance that had emanated in a different kind of logic in Nazi Germany. For Marcuse, modernization and technological development were leading to a mass, alienated, impersonal and post-modern society (whether East or West, communist or capitalist) characterized by rigidifying social hierarchies, increasing social domination and centralizing social and class controls over the lower strata of the population. In Marcuse's dyspeptic surmise, the 'logos of technics' did not produce the era of Reason, but a far more parlous reality in which social hierarchy and domination appeared to be part of the 'natural order of things'. Marcuse concluded that the technocratic elite was simply a new ruling class, perhaps even more dangerous than previous ruling classes since it represented its work as 'rational', not accountable to a public because its decisions were defended as purely technical and 'above' politics. Marcuse could not help but wonder why a society that had become so productive, a virtual cornucopia, still required a dominant elite. Society had reached the point where future work could readily be turned into creative play and leisure. That it had not done so, Marcuse argued, was proof that the politics of domination lived on, that 'the liberating force of technology' was nothing but a new form of servitude. George Lichtheim's masterful summary of technocratic ideology pointed out the reasons for Marcuse's urgent warnings, and why Marcuse felt it necessary to re-emphasize the liberating potential of Utopia against the claims of Technocracy:

> Human societies exist for the purpose of developing and for no other; nature having been tamed by science, the task remains, with the help of the 'human sciences', to develop the techniques necessary to master human relations; industrial civilization levels the barriers between classes, races and traditional cultures; the only remaining social stratification is a meritocratic one based on productivity and competence; the ancient political cleavages between parties, between liberalism and conservatism, capitalism and socialism, are outdated and linked to dead ideologies; the system of boundless wealth-production marks the end of ideology and the de-politicization of society; the age of automation leaves only one opposition: that between the planners and the planned.[9]

Not surprisingly, neither dissent nor utopianism disappeared in the decades of the 'cornucopia'. When George Lichtheim wrote in the early 1970's, the social upheavals of 1968, from Paris to Berkeley, were still 'visible', moving him to note that public dissent was not only extant at the margins of society but was very much present among the masses of middle-class wage-earners as well. This was precisely because of the problems that remained unsolved – or were sometimes generated by – the so-called rational Technocracy. Radical criticism, Lichtheim surmised, would spread from the privileged minorities of the universities to the general public "because everyone suffers from the operation of a system which literally poisons the atmosphere."[10]

Lichtheim acknowledged that such problems as industrial pollution and waste could be viewed as technical problems whose solution was to be found in science, not politics. He did not even dispute that the West had met the elemental and material needs of its citizens. But in the terms of political discourse in the West, in both Europe and America, he feared something far more insidious. Technocracy and the classical meaning of democracy were incompatible. In technocratic Utopia "what counts . . . is no longer the will of a politically mature citizenry, but the programmed reaction of consumers to the manipulations of those in control."[11] Lichtheim seemed to be repeating the pessimism of writers like Orwell and Aldous Huxley in an earlier generation, and for many of the same reasons:

> With the best will the rulers of a major industrial country are constantly obliged to take decisions over a wide range of subjects which are not really amenable to public control because the individual citizen is no longer able to assess the merits of the case. To take an extreme instance, the proper balance between nuclear and conventional forces simply cannot be judged by the electorate, although the voters can (and should) decide whether their country ought to possess nuclear arms at all. To the extent that the exercise of judgment is still possible, it devolves for the most part upon organized bodies advised by professional experts: political parties, corporations, trade unions and the like.[12]

Lichtheim concluded that the social and political lines of demarcation no longer were between socialists and conservatives, but between technocrats and democrats, between those who claimed a superior political wisdom and those who demanded public accountability. To some radical theoreticians the differences could be framed as the struggle between scientism and humanism. German critical theorists Max Horkheimer, Theodor Adorno and Jurgen Habermas claimed that science, far from being in service to a higher rationality, to Reason, had been severed from its humanistic basis and had been instrumentalized by the requirements of technical proficiency and profitability. But Habermas believed it was possible to reattach science to more rational and authentically human purposes because scientists were also citizens whose self-interest, the creation of a conflict free society, coincided with the general interests of society and of humanity.[13]

To the extent that science had not achieved such humanistic aims, there remained a gap between existing reality and the kind of life implicitly promised by the advances of science. Utopia, in other words, and utopian vision, was likely to persist even through the 'cornucopian' age. It was clear that the inequalities and social deformations that still persisted from the past had not been transcended by the technocratic claims of a higher rationality. The technocratic faith, which explicitly claimed a de-politicized paradise for the future, was implicitly an authoritarian creed. If ideology no longer delineated the global order, especially after 1989, neither did the technocratic vision of the West prevail as the illuminating vision of a utopian future. The old Wellsian vision of society as a well-oiled machine, as a mechanism subject to social engineering by a scientific and neutral value-free elite, was not credible. Technical or scientific advance was not synonymous with historical Progress. Technocracy was not compatible with Democracy.

In the 1980's, Andre Gorz took the debate in a new direction, building on the ideas of the utopian Marx as he, Gorz, traveled the road from Red to Green. Gorz projected an ecotopian future, an eco-socialist society that anticipated post-industrial socialism and a world in which humanity had been liberated from the formal economy of production. A utopian world, in other words, in which human beings no longer had to work, or had to work only minimally. The conversion of work time into leisure, Gorz argued, made it possible for individuals to concentrate on personal fulfillment and pleasure. He anticipated a future in which there was no need for a so-called neutral elite of planners; a liberated society was about much more than meeting needs through the production and allocation of goods and services to minimize unmet desire. In Gorz's dual society, individuals would move between the sphere of heteronomy and autonomy, between wage-based labor which was becoming increasingly minimal, and obsolete, and the sphere of autonomy in which people could define themselves in self-designated leisure-work and in which life could become an end in itself. Freed of the demands of production, individuals had at last come to the brink of the realm of freedom. Necessary work would now give way to the pursuit of cultural, educational and communal activities that were self-fulfilling and intrinsically satisfying.[14] Far from abandoning Utopia, Gorz optimistically hoped it had at last arrived.

What's Left?

Andre Gorz understood the limits of planning, and the dangers of Technocracy. His vision of ecotopia was about human liberation and the realm of human autonomy, but it was an implicit warning also about the limits of growth and the absurdity of insisting on illimitable development, whether of really existing capitalism or socialism. In saying this, Gorz was not abandoning socialism. He was simply reminding his public that human beings were capable of living in radically different ways and in radically different social orders. Socialism, in other words, and the utopian impulse, remained vivid and hopeful in Gorz.

Like Gorz, British philosopher Raymond Williams, in his utopian-minded *Towards 2000*, insisted that only utopian (socialist) thinking had been concerned with human possibilities and the radically different ways in which human beings could live. Utopian thought, Williams argued eloquently, refused to resign itself to endless crises and wars. As such, Williams believed that the utopian impulse was at the heart of the human essence, and it provided a necessary critique of the inherent weaknesses of a 'libertarian capitalist cornucopia'.[15] Utopia's "strongest center [was] still the conviction that people can live very differently, as distinct both from having different things and from becoming resigned to endless crises and wars. In a time of scarce resources . . . there can be no question of dispensing with it."[16]

Williams wrote with considerable passion as both utopian and Marxist. Ironically, he wrote at a time when much of the world, certainly in the West,

already had dispensed with Utopia and had settled back into a more or less comfortable and pragmatic acceptance of capitalism, whether in its social democratic
or liberal American versions. Moreover, within several years of Williams' utopian speculations in *Towards 2000*, which appeared in 1983, the Soviet Union
collapsed, as did communism in Russia. In the same period Chinese communism
became more and more market oriented as Maoist utopian engineering receded
into oblivion. Other communist stalwarts, Cuba and Vietnam, hardly excited the
kind of utopianism that Williams was discussing. Neither projected an image
that was likely to inspire the kind of utopian longing that had moved so many in
the first half of the twentieth-century when thousands of Westerners made the
proverbial trip to Russia and China to build a paradaisical future.

And yet, as the world entered a new millennium, Western democracies had
not made good on many the promises once heralded in the name of democracy.
Neither Europe nor America was able to articulate a vision of a future that was
inclusive of all social constituencies, nor to create anything like a new global
order that could erase all the disparities and anomalies of wealth and power that
had previously defined the era of high imperialism.

Thus, despite the many advances of the United States in the post-war period, as America approached the millennium, serious social pathologies remained. In 1995 the richest 1 percent of Americans owned 40% of American
wealth. Several years later, in 2001, some 3 percent of the American population
owned more than 90% of the total value held in stocks.[17] Yet as wealth became
ever more concentrated, about 45 million Americans had no health insurance
while many elderly, protected in theory by Medicare, had to make hard decisions about whether to buy food or medicine. Meanwhile, in Europe, as the EU
pushed further and further to the East, preparing to absorb many erstwhile communist countries like Poland and Hungary, the immigrant populations from former Western empires were swelling the neighborhoods of European capitals.
Not only were these populations not assimilating, the new strains on neighborhoods, schools and the Welfare State itself defied efforts at 'rational planning'.
Even worse, the renewed stresses were reviving xenophobia and some of the old
paranoia about foreign cultures and foreigners. With the awakening of the Mus-
lim world, as tens of thousands of Muslims transplanted themselves into England, France and the West, outright racism was appearing even in respectable
political parties like the Conservative Party in Britain. Moreover, as the EU prepared to expand into the Balkans, erstwhile communist countries like Romania
and Bulgaria were set to join by 2006, foundation countries like France and England readied themselves to suffer the reverse of two centuries of gains for their
working classes. The expansion of the EU toward the east took on the look of
neo-imperialism as tens of thousands of jobs were ready to be exported to the
cheap-labor countries of Eastern Europe. French workers were invited to mi-
grate with their companies to Romania in one case, but for a salary of $140 per
month, 10 percent of what they made in France. There was little wonder that the
EU was not certain if France would even ratify the new EU constitution in 2005
(it didn't). Meanwhile, other European countries, less sanguine than France
about the passage of the new constitution if it had to be ratified by popular vote,

prepared to send the document to their respective parliaments for ratification where, success was far more likely.

None of this means that Utopia will revive or endure. But it does suggest that Western democracy is deficient and will probably suffer serious challenges ahead. Moreover, the revival of racism due to in-migration from Eastern Europe and continuing migration from former empire states, could lead to a kind of recidivism and enhance ethnic tensions that once produced decades of chaos and worse. Nobody is predicting a resurgence of neo-nationalism that scarred Europe for centuries, but Europe today is less white, less Christian and less 'European'. For the future it seems that Europe will look backward as much as it will look forward. And Utopia will loom large in its memory when it does.

Notes

Preface

1. Leon Baradat, *Political Ideologies. Their Origins and Impact*, 8th ed. (Upper Saddle River, NJ: Prentice Hall, 2003), 223.
2. Vincent Geoghegan, *Utopianism and Marxism* (London: Methuen, 1987), 4.
3. *Ibid.*
4. J. L. Talmon, *The Origins of Totalitarian Democracy* (New York: W. W. Norton, 1970), 249-52.
5. Plato, *The Republic*, trans. Robin Waterfield (New York: Oxford University Press, 1993), 227-49.
6. Thomas More, *Utopia* (Harmondsworth: Penguin, 1965), 128-31.
7. *Ibid.*
8. Thomas Campanella, *The City of the Sun*, trans. Daniel J. Donno (Berkeley: University of California Press, 1981), for a complete description.
9. Denis Diderot, *Supplement au Voyage de Bougainville* (Paris: E. Droz, 1935).
10. Jean-Jacques Rousseau, *The Social Contract*. ed. Roger D. Masters and ChristopherKelly, trans. Judith R. Bush, Roger D. Masters and Christopher Kelly, *Collected Writings of Rousseau*, vol. 4 (Hanover, NH: University Press of New England, 1994), 131-9. See also the commentary of Judith N. Shklar in *Men and Citizens· A Study of Rousseau's Social Theory* (Cambridge: Cambridge University Press, 1969); and Krishan Kumar, *Utopia and Anti-Utopia in Modern Times* (Oxford: Basil Blackwell Ltd., 1987), 37.
11. Rousseau, *Social Contract*, 131-9.
12. Henri de Saint-Simon, "Declaration of Principles," in Keith Taylor, trans. and ed., *Henri Saint-Simon· Selected Writings on Science, Industry and Social Organization* (New York: Holmes and Meier Publishers, Inc., 1975), 158-61.
13. *The Utopian Vision of Charles Fourier Selected Texts on Work, Love and Passionate Attraction*, ed. and trans. Jonathan Beecher and Richard Beinvenu (Boston: Beacon Press, 1971), 215-24, 274-96, 311-22.
14. Geoghegan, *Utopianism and Marxism*, 18-19.
15. Karl Marx, *Economic and Philosophical Manuscripts of 1844*, in Erich Fromm, *Marx's Concept of Man*, trans. T. Bottomore (New York:Frederick Ungar Publishing, 1961), 168.
16. Marx, *Philosophical Manuscripts*, 111; see Fromm's commentary in his essay *Marx's Concept of Man*, 56.
17. Marx, *Philosophical Manuscripts*, 144.

18. Cited in Fromm, *Marx's Concept of Man*, 59. The original may be found in Paul Tillich, *Protestantische Vision* (Stuttgart.Ring Verlag, 1952), 6.
19. See the comments of Erich Fromm, *Marx's Concept of Man*, 60.
20. Cited in Raya Dunayevskaya, *Marxism and Freedom* (New York: Bookman Associates, 1958), 19.
21. Fromm, *Marx's Concept of Man*, 64-5.
22. *Ibid.*, 66.
23. Kumar, *Utopia and Anti-Utopia*, 29.

Chapter 1

1. Maurice Meisner, *Marxism, Maoism and Utopianism   Eight Essays* (Madison, WI: University of Wisconsin Press, 1982), 3.
2. Herbert Marcuse, *Eros and Civilization   A Philosophical Inquiry into Freud* (London: Ark Paperbacks, 1987), 110.
3. Vincent Geoghegan, *Utopianism and Marxism*, 1-2.
4. Norman Cohn, *The Pursuit of the Millennium* (New York: Harper and Row, 1961), 308- 9.
5. Adam Ulam, "Socialism and Utopia," *Daedalus* 94, no. 2 (Spring 1965): 392.
6. *Ibid.*, 399.
7. J. L. Talmon, *The Origins of Totalitarian Democracy* (New York: W. W. Norton & Company, Inc.), 251-2.
8. *Ibid.*, p.252.
9. *Ibid.*
10. Meisner, *Maoism and Utopianism*, 18.
11. *Ibid*, 18-20.
12 George Lichtheim, *New York Review of Books*, 16 September 1965, 14.
13. Meisner, *Maoism and Utopianism*, 24.
14. Georg Wilhelm Friedrich Hegel, *The Philosophy of History*, tr. J. Sibree (New York: Dover Publications, Inc., 1956), 442-57.
15. Krishan Kumar, *Utopia and Anti-Utopia*, 55.
16. Karl Marx, *Economic and Philosophical Manuscripts,* in Tom Bottomore, ed., *Karl Marx   Early Writings* (New York: McGraw Hill, 1964), 128.
17. *Ibid.*, 155.
18. Karl Marx, *Capital*, III, trans. Ernest Untermann (Chicago: Charles H. Kerr & Co., 1909), 954-5.
19. Kumar, *Utopia and Anti-Utopia*, 57.
20. Karl Marx, *The German Ideology* (Moscow: International Publishers 1947), 22.
21. Karl Marx, "Excerpt Notes of 1844," in David Easton and Kurt H. Guddat, eds., *Writings of the Young Marx on Philosophy and Society* (Garden City, NY: Anchor Books, 1967), 281.
22. Karl Marx, *Grundrisse*, trans. Martin Nicolaus (Harmondsworth: Penguin Books, 1973), 705-6.
23. Marx, *Economic and Philosophical Manuscripts*, 155.
24. *Ibid.*, 156-7.

Chapter 2

1. Cited in M. Salvadori, *Karl Kautsky and the Socialist Revolution, 1880-1938* (London: New Left Books, 1979), 66.
2. *Ibid.*, 76. See also Karl Kautsky, *The Social Revolution* (Chicago: Kerr & Co., 1916), 103-4.
3. Karl Marx, *Theses on Feurbach*, in Karl Marx and Frederick Engels, *Collected Works*, vol. V, trans. Richard Dixon et al (London: Lawrence and Wishart, 1975), 4.
4. Geoghegan, *Utopianism and Marxism*, 39.
5. P. Goode, ed., *Karl Kautsky, Selected Political Writings* (London: Macmillan, 1983), 133.
6. Karl Kautsky, *The Social Revolution*, 103-4.
7. V. I. Lenin, *What is to be Done?* Ed. S. V. Utechin, trans. Patricia and S. V. Utechin (Oxford: Clarendon Press, 1963), 58-71, 105-16, 183-8.
8. *History of the Communist Party of the Soviet Union (Bolsheviks) Short Course* (Toronto, Francis White Publishers, Ltd., 1939), 37.
9. *Ibid.*, 114.
10. *Ibid.*, 115.
11. Fernando Claudin, *The Communist Movement· From Comintern to Cominform*, vol. I, tr. Brian Pearce (New York: Monthly Review Press, 1975), 118.
12. Leon Trotsky, *The Permanent Revolution* (London: New Park Publications, 1962), 27.
13. Cited in Claudin, *Communist Movement*, 121-2.
14. Milovan Djilas, *Rise and Fall* (Basingstoke: Macmillan, 1985), 238.
15. Cited in Robert Tucker, *Stalin in Power· The Revolution from Above, 1928-1941* (New York: W. W. Norton & Company, Inc., 1992), 89.
16. Robert Tucker, *The Marxian Revolutionary Idea* (New York: W. W. Norton & Company, Inc. 1969), 138-9.
17. *Ibid* , 140.
18. Cited in Tucker,*Marxian Revolutionary Idea*, 141.
19. *Communist Party*, 114-5.
20. Geoghegan, *Utopianism and Marxism*, 76-7.
21. David Caute, *The Fellow Travelers A Postscript to the Enlightenment* (New York: Macmillan, 1973), 36. I am indebted to David Caute for much of the following account and for leading me to a number of sources.
22. Cited in Caute, *Fellow Travelers*, 37.
23. *Ibid* , 38.
24. *Ibid.*, 39.
25. Cited in Caute, *Fellow Travelers*, 62.
26. Theodore Dreiser, *Dreiser Looks at Russia* (New York: H. Liveright, 1928), 32.
27. Sean O'Casey, *Mirror in My House Autobiographies*, vol. 2 (New York: Macmillan, 1956), 222.
28. Caute, *Fellow Travelers*, 66.
29. Corliss Lamont, *Soviet Civilization* (New York: Philosophical Library, 1952), 198-9.
30. Maurice Hindus, *The Great Offensive* (London: Gollancz, 1933), 42.
31. Sidney and Beatrice Webb, *Soviet Communism: A New Civilization?*, vol. I (London: Longmans, Green and Co., 1936), 430.
32. Caute, *Fellow Travelers*, 81.
33. Geoghegan, *Marxism*, 73-7.
34. Anna Louise Strong, *The New Soviet Constitution* (New York: H. Holt and Co., 1937), 47.
35. Bernard Pares, *Russia and the Peace* (New York: Penguin, 1944), 11.

36. Hewlett Johnson, *Searching for Light* (London: Joseph, 1968), 228-9.
37. Walter Duranty, *Stalin & Co   The Politburo – the Men Who Run Russia* (New York: William Sloane Associates, Inc., 1949), 85-6.
38. *Ibid.*, 86.
39. Hewlett Johnson, *The Socialist Sixth of the World* (London. Gollancz, 1939), 355-6.
40. *Ibid.*, 349.
41. Cited in Caute, *Fellow Travelers*, 107.
42. *Ibid.*, 114.
43. George Orwell, *The Collected Essays, Journalism and Letters of George Orwell*, ed. Sonia Orwell and Ian Angus, vol. 1 (Harmondsworth: Penguin, 1970), 370
44. *Ibid*, vol. 3, 273.
45. Geoghegan, *Utopianism and Marxism*, 83.
46. In Richard Crossman, ed., *The God That Failed* (London: Hamish Hamilton, 1950), 82.
47. Douglas Hyde, *I Believed· The Autobiography of a Former British Communist* (London: Heinemann, 1951). For background see Geoghegan, *Utopianism and Marxism*, 83.
48. E. P. Thompson, "Through the Smoke of Budapest," *The Reasoner*, 3 (Nov. 1956: Supplement 6).
49. Geoghegan, *Utopianism and Marxism*, 85.
50. Cited in Bernard Crick, *George Orwell A Life* (Boston: Little, Brown and Co., 1980), 507. Orwell's original statement may be found in "What is Socialism?" in *Manchester Evening News*, 31 Jan. 1946. This essay was omitted from Orwell's *Collected Essays*.

Chapter 3

1. Von Laue, *World Revolution*, 121.
2. Cited in Stuart R. Schram, *The Political Thought of Mao Tse-tung* (Harmondsworth: Penguin, 1974), 290.
3. Theodore H. Von Laue, *The World Revolution of Westernization The Twentieth Century in Global Perspective* (New York: Oxford University Press, 1987), 276.
4. Cited in Paul Johnson, *Modern Times The World from the Twenties to the Eighties* (New York: Harper & Row, Publishers, 1983, 546.
5. Stuart R. Schram, *Mao Tse-tung* (New York: Simon & Schuster, 1966), 271, footnote. See also Johnson, *Modern Times*, 548.
6. Ross Terrill, *Mao· A Biography* (New York: Harper & Row, Publishers, 1980), 216-7.
7. Schram, *Mao*, 271. See also Johnson, *Modern Times*, 549.
8. *Ibid* , 267.
9. Terrill, *Mao*, 217-8.
10. Cited in Schram, *Political Thought of Mao*, 346.
11. *Ibid.*
12. Cited in Han Suyin, *Wind in the Tower. Mao Tse-tung and the Chinese Revolution, 1949-1975* (Boston: Little, Brown & Company, 1976), 53.
13. Paul Johnson, *Modern Times*, 549.
14. Maurice Meisner, *Maoism and Utopianism*, 67.
15. Von Laue, *World Revolution*, 284.
16. Johnson, *Modern Times*, 550.
17. Von Laue, *World Revolution*, 283-4.
18. *Ibid.*, 284.

19. Cited in Schram, *Mao*, 273.

20. Cited in Schram, *Mao, 273*

21. Meisner, *Maoism and Utopianism*, 198.

22. Cited in Meisner, *Maoism and Utopianism*, 198.

23. *Ibid*, 118-9.

24. Mao-Tse-tung, "In Memory of Norman Bethune," *Peking Review* (17 February 1967): 5.

25. Meisner, *Maoism and Utopianism*, 120-9.

26. Von Laue, *World Revolution*, 284; and Terrill, *Mao*, 269-70.

27. Von Laue, *World Revolution*, 285.

28. Cited in Terrill, *Mao*, 270-1.

29. Mao Tse-tung, *On the Correct Handling of Contradictions among the People* (Peking: Foreign Language Press, 1957), 9, 49-58.

30. Edgar Snow, *The Long Revolution* (New York: Random House, 1972), 68-9.

31. Meisner, *Maoism and Utopianism*, 167.

32. Mao Tse-tung, *Chairman Mao Talks to the People Talks and Letters, 1956-1971* (New York: Pantheon Books, 1974), 203, 205. 207.

33. Cited in Terrill, *Mao*, 315.

34. Cited in Johnson, *Modern Times*, 555.

35. *Ibid.*, 556.

36. Cited in Jack Chen, *Inside the Cultural Revolution* (London: Sheldon Press, 1976), 221-4.

37. Johnson, *Modern Times*, 558-9.

38. David Milton, Nancy Milton and Franz Schurmann, eds., *The China Reader People's China* (New York: Vintage, 1974), 285.

39. *Ibid.*, pp. 269-70.

40. Milton, *China Reader*, 271.

41. Von Laue, *World Revolution*, 290.

42. Mao Tse-tung, *Quotations from Chairman Mao* (Peking: Foreign Language Press, 1966), 179, 204-5.

43. *Ibid.*, pp. 204-5.

44. Bernard Frolic, "Reflections on the Chinese Model of Development," *Social Forces* (December 1978): 384-6. I am indebted to Paul Hollander, *Political Pilgrims Travels of Western Intellectuals to the Soviet Union, China and Cuba* (Lanham, MD: University Press of America, 1990), for leading me to this and many of the following sources.

45. Ibid., 290.

46. Staughton Lynd and Tom Hayden, *The Other Side* (New York: New American Library, 1966), 39-40.

47. Hewlett Johnson, *The Upsurge of China* (Peking: New World Press, 1961), 368.

48. Hewlett Johnson, *China's New Creative Age* (New York: International Publishers, 1953), 184.

49. Simone de Beauvoir, *The Long March* (New York: World Publishing Co., 1958), 164.

50. John K. Fairbank, "The New China and the American Connection," *Foreign Affairs* 51, no. 1 (October 1972): 36-7.

51. *Ibid.*, 41

52. Peter Worsley, *Inside China* (London: Allen Lane, 1975), 20.

53. *Ibid.*, 129.

54. *Ibid.*

55. Maria Macciocchi, *Daily Life in Revolutionary China* (New York: Monthly Review Press, 1972), 314.

56. Felix Greene, *Awakened China The Country Americans don't Know* (Garden City, NY: Doubleday, 1961), 221.
57. John Kenneth Galbraith, *A China Passage* (Boston: Houghton-Mifflin, 1973), 120.
58. Martin King Whyte, " Inequality and Stratification in China," *China Quarterly* (December 1975): 685, 692.
59. Donald S. Zagoria, "China by Daylight," *Dissent* (spring 1975): 138-9.
60. Edgar Snow, *Red China Today* (New York: Random House, 1970), 285.
61. Cited in Hollander, *Political Pilgrims*, p. 317.
62. Mao Tse-tung, *Chairman Mao Talks to the People*, 274.
63. Von Laue, *World Revolution*, 292.
64. Zbigniew Brzezinski, *The Grand Failure The Birth and Death of Communism in the Twentieth Century* (New York: Collier Books, 1989), 148.
65. *Ibid.* 149.

Chapter 4

1. Howard Eiland and Kevin McLaughlin, "Foreword," in Walter Benjamin, *The Arcades Project*, ed. Rolf Tiedemann, trans. Howard Eiland and Kevin McLaughlin (Cambridge, MA: The Belknap Press of Harvard University Press, 1999), x.
2. *Ibid.*, xi-xii.
3. Walter Benjamin, "Hashish in Marseilles," *One Way Street and Other Writings*, trans. Edmund Jephcott and Kingsley Shorter (London: Verso, 1979), 215.
4. *Ibid.*, 220.
5. *Ibid.*, 220-1.
6. *Ibid.*, 221.
7. *Ibid.*
8. Benjamin, "Surrealism," *One Way Street*, 226.
9. *Ibid.*, 225-6.
10. *Ibid.*, 228.
11. *Ibid.*, 229.
12. *Ibid.*, 230-1.
13. *Ibid.*, 231.
14. *Ibid.*, 234-5.
15. *Ibid.*, 235.
16. *Ibid.*, 236.
17. *Ibid.*
18. *Ibid.*
19. Walter Benjamin, "A Berlin Chronicle," *Reflections· Essays, Aphorisms, Autobiographical Writings*, ed. Peter Demetz, trans. Edmund, Jephcott (New York: Schocken Books, 1986), 3-60.
20. Benjamin, "Surrealism," *One Way Street*, 238.
21. *Ibid.*
22. Walter Benjamin, "One Way Street," *One Way Street and Other Writings*, 45-6.
23. Benjamin, "Berlin Chronicle," *Reflections*, 6
24. *Ibid.*, 11.
25. *Ibid.*
26. *Ibid.*
27. *Ibid.*, 18.
28. *Ibid.*, 25-6.
29. *Ibid.*, 28.
30. *Ibid.*, 40.

31. *Ibid.*, 38-40.
32. Walter Benjamin, "The Image of Proust," *Illuminations*, ed. Hannah Arendt (Schocken Books: New York, 1969), 207-8.
33. *Ibid.*, 208.
34. *Ibid.*, 209.
35. *Ibid.*, 210.
36. *Ibid.*, 210-1.
37. *Ibid.*, 210-3.
38. *Ibid.*, 210-1.
39. Rolf Tiedemann, "Dialectics at a Standstill," in Benjamin, *The Arcades Project*, 933.
40. Benjamin, *The Arcades Project*, 838, 844, 863.
41. *Ibid.*, p. 844.
42. *Ibid*; and Tiedemann, "Dialectics," *Arcades Project*, 934.
43. Benjamin, *The Arcades Project*, 846. See the illuminating comments of John Berger, *Ways of Seeing* (London: Penguin, 1972), 14-16.
44. Benjamin, *The Arcades Project*, 846.
45. *Ibid.*
46. *Ibid.*
47. *Ibid.*, 464.
48. Tiedemann, "Dialectics," *Arcades Project*, 939.
49. Benjamin, *The Arcades Project*, 13.
50. Benjamin, "The Author as Producer," *Reflections*, 226-7.
51. *Ibid.*, 229.
52. *Ibid.*, 230.
53. *Ibid.*, 230-2.
54. *Ibid.*, 235-6.
55. *Ibid.*, 236.
56. Benjamin, "The Work of Art in the Age of Mechanical Reproduction," *Illuminations*, 217-51.
57. *Ibid*, 223-4.
58. *Ibid.*, 234.
59. *Ibid.*, 238.
60. *Ibid.*
61. *Ibid.*, 239-41.
62. Benjamin, *The Arcades Project*, 239. For further comments on Baudelaire, see also Walter Benjamin, *Charles Baudelaire A Lyric Poet in the Era of High Capitalism*, trans. Harry Zohn (London: Verso, 1983).
63. Benjamin, *The Arcades Project*, 265.
64. *Ibid.*, 298.
65. *Ibid.*, 314.
66. *Ibid.*, 314-8.
67. *Ibid.*, 339.
68. *Ibid.*, 343-8.
69. *Ibid.*, 361.
70. *Ibid.*, 389.
71. *Ibid.*
72. *Ibid.*
73. Cited in Tiedemann, "Dialectics," *Arcades Project*, 944.
74. *Ibid.*, 944.
75. Benjamin, "Theses on the Philosophy of History," *Illuminations*, 254. This was written in spring 1940, shortly before Benjamin's death.
76. *Ibid.*, 255.

77. *Ibid.*
78. *Ibid.*
79. *Ibid.*, 292-3.

Chapter 5

1. E. J. Hobsbawm, "The Principle of Hope," *The Times Literary Supplement*, 31 March 1961, 194.
2. Wayne Hudson, *The Marxist Philosophy of Ernst Bloch* (New York: St. Martin's Press, 1982), 12.
3. *Ibid.*, 31-2; and Ernst Bloch, *The Spirit of Utopia*, trans. Anthony A. Nassar (Stanford, CA: Stanford University Press, 2000), 10-26.
4. *Ibid.*, 25-6.
5. *Ibid.*, 243.
6. *Ibid.*, 40.
7. Ernst Bloch, *Man on His Own Essays in the Philosophy of Religion*, trans. E. B. Ashton (New York: Herder and Herder, 1970), 35.
8. *Ibid.*, p. 37.
9. *Ibid.*, p. 39. See also Hudson, *Bloch*, p. 34.
10. Ernst Bloch, "Nonsynchronism and the Obligation to its Dialectics," *New German Critique* 11 (Spring 1977): 22-38.
11. Ernst Bloch, *The Principle of Hope*, trans. Neville Plaice, Stephen Plaice and Paul Knight, 3 vols. (Cambridge, Mass.: The MIT Press, 1986). See especially vol. 2, 471-624, for these themes. See also Hobsbawm, "Hope," 193.
12. Jack Zipes, "Introduction," in Ernst Bloch, *The Utopian Function of Art and Literature Selected Essays*, trans. Jack Zipes and Frank Mecklenburg (Cambridge, MA: 1988), xxvii. For Bloch's comments see his 1931 essay, "Poesie im Hohlraum," in *Literarische Aufsatze, Gesamtausgabe*, vol. 9 (Frankfurt am Main: Suhrkamp, 1977), 119.
13. Bloch, *Principle of Hope*, vol. 1, p. 146.
14. *Ibid.*, 5.
15. *Ibid.*
16. *Ibid.*
17. *Ibid.*, 11.
18. *Ibid.*, 9, 12.
19. *Ibid.*, 35.
20. *Ibid.*
21. *Ibid.*
22. *Ibid.*, 51.
23. *Ibid.*
24. *Ibid.*, 56.
25. *Ibid.*
26. *Ibid.*,64.
27. *Ibid.*
28. *Ibid.*, 66.
29. *Ibid.*, 69.
30. *Ibid.*, 76.
31. *Ibid.*
32. *Ibid.*, 77.
33. *Ibid.*, 84-5.

34. *Ibid.*, 94.
35. *Ibid.*, 95.
36. *Ibid.*
37. *Ibid.*
38. *Ibid.*, 116.
39. *Ibid.*, 124.
40. *Ibid.*, 125.
41. *Ibid.*, 126-7.
42. Ibid., 144; see also Vince Geoghegan, *Utopianism and Marxism*, 90-1
43. Bloch, *Hope*, vol. 1, 158, 163.
44. *Ibid.*, 163.
45. *Ibid.*
46. *Ibid.*
47. Zipes, "Introduction," *Utopian Function,* xxix-xxx.
48. *Ibid.*
49. *Ibid.*, xxxii.
50. Bloch, *Principle of Hope*, 214.
51. *Ibid.*, 214-5.
52. Zipes, Introduction, xl.
53. Fredric Jameson, *Marxism and Form. Twentieth-Century Dialectical Theories of Literature* (Princeton, NJ: Princeton University Press, 1971), 145; see also Ernst Bloch, "Recollections of Walter Benjamin," in G. Smith, ed., *On Walter Benjamin Critical Essays and Recollections* (Cambridge, MA: MIT Press, 1988), pp. 338-345.
54. Bloch, *Hope*, vol. 2, 479.
55. *Ibid.*, 451.
56. *Ibid.*, 496.
57 *Ibid.*
58. *Ibid*
59. I Sam. 1, 2; II Kings 1, 8; Luke 1, 15 KJ
60. Bloch, *Principle of Hope*, II, 497.
61. *Ibid.*
62. *Ibid.*
63. *Ibid.*
64. Is. 55, 1 KJ
65. Cited in Bloch, *Principle of Hope*, II, 498.
66. Bloch, *Principle of Hope*, II, 497-8.
67. Is. 54, 14 KJ
68. Mat. 3, 10 KJ
69. Bloch, *Principle of Hope*, vol. 2, 499.
70. *Ibid.*
71. *Ibid.*
72. *Ibid.*, 500.
73. Ernst Bloch, *Atheism in Christianity The Religion of the Exodus and the Kingdom*, trans. J. T. Swann (New York: Herder and Herder, 1972), 268. See also Vincent Geoghegan, *Ernst Bloch* (London: Routledge, 1996), 87-8 for further discussion of this point. Bloch's notion of a revolutionary Christ founded on the social gospel was already worked out in *The Principle of Hope*, vol. III, 1199-1200.
74. Mat. 25, 40 KJ; see Bloch, *Principle of Hope*, II, 500.
75. *Ibid* , II, 501.
76. *Ibid.*, 501-2.
77. *Ibid.*, 502.
78. *Ibid.*

79. *Ibid.*
80. *Ibid.*, 507-8.
81. *Ibid.*, 509.
82. *Ibid.*
83. *Ibid.*
84. *Ibid.*, 510-1.
85. *Ibid.*, 511.
86. *Ibid.*, 512.
87. *Ibid.*
88. *Ibid.*, 513.
89. *Ibid.*, 514.
90. *Ibid.*
91. *Ibid.*
92. *Ibid.*, 515.
93. Geoghegan, *Bloch*, 79.
94. *Ibid.*, 81.
95. Bloch, *Principle of Hope*, III, 1199-1201.
96. Geoghegan, *Bloch*, 82.
97. Cited in Bloch, *Principle of Hope*, II, 515.
98. Bloch, *Principle of Hope*, II, 560-1.
99. *Ibid.*, II, 568.
100. *Ibid.*
101. *Ibid*, 577-8.
102. *Ibid.*, 582.
103. *Ibid.*
104. *Ibid.*, 583.
105. *Ibid.*, III, 947.
106. *Ibid.*, 968.
107. *Ibid.*
108. Jack Zipes, "Introduction," *Utopian Function*, xxiii.
109. *Ibid.*, 1063.
110. *Ibid.* This cantata, number 53, was incorrectly attributed to Bach when Bloch wrote about it.
111. *Ibid.*, 1088-9.
112. *Ibid.*, 1102.
113. *Ibid.*, 1103.
114. Geoghegan, *Bloch*, 89; and Bloch, *Principle of Hope*, III, 1103-16.
115. *Ibid.*, 1260-71; and Geoghegan, *Bloch*, 89.
116. Bloch, *Principle of Hope*, III, 1273.
117. *Ibid.*
118. *Ibid.*
119. *Ibid.*, 1199-1200.
120. *Ibid.*, 1199.
121. *Ibid.*
122. *Ibid.*, 1201.
123. *Ibid.*, 1357.
124. *Ibid.*, 1367.
125. *Ibid.*, 1368-73.
126. *Ibid.*, 1367.
127. *Ibid.*, p. 1368; and Geoghegan, *Bloch*, 119.
128. Bloch, *Principle of Hope*, III, 1358.
129. *Ibid.*, 1357.

130. *Ibid.*, pp. 1357-58; on this point see the comments of Geoghegan, *Bloch*, 120.
131. Bloch, *Principle of Hope*, III, 1358.
132. *Ibid.*
133. *Ibid.*, 1359.
134. Marx's letter cited in Bloch, *Principle of Hope*, III, 1363.
135. *Ibid.*
136. Ernst Bloch, *On Karl Marx*, trans. J. Maxwell (New York: Herder and Herder, 1970), 108.
137. Bloch, *Principle of Hope*, III, 1370.
138. *Ibid.*, I, 174.
139. *Ibid.*, 249.
140. Ernst Bloch, "A Jubilee for Renegades," *New German Critique* 4 (1975): 18. See Geoghegan, *Utopianism and Marxism*, 96.
141. Ernst Bloch, *Heritage of Our Times*, trans. N. and S. Plaice (Oxford: Polity, 1991), 4.
142. *Ibid.*
143. Bloch, *Principle of Hope*, II, 595.
144. Zipes, "Introduction," *Utopian Function*, xxi.
145. Cited in Geoghegan, *Bloch*, 127.
146. Zipes, "Introduction," *Utopian Function*, xxii.
147. Geoghegan, *Bloch*, 128.
148. Cited in Geoghegan, *Bloch*, 128.
149. *Ibid.*, 129.
150. Bloch, *Principle of Hope*, II, 622.
151. *Ibid.*, 691.
152. *Ibid.*
153. Geoghegan, *Marxism and Utopianism*, 97.

Chapter 6

1. Kumar, *Utopia and Anti-Utopia*, 394.
2. Herbert Marcuse, *Eros and Civilization: A Philosophical Inquiry into Freud* (London: Ark Paperbacks, 1956), 3-4.
3. *Ibid.*, 201.
4. Kumar, *Utopia and Anti-Utopia*, 396.
5. Marcuse, *Eros*, 140. See Sigmund Freud, *Collected Papers*, vol. IV (London: Hogarth Press, 1950), 16-17.
6. This was the general argument in Sigmund Freud, *Civilization and Its Discontents and Other Works* (Harmondsworth: Penguin, 1985).
7. Geoghegan, *Utopianism and Marxism*, 99; and Marcuse, *Eros*, 142.
8. *Ibid.*, 141-2.
9. *Ibid.*, 142.
10. *Ibid.*
11. *Ibid.*, 143.
12. *Ibid.*
13. *Ibid.*
14. *Ibid.*, 144.
15. *Ibid.*, 145-6.
16. Geoghegan, *Marxism and Utopianism*, 101; on this point see Freud, *Civilization and Its Discontents*, 73.

17. Marcuse, *Eros*, 231.
18. *Ibid.*, 232.
19. *Ibid.*
20. *Ibid.*
21. *Ibid.*, 19. See Barry Katz, *Herbert Marcuse and the Art of Liberation An Intellectual Biography* (London: Verso, 1982), 150.
22. Marcuse, *Eros*, 18-19.
23. *Ibid.* 19.
24. *Ibid.*, 233.
25. Ibid., 140.
26. *Ibid.*, 56.
27. Ibid., 63.
28. *Ibid.*, 63-7.
29. Ibid., 65; and Geoghegan, *Utopianism and Marxism*, 101.
30. Marcuse, *Eros*, 73.
31. *Ibid.*, 56-61.
32. *Ibid.*, 69-70.
33. *Ibid.*, 70.
34. *Ibid.*, 71-3.
35. Katz, *Marcuse*, 149-53.
36. *Ibid.*, 149-53.
37. *Ibid.*, 152-3.
38. Marcuse, *Eros*, 12.
39. *Ibid.*, 50-61. See also the comments of Katz, *Marcuse*, 152-3.
40. Marcuse, *Eros*, 18.
41. *Ibid.*, 55-65, 73-5 for the priority of memory and its relationship to the archaic heritage.
42. Ibid., 83-4. For insights into the relationship between Freud's performance principle, Marx's theory of alienation and Marcuse's notion of instinctual rebellion, see H. Stuart Hughes, *The Sea Change The Migration of Social Thought, 1930-1965* (New York: Harper and Row, 1975), 177.
43. Marcuse, *Eros*, 48-9.
44. Hughes, *Social Thought*, 178.
45. Marcuse, *Eros*, 197-213.
46. Kumar, *Utopia and Anti-Utopia*, 396-7.
47. Herbert Marcuse, *One Dimensional Man* (Boston: Beacon Press, 1966), 1.
48. *Ibid.*, "Preface," xiii.
49. *Ibid*, 16-18, 57.
50. *Ibid.*, 57.
51. *Ibid.*, 7.
52. Kumar, *Utopia and Anti-Utopia*, 397.
53. *Ibid.* See C. W. Mills, *The Power Elite* (New York: Oxford University Press, 1957); David Riesman, *The Lonely Crowd A Study of the Changing American Character* (New Haven, CT: Yale University Press, 1950); and William Whyte, *The Organization Man* (New York: Simon & Schuster, 1956).
54. Marcuse, *One Dimensional Man*, 7.
55. *Ibid.*, "Preface," xvi and 18.
56. *Ibid.*, 256-7.
57. Kumar, *Utopia and Anti-Utopia*, 398.
58. Hughes, *Social Thought*, 181.
59. Kumar, *Utopia and Anti-Utopia*, 398.
60. Herbert Marcuse, "The End of Utopia," *Five Lectures* (Boston: Beacon Press, 1970),

64. See also Geoghegan, *Utopianism and Marxism*, 107.
61. Marcuse, "The End of Utopia," *Five Lectures.*, 63
62. Kumar, *Utopia*, 398-9.
63. Cited in Kumar, *Utopia and Anti-Utopia*, 399. See also Herbert Marcuse, "Liberation from the Affluent Society," in David Cooper, ed., *The Dialectics of Liberation* (New York: Collier Books, 1968), 175-92, for the entire text.
64. Kumar, *Utopia and Anti-Utopia*, 399-400.
65. *Ibid.*, 402.
66. Herbert Marcuse, *An Essay on Liberation* (Boston: Beacon Press, 1969), 3.
67. *Ibid.*, 4.
68. *Ibid.*, 5
69. *Ibid.*
70. *Ibid.*, 9-11.
71. *Ibid.*, 26.
72. *Ibid.*, 27.
73. *Ibid.*, 29.
74. *Ibid.*, 31.
75. *Ibid.*
76. *Ibid.*, 30-36.
77. Kumar, *Utopia*, 400.
78. *Ibid* , 400-1.
79. Katz, *Marcuse*, 186-8.
80. *Ibid.*, 187.
81. Marcuse, *Essay on Liberation*, 22.
82. *Ibid.*, p. 24; see also Marcuse, *Eros*, 180-83.
83. Marcuse, *Essay on Liberation*, vii.
84. *Ibid.*
85. *Ibid.*, viii.
86 *Ibid.*
87. *Ibid.*
88. *Ibid.*, ix.
89. Hughes, *Social Thought*, 182.

Chapter 7

1. Andre Gorz, *Ecology as Politics*, trans. Patsy Vigderman and Jonathan Cloud (London: Pluto Press, 1987), 12-16.
2. Geoghegan, *Utopianism and Marxism*, 128.
3. Gorz, *Ecology*, 19.
4. *Ibid.*
5. *Ibid* , 20.
6. *Ibid.*, 42-50.
7. *Ibid.*, 20.
8. *Ibid.*, 37.
9. Ibid., 38-40.
10. Stanley Aronowitz, *The Crisis in Historical Materialism: Class, Politics and Culture in Marxist Theory* (New York: Praeger, 1982), 54.
11. *Ibid.*
12. Gorz, *Ecology*, pp55-63.
13. Andre Gorz, *Farewell to the Working Class An Essay on Post-Industrial Socialism*,

trans. Michael Sonenscher (London: Pluto Press, 1982), 7.
14. *Ibid.*
15. *Ibid.*
16. *Ibid.*, 10.
17. *Ibid.*, 11
18. *Ibid.*
19. *Ibid.*
20. *Ibid.*, 13.
21. *Ibid.*, 75.
22. *Ibid.*, 8, 75.
23. *Ibid.*, 75.
24. Andre Gorz, *Paths to Paradise On the Liberation from Work*, trans. Malcolm Imrie (London: Pluto Press, 1985), vi.
25. *Ibid.*, vii.
26. *Ibid.*, 1.
27. *Ibid.*,
28. *Ibid.*, 30.
29. *Ibid.*, 32.
30. *Ibid.*, 40-41.
31. *Ibid.*, 41.
32. *Ibid.*
33. *Ibid.*, 42.
34. *Ibid.*, 42-4.
35. *Ibid.*, 44.

Chapter 8

1. Kumar, *Utopia and Anti-Utopia*, 421.
2. See C. W. Mills, *The Power Elite* (New York: Oxford University Press, 1957), 123, for criticism of Technocracy.
3. John Kenneth Galbraith, *The New Industrial State* (Boston: Houghton-Mifflin, 1969), 71.
4. George Lichtheim, *Europe in the Twentieth Century* (New York: Praeger, 1972), 336.
5. *Ibid.*, 339.
6. Stephen Kotkin, *Armageddon Averted the Soviet Collapse, 1970-2000* (New York: Oxford University Press, 2001), 20.
7. Marcuse, *One Dimensional Man*, 144.
8. *Ibid.*
9. Lichtheim, *Europe*, 335.
10. *Ibid.*, 338.
11. *Ibid.*
12. *Ibid.*, 353.
13. *Ibid.*, 342.
14. Gorz developed this argument in both *Farewell to the Working Class* and *Paths to Paradise*.
15. Raymond Williams, *Towards 2000* (New York: Pantheon books, 1983), 11-18, 243-69.
16. *Ibid.*, 14.
17. Baradat, *Political Ideologies*, 92-3.

Bibliography

Aronowitz, Stanley. *The Crisis in Historical Materialism Class, Politics and Culture in Marxist Theory* New York: Praeger, 1982.

Baradat, Leon. *Political Ideologies Their Origins and Impact*, 8th ed. Upper Saddle River, N.J.: Prentice Hall, 2003.

Beauvoir, Simone de. *The Long March*. New York: World Publishing Co., 1958.

Benjamin, Walter. *The Arcades Project*. With a foreword by Howard Eiland and Kevin McLaughlin. Edited by Rolf Tiedemann. Translated by Howard Eiland and Kevin McLaughlin. Cambridge, Mass.: The Belknap Press of Harvard University Press, 1999.

————. *Charles Baudelaire A Lyric Poet in the Era of High Capitalism*. Translated by Harry Zohn. London: Verso, 1983.

————. *Illuminations* Edited and with an introduction by Hannah Arendt. New York: Schocken Books, 1969.

————. *One Way Street and Other Writings*. Translated by Edmund Jephcott and Kingsley Shorter. London: Verso, 1979.

————.*Reflections Essays, Aphorisms, Autobiographical Writings*. Edited and with an introduction by Peter Demetz. Translated by Edmund Jephcott. New York: Schocken Books, 1986.

Berger, John. *Ways of Seeing* London: Penguin, 1972.

Bloch, Ernst. *Atheism in Christianity: The Religion of the Exodus and the Kingdom* Translated by J. T. Swann. New York: Herder and Herder, 1972.

————. *Heritage of Our Times*. Translated by N. and S. Plaice. Oxford: Polity, 1991.

————. "A Jubilee for Renegades," *New German Critique*, no. 4 (Winter 1975): 17-25.

————. *Man on His Own Essays in the Philosophy of Religion*. Translated by E. B. Ashton. New York: Herder and Herder, 1970.

————. "Nonsynchronism and the Obligation to its Dialectics." *New German Critique*, no. 11 (Spring 1977): 22-38.

————. *On Karl Marx*. Translated by J. Maxwell. New York: Herder and Herder, 1970.

————. "Poesie im Hohlraum." In *Literarische Aufsatze, Gesamptausgabe* Vol. 9. Frankfurt am Main: Suhrkamp, 1977.

————. *The Principle of Hope*. Translated by Neville Plaice, Stephen Plaice and Paul Knight. Vols. 1-3. Cambridge, Mass.: The MIT Press, 1986.

————. "Recollections of Walter Benjamin." In *On Walter Benjamin. Critical Essays and Recollections*. Edited by G. Smith. Cambridge, MA: MIT Press, 1988.

————. *The Spirit of Utopia*. Translated by Anthony A. Nassar. Stanford, CA: Stanford University Press, 2000.

————. *The Utopian Function of Art and Literature Selected Essays*. With an introduction by Jack. Zipes. Translated by Jack Zipes and Frank Mecklenburg. Cambridge, MA: The MIT Press, 1988.

Brzezinski, Zbigniew. *The Grand Failure The Birth and Death of Communism in the Twentieth Century* New York: Collier Books, 1989.

Campanella, Thomas. *The City of the Sun*. Translated by Daniel J. Donno. Berkeley: University of California Press, 1981.

Caute, David. *The Fellow Travelers A Postscript to the Enlightenment*. New York: Macmillan, 1973.

Chen, Jack. *Inside the Cultural Revolution* London: Sheldon Press, 1976.

Claudin, Fernando. *The Communist Movement From Comintern to Cominform*. Vol. 1. Translated by Brian Pearce. New York: Monthly Review Press, 1975.

Cohn, Norman. *The Pursuit of the Millennium*. New York: Harper and Row, 1961.

Crick, Bernard. *George Orwell. A Life*. Boston: Little, Brown and Co., 1980.

Crossman, Richard, ed. *The God That Failed* London: Hamish Hamilton, 1950.

Diderot, Denis. *Supplement au Voyage de Bougainville*. Paris: E Droz, 1935.

Djilas, Milovan. *Rise and Fall*. Basingstoke: Macmillan, 1985.

Dreiser, Theodore. *Dreiser Looks at Russia*. New York: H. Liveright, 1928.

Dunayevskaya, Raya. *Marxism and Freedom* New York: Bookman Associates, 1958.

Duranty, Walter. *Stalin & Co . The Politburo – the Men Who Run Russia*. New York: William Sloane Associates, Inc., 1949.

Fairbank, John K. "The New China and the American Connection," *Foreign Affairs* 51, no. 1 (October 1972): 31-43.

Fourier, Charles. *The Utopian Vision of Charles Fourier Selected Texts on Work, Love and Passionate Attraction*. Edited and translated by Jonathan Beecher and Richard Beinvenu. Boston: Beacon Press, 1971.

Freud, Sigmund. *Civilization and Its Discontents and Other Works* Harmondsworth: Penguin, 1985.

————. *Collected Papers*. Vol. 4. London: Hogarth Press, 1950.

Frolic, Bernard. "Reflections on the Chinese Model of Development," *Social Forces* 57, no. 2 (December 1978): 384-418.

Fromm, Erich. *Marx's Concept of Man*. Translated by T. Bottomore. Frederick Ungar Publishing, 1961.

Galbraith, John Kenneth . *A China Passage* Boston: Houghton-Mifflin, 1973.

————. *The New Industrial State*. Boston: Houghton-Mifflin, 1969.

Geoghegan, Vincent. *Ernst Bloch* London: Routledge, 1996.

————. *Utopianism and Marxism* London: Methuen, 1987.

Goode, P., ed. *Karl Kautsky, Selected Political Writings* London: Macmillan, 1983.

Gorz, Andre. *Ecology as Politics*. Translated by Patsy Vigderman and Jonathan Cloud. London: Pluto Press, 1987.

————. *Farewell to the Working Class An Essay on Post-Industrial Socialism*. Translated by Michael Sonenscher. London: Pluto Press, 1982.

————. *Paths to Paradise· On the Liberation from Work*. Translated by Malcolm Imrie. London: Pluto Press, 1985.

Greene, Felix. *Awakened China· The Country Americans don't Know*. Garden City, NY: Doubleday, 1961.

Hegel, Georg Wilhelm Friedrich. *The Philosophy of History*. Translated by J. Sibree. New York: Dover Publications, Inc., 1956.

Hindus, Maurice. *The Great Offensive*. London: Gollancz, 1933.

History of the Communist Party of the Soviet Union (Bolsheviks) Short Course Toronto: Francis White Publishers, Ltd., 1939.

Hobsbawm, E. J. "The Principle of Hope." *The Times Literary Supplement*, 31 March 1961, 194.

Hollander, Paul. *Political Pilgrims· Travels of Western Intellectuals to the Soviet Union, China and Cuba* Lanham, MD: University Press of America, 1990.

Hudson, Wayne. *The Marxist Philosophy of Ernst Bloch*. New York: St.Martin's Press, 1982.

Hughes, H. Stuart. *The Sea Change The Migration of Social Thought, 1930-1965* New York: Harper and Row, 1975.

Hyde, Douglas. *I Believed The Autobiography of a Former British Communist*. London: Heinemann, 1951.

Jameson, Fredric. *Marxism and Form Twentieth-Century Dialectical Theories of Literature* Princeton, NJ: Princeton University Press, 1971.

Johnson, Hewlett. *China's New Creative Age* New York: International Publishers, 1953.

————. *Searching for Light*. London: Joseph, 1968.

————. *The Socialist Sixth of the World* London: Gollancz, 1939.

————. *The Upsurge of China*. Peking: New World Press, 1961.

Johnson, Paul. *Modern Times The World from the Twenties to the Eighties* New York: Harper & Row, Publishers, 1983.

Katz, Barry. *Herbert Marcuse and the Art of Liberation An Intellectual Biography*. London: Verso, 1982.

Kautsky, Karl. *The Social Revolution*. Chicago: Kerr & Co., 1916.

Kotkin, Stephen. *Armageddon Averted the Soviet Collapse, 1970-2000* New York: Oxford University Press, 2001.

Kumar, Krishan, *Utopia and Anti-Utopia in Modern Times*. Oxford: Basil Blackwell, Ltd., 1987.

Lamont, Corliss. *Soviet Civilization*. New York: Philosophical Library, 1952.

Lenin, V. I. *What is to be Done?* Edited by S. V. Utechin. Translated by Patricia and S. V. Utechin. Oxford: Clarendon Press, 1963.

Lichtheim, George. *Europe in the Twentieth Century* New York: Praeger, 1972.

Lynd, Staughton and Tom Hayden. *The Other Side* New York: New American Library, 1966.

Macciocchi, Maria. *Daily Life in Revolutionary China* New York: Monthly Review Press, 1972.

Mao Tse-tung. *Chairman Mao Talks to the People Talks and Letters, 1956-1971* New York: Pantheon Books, 1974.

————. "In Memory of Norman Bethune." *Peking Review*, 17 February 1967, 5.

————. *On the Correct Handling of Contradictions among the People* Peking: Foreign Language Press, 1957.

————. *Quotations from Chairman Mao* Peking: Foreign Language Press, 1966.

Marcuse, Herbert. *Five Lectures* Boston: Beacon Press, 1970.

————. *Eros and Civilization A Philosophical Inquiry into Freud*. London· Ark Paperbacks, 1987.

————. *An Essay on Liberation* Boston: Beacon Press, 1969.

————. "Liberation from the Affluent Society." In *The Dialectics of Liberation*, ed. David Cooper. New York: Collier Books, 1968.

————. *One Dimensional Man* Boston: Beacon Press, 1966

Marx, Karl. *Capital*. Vol. 3. Translated by Ernest Untermann. Chicago: Charles H. Kerr & Co., 1909.

————. *Economic and Philosophical Manuscripts*. In *Karl Marx Early Writings* Edited and translated by Tom Bottomore. New York: McGraw Hill, 1964.

————. "Excerpt Notes of 1844." In *Writings of the Young Marx on Philosophy and Society.* Edited by David Easton and Kurt H. Guddat. Garden City, NY: Anchor Books, 1967.

————. *The German Ideology.* Moscow: International Publishers, 1947.

————. *Grundrisse.* Translated by Martin Nicolaus. Harmondsworth: Penguin Books, 1973.

————. *Collected Works of Karl Marx and Frederick Engels* Vol. 5. *Theses on Feurbach.* Translated by Richard Dixon et al. London: Lawrence & Wishart, 1975-.

Meisner, Maurice. *Marxism, Maoism and Utopianism* Madison: The University of Wisconsin Press, 1982.

Mills, C. W. *The Power Elite* New York: Oxford University Press, 1957.

Milton, David, Nancy Milton and Franz Schurmann, eds. *The China Reader People's China* New York: Vintage, 1974.

More, Thomas. *Utopia* Harmondsworth: Penguin, 1965.

O'Casey, Sean. *Mirror in My House Autobiographies.* Vol. 2. New York: Macmillan, 1956.

Orwell, George. *The Collected Essays, Journalism and Letters of George Orwell.* Edited by Sonia Orwell and Ian Angus. Vol. 1. Harmondsworth: Penguin, 1970.

Pares, Bernard. *Russia and the Peace.* New York: Penguin, 1944.

Plato, *The Republic.* Translated by Robin Waterfield. New York: Oxford University Press, 1993.

Riesman, David, *The Lonely Crowd· A Study of the Changing American Character* New Haven, CT: Yale University Press, 1950.

Rousseau, Jean-Jacques. *The Social Contract.* In *The Collected Writings of Rousseau.* Edited by Roger D. Masters and Christopher Kelly. Translated by Judith R. Bush, Roger D. Masters and Christopher Kelly. Vol. 4. Hanover, NH: University Press of New England, 1994.

Saint-Simon, Henri de. "Declaration of Principles." In *Henri Saint-Simon Selected Writings on Science, Industry and Social Organization.* Edited and translated by Keith Taylor. New York: Holmes and Meier Publishers, Inc., 1975.

Salvadori, M. *Karl Kautsky and the Socialist Revolution, 1880-1938.* London: New Left Books, 1979.

Schram, Stuart R. *Mao Tse-tung* New York: Simon & Schuster, 1966.

————. *The Political Thought of Mao Tse-tung* Harmondsworth: Penguin, 1974.

Shklar Judith N. *Men and Citizens A Study of Rousseau's Social Theory.* Cambridge: Cambridge University Press, 1969.

Snow, Edgar. *The Long Revolution* New York: Random House, 1972.

————. *Red China Today* New York: Random House, 1970.

Strong, Anna Louise. *The New Soviet Constitution.* New York: H. Holt and Co., 1937.

Suyin, Han. *Wind in the Tower· Mao Tse-Tung and the Chinese Revolution, 1949-1975* Boston: Little, Brown & Company, 1976.

Talmon, J. L. *The Origins of Totalitarian Democracy.* New York: W. W.Norton, 1970.

Terrill, Ross. *Mao A Biography.* New York: Harper & Row, Publishers, 1980.

Thompson, E. P. "Through the Smoke of Budapest," *The Reasoner,* no. 3 (November 1956: Supplement 6).

Tiedemann, Rolf. "Dialectics at a Standstill." In Walter Benjamin, *The Arcades Project.* Edited by. Rolf Tiedemann. Translated by Howard Eiland and Kevin McLaughlin. Cambridge, MA: The Belknap Press of Harvard University Press, 1999.

Tillich, Paul. *Protestantische Vision* Ring Verlag: Stuttgart, 1952.

Trotsky, Leon. *The Permanent Revolution* London: New Park Publications, 1962.

Tucker, Robert. *The Marxian Revolutionary Idea*. New York: W. W. Norton & Co., 1969.

————. *Stalin in Power The Revolution from Above, 1928-1941*. New York: W. W. Norton & Co., 1992.

Ulam, Adam. "Socialism and Utopia," *Daedalus* 94, no. 2 (Spring 1965): 382-400.

Von Laue, Theodore H. The *World Revolution of Westernization: The Twentieth Century in Global Perspective*. New York: Oxford University Press, 1987.

Webb, Sidney and Beatrice. *Soviet Communism. A New Civilization?* Vol. 1 London: Longmans, Green and Co.,1936.

Whyte, Martin King. " Inequality and Stratification in China." *China Quarterly*. no. 64 (December 1975): 684-711.

Whyte, William. *The Organization Man*. New York: Simon & Schuster, 1956.

Williams, Raymond. *Towards 2000* New York: Pantheon Books, 1983.

Worsley, Peter. *Inside China* London: Allen Lane, 1975.

Zagoria, Donald S. "China by Daylight," *Dissent* (Spring 1975): 135-147.

Index

About the Author

Jack Luzkow was born in Detroit, Michigan, the son of first generation Jewish Americans. He was educated at Wayne State University, Washington University and Saint Louis University, receiving from the latter his M. A. and Ph D. degrees in modern European history. He has held various appointments in academia at Union College, Marycrest College and DePaul University, and is currently at Fontbonne University in Saint Louis, Missouri. He has served on the editorial board of the National Social Science Journal. Previous writings include a book, *The Revenge of History. A Critique of Francis Fukuyama*, and a number of articles on modern European history. He has also written several works of fiction. Jack Luzkow is married to Yelena Vardzigulova and is a frequent traveler to Russia, her native country.